# British Film
# Directors

# British Film Directors

*A Critical Guide*

## Robert Shail

Edinburgh University Press

© Robert Shail, 2007

Edinburgh University Press Ltd
22 George Square, Edinburgh

Typeset in 11 on 13 Ehrhardt
by Iolaire Typesetting, and
printed and bound in Great Britain by
Cromwell Press, Trowbridge, Wilts

A CIP record for this book is available from the British Library

ISBN 978 0 7486 2230 6 (hardback)
ISBN 978 0 7486 2231 3 (paperback)

# Contents

# Acknowledgements

I would like to thank the University of Wales, Lampeter for granting me research leave in which to complete this book and all of my colleagues in the Department of Film and Media for their support and patience in my absence. Its completion was also assisted by a grant from the University's Research Investment Fund. Many thanks to Edinburgh University Press, especially Sarah Edwards, for their support and to the Kobal Collection for supplying the photographs used.

My particular thanks go to Steve Gerrard, who acted as my research assistant on this project, and to my wife, Cerri, for proofreading, indexing and generally putting up with me.

# Illustrations

The following illustrations are provided as follows:

# Introduction

... consequently it is virtually impossible – despite the wealth of talent and occasional achievements of outstanding quality – to find a British film-making career that has the fullness of that of, say, Jean Renoir or Howard Hawks.[1] Roy Armes, *A Critical History of British Cinema*

There is little doubt that, in cinematic terms, we are living in the age of the director. A quick glance at the film pages in any of the national British broadsheet newspapers easily confirms this. The majority of reviews, even of mainstream commercial films, will make specific reference to the film's director and suggest how this film conforms or deviates from the established pattern of their work. Advertisements for the latest releases will often play heavily on the director's name and audiences are now familiar with opening credits which frequently include the claim that this is a film 'by' said director. Such status is afforded to even first-time directors or those with little interest in the artistic possibilities of the medium. The notion of the director as the key figure in the creative process of film-making, to the exclusion of other individuals or wider contextual factors, appears to be broadly established both as a critical mode and a marketing tool.

This development in film culture might usefully be dated from the arrival of the auteur theory in the late 1950s, a product of the young critics at the magazine *Cahier du Cinema*.[2] In claiming full artistic status for the modern era's most popular entertainment, they elevated the role of the director to become the equivalent of a painter, sculptor or poet. This individual was a visionary who could impose their own personal vision on even the most mundane commercial chore and thereby transform it into a work of art. Although the concept of an 'artist's film' predated the *Cahier* critics by a good forty years, it was a term that had been applied largely to the sphere of the European modernist avant-garde. Prior to the appearance of the auteur theory, very few mainstream directors had been afforded anything like this status, either from audiences or critics. Alfred

Hitchcock was one of the few directors whose name regularly appeared above the title, but this was as much a reflection of the fact that his name tended to guarantee a particular genre of entertainment as it was a testament to his cultural status. The *Cahier* critics used the theory principally to reassess the work of major American directors whose output had often been neglected by cultural commentators because they plied their trade in the heathen, capitalist world of Hollywood. Few would now argue with the artistic claims they made for Orson Welles, Howard Hawks, John Ford or Hitchcock, although the manner in which they chose to assign auteur status, or withhold it, often seemed a matter of personal taste. Don Siegel and Sam Fuller were in, but John Huston was definitely out. The elevation of a critic's idiosyncratic preferences to the point where they become orthodoxy is nowhere clearer than in the book *The Films in My Life* which collects together some of the critical writings of one of *Cahier*'s central figures, François Truffaut.[3] Here Truffaut trips from Billy Wilder to Robert Wise, and from Joshua Logan to Sidney Lumet, with little sense of the different contexts from which these varied film-makers emerged, even crediting Wise with the skilful editing of Orson Welles's, *The Magnificent Ambersons* (1942) with no apparent awareness of his role in butchering Welles's work on behalf of the studio that backed it.

Among the directors Truffaut discusses there are just four British-born film-makers: Charles Chaplin, Alfred Hitchcock, Charles Laughton and Norman McLaren. It is revealing to consider that Chaplin barely made any films in Britain, Hitchcock is best known for his Hollywood movies, Laughton's only film as a director was made in America and McLaren's most notable achievements were in Canada. Truffaut even manages to spell McLaren's surname incorrectly. British directors fared particularly badly from the prejudices of the *Cahier* critics and their followers. Famously, in his book-length interview with Hitchcock, Truffaut dismissed the merits of British cinema with barely disguised contempt, blaming an entire nation's 'incompatibility' with the world of cinema on such disparate factors as 'the English countryside, the subdued way of life, the stolid routine . . . the weather itself is anti-cinematic.'[4] He had obviously never seen the opening of David Lean's *Oliver Twist* (1948). Such attitudes are not far from the surface of Roy Armes' survey *A Critical History of British Cinema*. Armes at least attributes the creative failings of various British film-makers in part to the nature of the production context in which they have had to struggle: 'All the major directors of British cinema have had to find their own path between a degree of innovation which will render them unemployable and a conformist mediocrity which will deprive their work of all interest.'[5] Quite why such strictures don't apply to other national cinemas remains unclear. Critical opinion within Britain itself has certainly not helped to alleviate this neglect of British directors. Notoriously, the influential film magazine *Movie*, which in the 1960s embraced the auteur theory wholeheartedly, could barely find any space for the work of British film-makers in its pages.

Sadly, a good deal of this neglect is attributable to ignorance and critical prejudice on the part of some of the commentators concerned. However, there are historical factors which need to be acknowledged and which, to be fair to Armes, he does point the reader towards. One factor was the development in Britain of a studio production system which drew on the models established by Hollywood and which consequently tended to place considerable power in the hands of executives and line producers. The names of companies like Rank, Ealing, British Lion and ABPC figure prominently in any history of the industry and some of its most productive, charismatic figures have been producers such as Michael Balcon, Alexander Korda and David Puttnam. This was reflected in the literature available to Armes at the time he wrote his study when monographs on British directors were few and far between. Ealing provides a particularly appropriate case study in that the work of talented directors like Robert Hamer and Alexander Mackendrick was easily overshadowed by the trademark house style which developed at Ealing under the leadership of Balcon. Appropriately, Armes' chapter on this topic is called 'Balcon at Ealing' and is at some pains to indicate the ways in which Hamer and Mackendrick were able to impose some form of personal vision on their work, going against the grain of the prevailing studio ethos. This production system prevailed from the 1930s through to the economic decline of the 1970s. It could even be argued that it has now re-emerged via the franchise system adopted by the UK Film Council. This operates by distributing Lottery monies to three chosen companies, or 'franchises', and clearly reflects the view that the creative future of British cinema lies in sponsoring production outfits rather than individual film-makers.

This overview is perhaps slightly monolithic in that there have been some notable exceptions. In the 1940s the 'umbrella' system operated by the Rank Organisation allowed some independence to directors who, like Powell and Pressburger, were able to form their own production companies within the Rank set-up.[6] During the 1960s the massive injection of funding from Hollywood tended to be focused on individual directors such as Richard Lester and Tony Richardson whose more individualistic style was seen as offering the best chance of substantial box-office returns.[7] Both periods were relatively buoyant in production terms and this certainly led to a greater sense of self-confidence and risk-taking. Nonetheless, the dominant production mode in British cinema tended to define the director as a technician or craftsperson whose job it was to ensure the smooth transition from script to screen while conforming to the commercial requirements established by the production company concerned. A leaning toward personal creativity was often viewed with suspicion, as Powell and Pressburger were to discover.

It can also be argued that the pre-eminence in British film culture of two stylistic approaches, documentary realism and, as Armes calls it, 'literary cinema', has not done the director any great favours. Literary cinema, from David Lean's adaptations of Dickens and Anthony Asquith's versions of Shaw and Wilde to the contemporary Heritage films of Merchant-Ivory, has, unsurprisingly, placed greater emphasis on writing and adaptation. It has also tended to foreground actors in both marketing strategies and in maintaining the 'quality' of such films. A video release of Lean's versions of *Great Expectations* and *Oliver Twist* in the late 1980s actually packaged the tapes as if they were the original books by Dickens. The influence of the theatre on British cinema will be evident enough from many of the entries in this book and has led to often repeated allegations that directors drawn from the theatre consequently lack a real cinematic sense and have been more concerned with coaxing fine performances from their actors. The documentary-realist tradition can also be seen as operating with a conceptual framework designed to limit the role of the director to that of a technician tasked with recording the given nature of actuality, although the highly individualistic work of film-makers like Humphrey Jennings tends to contradict this. Armes concludes that both stylistic traditions are furthermore inherently conservative:

> The conservative tendency embraces both the documentary movement (which has traditionally seen its role as that of reflecting the ethos of the ruling class, not that of questioning the structures of society) and the prestige feature production which has customarily adapted its subjects from literature. As a result, there is a striking paucity of stylistic experiment in both areas.[8]

The picture needn't seem quite as dark as Armes painted it in 1978. Erik Hedling has traced the roots of an alternative tradition of British art cinema which finally emerged into the public gaze in the 1980s with the work of Derek Jarman and Peter Greenaway.[9] Hedling identifies its origins as lying back in the late 1950s with the appearance of the British New Wave and specifically highlights the contribution of Lindsay Anderson, both as a film-maker and a polemicist for a British auteur tradition. Of course Anderson himself suggested a lineage going further back again to the films of documentarists like Humphrey Jennings.[10] It's not difficult to broaden this out to include other directors of the 1960s such as John Boorman and Ken Russell, as well as those who settled in Britain from abroad during that period like Joseph Losey and Stanley Kubrick. It could be widened still further to encompass maverick figures who frequently found themselves at odds with the British studio system but who still managed to carve out interesting careers for themselves. Powell and Pressburger might be at the top of such a list, but it could also include John Baxter, Alberto Cavalcanti or Thorold Dickinson among others. Armes himself acknowledges Jennings, Powell and Dickinson among the handful of directors who he believed had achieved real artistic status.

The situation in the last ten years couldn't have changed more radically. Armes suggested that a number of British directors had been neglected by film historians. If that was the case in the late 1970s it has subsequently been rectified to a considerable degree. Many of the major directors in British cinema have been subject to substantial critical re-evaluations, none more so than Michael Powell. The *British Film Makers* series recently published by Manchester University Press is a fine example of this sea-change. Its titles include obvious candidates for reconsideration like Carol Reed, but also cover directors like J. Lee Thompson and Roy Ward Baker whose work was largely in commercial, mainstream genre films. The list even includes relatively obscure figures like Lance Comfort. This change in critical perspective might be best illustrated by the case of Hammer's prince of horror, Terence Fisher, a director whom Armes dismissed as 'a plodding and conventional director who, whatever the state of the British film industry, keeps in business for some twenty-five years by always safely fulfilling his contract',[11] but who is recognised now as, in the words of Wheeler Winston Dixon, 'arguably the most important director of the Gothic cinema in the second half of the 20th century.'[12] Central to this re-assessment has been a long overdue recognition that British directors are as capable of imposing a personal vision on their work, even in the face of a highly commercial, conformist industry, as film-makers in America or France.

This book attempts to bring together the work of one hundred disparate British film directors whose output is remarkable, not least for its sheer variety. In selecting these from an original list that was much, much longer, a few basic criteria were applied. This is a book about directors whose films have largely been made in Britain. Most of these directors were also born in the UK, but some, like Losey, Cavalcanti and Roman Polanski, were born elsewhere and then came to Britain to make some or all of their films. Conversely, this means that some British-born directors who have completed most, if not all of their work outside of the UK have consequently been excluded. Hence, no Ridley Scott or Charles Chaplin. The majority of the directors included have amassed a substantial body of work over a number of years, but some have been included even though their output has been small because they have made a particularly distinctive contribution to the national film culture. This accounts for the presence of Donald Cammell, Philip Leacock and Michael Reeves. With a finite number of entries there have inevitably been exclusions. Areas such as silent cinema, the documentary movement and animation have, I will confess, only been represented by a small selection of key figures as this is all that space would allow. Young filmmakers have also been rather harshly treated, so that only one or two who have already made quite a significant impact (such as Michael Winterbottom and Gurinder Chadha) have found their way in. There is a great deal of new talent out there and it can only be hoped, if this volume ever reaches further editions, that film-makers like Marc Evans, Stephen Daldry, Peter Mullan, Patrick Kieller, Peter Cattaneo and Antonia Bird may well find their way in.

The principle intention of this book is, obviously enough, to provide a reference guide for the film enthusiast and student of British cinema to the work of one hundred directors who have made a notable contribution to British film culture. However, in doing this the book also reveals a number of interesting patterns which help to distinguish that culture. Compiling the entries, it is clear enough that Roy Armes' contention that British cinema has been dominated by two opposing traditions, one literary, the other based on documentary-realism, still holds considerable weight. It is also the case that a populist genre cinema, where crime, horror and comedy have often been pre-eminent, emerges strongly. The work of these directors helps to illustrate the rise and fall of key studios like Hammer, Ealing, Rank and Goldcrest. The economic and creative fluctuations of the industry are evident through careers which had to negotiate the boom of the 1940s, the comparative caution of the 1950s and the reinvigoration of the 1960s, along with the more recent cycle of decline and restructuring since the 1970s. The influence of Hollywood often looms large as directors who struggle to survive in the austere climate of the British industry frequently find a sunnier outlook in the States. European connections also appear, not just in the number of Continental directors who have based themselves in Britain, but also in the impact of stylistic and thematic innovations drawn from European cinema. These are often careers in which restraints, cultural and economic, have been the instigators for creativity and imagination, so that the tension between conformism and subversion has been a recurring motif.

There are also recurring patterns in the career pathways of these directors. It is noticeable just how many of the directors to emerge in the 1930s and 1940s have their background in the theatre, classical or popular, frequently as struggling actors rather than directors. This is a pattern which has diminished, but not vanished. In the 1960s a new generation who had cut their teeth working in television appears, followed by the generation of the 1970s, such as Alan Parker and Hugh Hudson, whose background was in advertising. More recently the world of pop music promos has fostered film-makers like Guy Ritchie. If career pathways have changed, then the geographical map has altered more slowly. Lindsay Anderson claimed that British cinema was dominated by London and this tends to be born out by the entries in this book, although the provinces do begin to appear more among directors born since the 1930s.[13] Anderson also pointed towards a middle-class bias in British cinema and this also tends to be born out, with a striking number following a route from public school to Oxbridge and on into the industry – not an encouraging precedent for aspiring film-makers from the non-metropolitan working class. Another feature is the fragmentation which has removed the reasonably reliable career paths which dominated until the 1950s. The natural progression from runabout to editor to director, typified by David Lean and many others, has largely gone, to be replaced by far more wayward progression in which the budding director must be willing to work in whatever format or medium offers the opportunity for some employment.

Hopefully this volume will join with the others published in more recent years and help in the general reassessment of British cinema which has occurred. It should provide some kind of antidote to the pessimism exhibited by Roy Armes back in 1978 by showcasing the wide variety of achievements attained by British film-makers. The careers outlined here may show recurrent patterns, some of which confirm the conservatism of Britain's film industry and cinema culture, but there is much here to contradict that. These film-makers have shown that it is possible to produce in Britain work of genuine imagination, passion and cinematic fluency while still reflecting aspects of British social life familiar to audiences. This book is a small celebration of that achievement.

## How to Use This Guide

The one hundred entries in the Guide are arranged alphabetically by surname. Each entry focuses on that film-maker's career within the British industry. For directors who have spent periods working outside of the UK, that portion of their career is indicated briefly, but in much less detail than the work they have undertaken in Britain. Consequently, each filmography lists only their British feature films and does not include non-British productions or non-feature films, although these may be referred to in the main text. Defining what constitutes a British film can be exceedingly difficult. A film might be made in Britain with funding from elsewhere or perhaps the funding is British but the setting is abroad. The career of Stanley Kubrick poses particular problems here. I have adopted two guiding principles: all films which might be defined as 'culturally' British have been included and, where any doubt occurs, I have tended to err on the generous side. If this means that I have included some films whose British credentials seem tenuous, I apologise.

Each entry includes some basic biographical information, although this is usually limited to material which has had some impact on the director's film career. Those seeking revelations about private lives need to look elsewhere. This is a 'critical' guide and each entry offers some commentary on the quality of the director's achievements. The intention has been to summarise for the reader the existing critical debates about an individual film-maker's work. As an example, the entry on Ken Russell hopefully reflects the views of those who relish his colourful contribution to British cinema, along with those who would happily see his films burnt. I have tried to restrain imposing my own views too extensively, but inevitably they do appear. My reason is that this has mainly been to advocate the work of film-makers who remain unjustifiably neglected. The bibliographies are intended as a starting point for the film student, suggesting key sources from which to take their studies further.

Inevitably, in a volume such as this, the reader is likely to feel that some of the directors included didn't warrant an entry and that other crucial names are missing. Left to my own devices this book might have been three times as long. I hope I have checked my information diligently, but it is remarkable, and frustrating, just how often dates of birth or other basic pieces of factual information can vary depending on the sources used. Any suggestions and corrections will be gratefully received.

## Notes

1. Roy Armes, *A Critical History of British Cinema* (London: Secker & Warburg, 1978), p. 335.
2. See François Truffaut, 'A Certain Tendency of the French Cinema', originally published in *Cahiers du Cinema*, no. 31 (January, 1954) and reprinted in Bill Nichols (ed.), *Movies and Methods, Volume 1* (Berkeley and Los Angeles: University of California Press, 1976), pp. 224–37.

3. François Truffaut, *The Films in my Life* (London: Allen Lane, 1980).
4. François Truffaut, *Hitchcock* (London: Paladin, 1978), p. 140.
5. Armes, *A Critical History of British Cinema*, p. 3.
6. See Geoffrey Macnab, *J. Arthur Rank and the British Film Industry* (London and New York: Routledge, 1993).
7. For a detailed account of the 'American invasion' see Alexander Walker, *Hollywood, England* (London: Orion, 2005).
8. Armes, *A Critical History of British Cinema*, p. 334.
9. Erik Hedling, 'Lindsay Anderson and the Development of British Art Cinema', in Robert Murphy (ed.), *The British Cinema Book* (London: BFI, 2001).
10. Lindsay Anderson, 'Only Connect: Some Aspects of the Work of Humphrey Jennings', originally published in *Sight and Sound* (Spring, 1953) and reprinted in Paul Ryan (ed.), *Never Apologise: The Collected Writings of Lindsay Anderson* (London: Plexus, 2004).
11. Armes, *A Critical History of British Cinema*, p. 252.
12. Wheeler Winston Dixon's entry for Terence Fisher in Brian McFarlane, *The Encyclopedia of British Cinema* (London: Methuen, 2003), p. 224.
13. Lindsay Anderson, 'Get Out and Push!', originally published in *Declaration*, edited by Tom Maschler (1957) and reprinted in Paul Ryan (ed.), *Never Apologise: The Collected Writings of Lindsay Anderson*.

British Film Directors

# A

## Birt ACRES

Birt Acres was one of the key figures in the early development of cinema in Britain. His inventions were central in introducing the basic apparatus of cinema, from cameras and projectors to film stock itself. He was also a cameraman and director of considerable significance, whose films are landmarks in establishing a tradition for film-making in Britain.

Acres was born on 23 July 1854 in Richmond, Virginia, of English parents. When he came to Britain in the 1880s he was already an accomplished stills photographer (he was later to become a fellow of the Royal Photographic Society) and had considerable expertise in the whole process of making photographic prints. In 1892 he became the manager of Elliott and Sons Ltd of Barnet, a firm renowned for the manufacture of photographic plates. During the early 1890s he patented a number of photographic inventions culminating in 1896 with Britain's first fully functioning cinematograph camera, the Kineopticon.

In late 1894 Acres had started to work with another pioneer, Robert William Paul. By June 1895 they had manufactured their own camera and produced about a dozen short films together, with Acres usually acting as cameraman. These films recorded such actuality subjects as the Henley Royal Regatta, the Oxford and Cambridge University Boat Race and the Derby, as well as famously capturing *Rough Sea at Dover*. These films may well qualify Acres as the first news reportage cameraman in Britain. After parting company with Paul he made a number of films in Germany, including filming the opening of the Kiel Canal and Kaiser Wilhelm inspecting his troops.

Several of his films were included in Edison's first film show in April 1896 and Acres himself arranged what is probably the first public film screening in Britain at the Lyonsdown Amateur Photographic Association in Barnet, January 1896. On 14 January that year, at almost the same time the Lumières were giving their first film show in London, he gave a public screening at the Royal Photographic Society of his 'animated photography'. During 1896 he began to extend the range of his subjects to cover fictional comedies and dramas, such as *The Arrest of a Pickpocket*, in addition to his actuality films. That year he also set up the Northern Photographic Works at Hadley in order to market his films and equipment.

Acres seems to have been less interested in the commercial possibilities of public film shows than other pioneers and focused more on private screenings. He gave the inaugural Royal Command Film Performance for the Prince of Wales and seventy-five other members of European royalty at Marlborough House on 21 July 1896. Acres had previously filmed the Prince of Wales in Cardiff, making him the first British royal to be captured on celluloid. Having shot more than thirty shorts, Acres ceased making films in 1900 to concentrate on his film developing and printing business. Among his later achievements is the invention of the Birtac, a 17.5 mm camera/projector which was the first designed specifically for home use. After his death in 1918 he became a rather forgotten figure, but is now acknowledged as one of the founding fathers of British cinema.

**Bibliography:** Richard Brown, 'Birt Acres', in Stephen Herbert and Luke McKernan (eds), *Who's Who of Victorian Cinema: A Worldwide Survey* (London: British Film Institute, 1996).

## Lindsay ANDERSON

In a national cinema where conformism has often been seen as a virtue, Anderson stands out as a true individualist. His is a maverick voice, whether in the handful of feature films he directed or in the variety of other work (short films, documentaries, essays and criticism) he completed. He was frequently at odds with what he saw as a moribund British film establishment and therefore became something of a champion for British cinema's malcontents.

Ironically Anderson's own background could hardly have been more establishment. He was born on 17 April 1923 in Bangalore, India, the son of a major-general. His education took him from public school to Wadham College, Oxford. It was here that his interest in cinema found its first expression through the magazine *Sequence* which he co-founded and co-edited through fourteen issues between 1947 and 1952. Throughout the 1950s he continued to write essays, film reviews and polemics for publications such as *Sight and Sound*, *New Statesman* and *The Observer*. He developed an idiosyncratic, but influential, agenda which argued for a cinema of social relevance, while celebrating the medium's status as an art form. In key essays like *Get Out and Push!* (1957) Anderson rails at the timidity of British film-making, with its backward-looking nostalgia and reliance on narrowly middle-class values. His vocal expression of these concerns made him a figurehead for the New Wave in British film-making.

His chance to put his ideas into practice came first with a series of

documentary shorts. These were made for a variety of producers including the NSPCC, the Fuel Efficiency Service and the Wakefield engineering firm of Richard Sutcliffe Ltd, as well as for the BFI. He helped to organise the series of six 'Free Cinema' programmes shown between 1956 and 1959 at the National Film Theatre, which included some of his own shorts. Three of his 1950s documentaries are of particular interest: *Thursday's Children* (1953) is a sympathetic account of a school for deaf children which won him an Oscar; *Everyday Except Christmas* (1957) provides a semi-poetic impression of the workers in Covent Garden Market but doesn't completely avoid patronising them; and *O Dreamland* (1953), which offers a more overtly disparaging view of the amusement arcades of Margate and their clientele. Anderson's apparent sense of distance from the working-class lives he often captures was to become a frequent criticism of his early film-making.

He finally made his feature debut in 1963 with an adaptation of David Storey's novel *This Sporting Life*. Although the film bears many hallmarks of the New Wave in its gritty depiction of lives stunted by social conditions, it also indicates Anderson's desire to go beyond the limitations of a strictly naturalistic style. It does this through its use of a complex flashback structure and in its concern for psychological depth. The performances of Richard Harris as the former miner turned professional rugby player, Frank Machin, and of Rachel Roberts as his painfully repressed landlady Mrs Hammond, remain vividly compelling.

It was five years before Anderson made his second feature film, but in between came two short films. *The Singing Lesson* (1967) is a relatively minor documentary recording a class at the Warsaw Dramatic Academy, whereas *The White Bus* (1966) is more substantial. Written by Shelagh Delaney, it was intended as one segment of a three-part feature to be called *Red, White and Zero* (the other parts to be directed by Tony RICHARDSON and Peter Brook) which was never released. Its elements of satire and surrealism prefigure Anderson's second feature, *If.* . . (1968). Probably his most successful film, winning the Palme d'Or at Cannes, this scurrilous attack on the absurdities of the public school system (partially filmed at Anderson's old school, Cheltenham College) combines an observational style with modernist techniques (Brechtian chapter headings, abrupt jumps between colour and monochrome) and a gradual shift into fantasy. Taking the students' rebellion as a metaphor for the wider British society, the film could not have been better timed, coinciding as it did with the Paris uprising.

The film's central character, Mick Travis (Malcolm McDowell), appeared in two further films which, together with *If.* . ., form a kind of 'state of the nation' trilogy. *O Lucky Man!* (1973) uses an episodic structure, as Travis wanders Britain encountering corruption at every level, from a northern working-men's club to a corporate boardroom. The film's experimental devices include the use of the same actors in various roles, musical interludes by Alan Price and the appearance of Anderson himself as the film's own director. The final part of the trilogy, *Britannia Hospital* (1982), met with considerable critical hostility. Here Anderson's social critique uses the parlous state of the National Health Service as a metaphor for Britain's decline. Anderson was accused by some on the Left of reversing his political position, replacing the youthful rebellion of his earlier work with middle-aged cantankerousness.

Anderson's intermittent film output was separated by periods of sustained work in the theatre, including succeeding Tony Richardson at the Royal Court. He worked a number of times with the playwright David Storey and filmed his play *In Celebration* in 1974 for the American Film Theatre, as well as making a television version of *Home* (1972). He worked occasionally in television directing a striking version of Alan Bennett's *The Old Crowd* (1979) and the Canadian-backed *Glory! Glory!* (1989) which satirised TV evangelism. His eclecticism is reflected in the breadth of his work, which also included occasional acting roles, most notably when cast ironically as an establishment academic in Hugh HUDSON's *Chariots of Fire* (1981). He is at the centre of his own 'mockumentary' in *Is That All There Is?* (1993), reviewing the achievements and battles which marked his career. Anderson's last feature before his death in August 1994 was the elegiac, American-made *The Whales of August* (1987) which showcased a range of fine performances from a cast of classic-era Hollywood stars including Lillian Gish, Bette Davis and Vincent Price.

Anderson is a contradictory figure in British film culture. His love of tradition, his poetic sensibility and dislike of fashionable critical theory made him sometimes appear to be the 'grumpy old man' of British films, but his dedication to a cinema of social relevance and visionary imagination also made him a focus for dissent. His lasting legacy, apart from the films themselves, may be as one of the instigators for a fully fledged British art cinema.

**British Feature Films:** *This Sporting Life* (1963); *If . . .* (1968); *O Lucky Man!* (1973); *In Celebration* (1974); *Britannia Hospital* (1982).

**Bibliography:** Paul Ryan (ed.), *Never Apologise: Lindsay Anderson, The Collected Writings* (London: Plexus, 2004); Paul Sutton (ed.), *The Diaries of Lindsay Anderson* (London: Methuen, 2004); Erik Hedling, *Lindsay Anderson: Maverick Film-Maker* (London: Continuum, 1998).

# Anthony ASQUITH

If British cinema has often been a literary cinema, then one of the finest exponents of this style was Anthony Asquith. The major achievements of his career include benchmark adaptations of Shaw and Wilde, as well as a number of collaborations with the playwright Terence Rattigan. The tasteful restraint of his approach and an unsurprising reliance on dialogue can easily obscure the fact that many of his films are also marked by an elegant craftsmanship and visual subtlety which mark them as genuinely cinematic.

The son of Lord (Herbert) Asquith, the Liberal Prime Minister, 'Puffin' Asquith (as he was affectionately known) was born on 9 November 1902 in London. After attending Winchester and Balliol College, Oxford, he went to Hollywood to learn film-making. Back in England, Asquith entered the industry with mundane jobs at British Instructional before making his debut as a director on *Shooting Stars* (1928, co-directed by A. V. Bramble). From the late 1920s he established himself as one of Britain's leading film-makers, exhibiting a fluency of technique unusual in British cinema of the period. His flair is already apparent in *Shooting Stars* which mocks the falsities of the film world by providing us with a glimpse behind the scenes in a film studio. Like Hitchcock, Asquith worked on German co-productions such as *The Runaway Princess* (1929); the influence of expressionism is evident in the stylish thrillers *Underground* (1928) and *A Cottage on Dartmoor* (1929) in their striking imagery. With the advent of sound, Asquith moved to Gaumont-British and then to London Films, but his career stalled, particularly with the derided *Moscow Nights* (1935). Although many of his early sound films are strictly within the routine studio format of the period, he demonstrated an eye for social observation in the comedy-drama *Dance Little Lady* (1932) which prefigures his later work.

*Pygmalion* (1938) and *French Without Tears* (1939) mark a watershed in Asquith's development. Adapted from George Bernard Shaw's play and co-directed by its star, Leslie Howard, *Pygmalion* provides a model for theatrical adaptations of its kind. An outstanding cast, including Wendy Hiller as Eliza Doolittle, are expertly handled so as to give full emphasis to the wit of Shaw's dialogue as well as to the sharpness of his class critique. *French Without Tears* is significant for first teaming Asquith with Terence Rattigan, the master of the 'well-made play', and already shows Asquith's adept touch in transferring Rattigan's West End success to the screen.

During the war period Asquith was recruited to aid the propaganda effort which he did with documentary shorts such as *Channel Incident* (1940) and fiction features, including the soberly realist *We Dive at*

*Dawn* (1943) and the quirkily humorous *The Demi-Paradise* (1943). The spy thriller *Cottage to Let* (1941) combines propaganda with a return to the expressive visual style of his earlier films, but his most flamboyant film of the period is the costume melodrama *Fanny by Gaslight* (1944) made for Gainsborough. This period of his career is neatly closed by *The Way to the Stars* (1945), a typically understated account of the war co-scripted by Rattigan and centred on life at a bomber station. Asquith handles familiar material with an obvious sympathy and focuses more on the human costs of the war than on heroics. The film remains moving and remarkably evocative of the period.

In the immediate postwar years Asquith made three films which seem to distill his distinctive qualities. Both *The Winslow Boy* (1948) and *The Browning Version* (1951) are adapted by Rattigan from his own plays and exhibit the strengths of his writing in their clearly delineated plots and well-drawn characters. Asquith draws touching performances from Robert Donat and Michael Redgrave and both films offer a gentle critique of middle-class England with its repressed emotions and social inequities. The high-water mark of Asquith's career, however, is his glorious version of Oscar Wilde's *The Importance of Being Earnest* (1952). Asquith foregrounds the theatricality of his material by book-ending the film with shots of the audience watching the play in a theatre, but his cinematic skill is also apparent in the evocative use of colour. He takes full advantage of a marvelous cast including Dorothy Tutin, Michael Redgrave and the imperious Edith Evans to provide what remains an object lesson in filming Wilde.

Theatrical adaptations continued to dominate Asquith's output throughout the rest of the 1950s. There were two further versions of Shaw, *The Doctor's Dilemma* (1958) and *The Millionairess* (1960), with its unlikely pairing of Sophia Loren and Peter Sellers. *The Final Test* (1953) was adapted from a television play by Rattigan and both *Carrington VC* (1954) and *Libel* (1959) are stagey courtroom dramas. *The Net* (1953) and *Orders to Kill* (1958), the only film of this period not to have a theatrical source, are low-key spy thrillers, but none of these films really contradicts the common view of British cinema of this period as dated and conformist.

His final films of the 1960s were a disappointing end to a distin-guished career. *Two Living, One Dead* (1961), which was co-produced in Sweden, did not get a British circuit release. *The VIPs* (1963) and *The Yellow Rolls-Royce* (1964) teamed Asquith with Rattigan once again, but despite starry casts and glossy cinematography both films are vacuous in comparison with Asquith's best work. In films like *Pyg-malion* and *The Importance of Being Earnest* he had shown a remarkable gift for drawing memorable performances from polished actors, as well as demonstrating a subtle, understated handling of cinematic technique which favoured craftsmanship over flamboyance. It is this work upon which his reputation rests. His commitment to the industry was also evident in his role as President of the film trade union ACCT, a post which he held from 1937 until his death from cancer in 1968.

**British Feature Films:** *Shooting Stars* (1928, co-directed with A. V. Bramble); *Underground* (1928); *The Runaway Princess* (1929); *A Cottage on Dartmoor* (1929); *Tell England* (1931, co-directed with Geoffrey Barkas); *Dance Pretty Lady* (1932); *The Lucky Number* (1933); *Unfinished Symphony* (1934, co-directed with Willy Forst); *Moscow Nights* (1935); *Pygmalion* (1938, co-directed with Leslie Howard); *French Without Tears* (1939); *Freedom Radio* (1940); *Quiet Wedding* (1941); *Cottage to Let* (1941); *Uncensored* (1942); *We Dive at Dawn* (1943); *The Demi-Paradise* (1943); *Fanny by Gaslight* (1944); *The Way to the Stars* (1945); *While the Sun Shines* (1947); *The Winslow Boy* (1948); *The Woman in Question* (1950); *The Browning Version* (1951); *The Importance of Being Earnest* (1952); *The Final Test* (1953); *The Net* (1953); *The Young Lovers* (1954); *Carrington VC* (1954); *Orders to Kill* (1958); *The Doctor's Dilemma* (1958); *Libel* (1959); *The Millionairess* (1960); *Two Living, One Dead* (1961); *Guns of Darkness* (1962); *The VIPs* (1963); *An Evening with the Royal Ballet* (1963, documentary); *The Yellow Rolls-Royce* (1964).

**Bibliography:** J. R. Minney, *Puffin Asquith: A Biography of the Hon. Anthony Asquith* (London: Leslie Frewin, 1973).

### Richard (Lord) ATTENBOROUGH

The influence of Richard Attenborough on British cinema spreads considerably beyond the eleven films he has directed. Apart from also being a producer and actor, he has held innumerable public offices. It's not unreasonable to suggest that he has been one of the most prominent voices in debates over the development of British film-making in the last forty-five years.

Attenborough was born in Cambridge on 29 August 1923 and first made his mark in British films as an actor. Following training at RADA, he made his film debut in Noël Coward and David LEAN's *In Which We Serve* (1942), cast as a nervy sailor who deserts his post. This was the first of a series of juvenile roles playing characters who are either delinquent or cowardly or both. The epitome of this is his unforgettable performance as Pinkie in the BOULTING Brothers' adaptation of *Brighton Rock* (1947). In later roles he developed into a useful character actor, notably as the murderer John Christie in *10 Rillington Place* (1971).

He said it was his inability to shake off the public's perception of him as a cherubic gangster that led him to a career behind the camera. He began in production, founding Beaver Films with Bryan FORBES in 1959. Showing the influence of the New Wave, their intention was to make films of social relevance as typified by *The Angry Silence* (1960, Guy Green). The film depicts the persecution by his workmates of a man (played by Attenborough) who refuses to take strike action and angered some on the Left for its alleged union bashing. Attenborough was producer for FORBES on three further films in the 1960s (*Whistle Down the Wind*, *The L-Shaped Room* and *Séance on a Wet Afternoon*) as well as on most of the films he directed himself.

Attenborough's debut as director was an adaptation of Joan Greenwood's stage success *Oh! What a Lovely War* (1969). Greenwood incorporated period songs and reportage into an impressionistic account of the horrors of the First World War and Attenborough retains many of these elements. The film matches its theatricality with cinematic flourishes like the final tracking shot back over the endless rows of war graves. The incorporation of many styles, from parody to the surreal, sometimes overloads the film's anti-war message but captures Greenwood's intentions. Two consistent elements have emerged in Attenborough's films: an eye for cinematic spectacle; and an interest in historical figures who uphold principles which, for Attenborough, make them heroic. The choice of Churchill in *Young Winston* (1972) might seem odd for such an overtly liberal film-maker, but this sympathetic account of Churchill's early years focuses on questions of personal morality and bravery rather than on Churchill's politics. *A Bridge Too Far* (1977) portrays the Allied attempt to secure bridges behind German lines in the Second World War. The film's attempt to mix the epic with the intimate results in a degree of confusion and the roster of stars is frequently distracting. The restaging of events for dramatic effect invited criticism from historians, as well as veterans, as to their accuracy. Nonetheless, some performances are striking and the film conveys the epic scale and chaos of proceedings.

*Magic* (1978), which was made in America, is a psychological horror on the familiar theme of a ventriloquist (Anthony Hopkins) whose dummy seems all too alive. The handling has panache, with both direction and central performance suitably overstated. Back in Britain Attenborough finally completed the film he had dreamt of directing for twenty years, *Gandhi* (1982). The film showcases sufficiently more of the director's virtues than his weaknesses to make it his most effective film. His feeling for spectacle is apparent in such brilliantly staged sequences as Gandhi's funeral procession and his skill with actors is rewarded in the performance of Ben Kingsley. Historians again didn't care for Attenborough's tendency to reshape the complexities of Indian history into an audience-pleasing drama, but no one would question the director's sincerity. The film was an international success, garnering the Oscar for Best Picture.

His following film was almost bound to pale in comparison, which at least partly explains the critical hostility which met *A Chorus Line* (1985), an uncertain adaptation of the popular Broadway musical. With *Cry Freedom* (1987) Attenborough returned to more familiar ground, recounting the story of the murdered South African anti-apartheid activist Steve Biko (Denzel Washington). Attenborough's desire to reach a wide audience led to criticisms that he had compromised the film's political edge by portraying events through the eyes of the white reporter Donald Woods (Kevin Kline). Nonetheless, the film is compelling, bolstered by strong performances and provides another example of Attenborough's ability to organise cinematic spectacle, here in the form of Biko's funeral.

Attenborough turned to another of his heroes in *Chaplin* (1992). The film attempts the impossible in trying to cover one of the most extraordinary twentieth-century lives. It does showcase another fine performance, from Robert Downey Jr, and manages a reasonably balanced summation of a complex man. He elicits another striking performance, this time from Anthony Hopkins, in *Shadowlands* (1993). This is an uncharacteristically low-key drama of loss and grief, with Hopkins as the writer C. S. Lewis. The film shows a degree of sensitivity not always apparent in Attenborough's work. His more recent directorial entries suggest a decline. *In Love and War* (1996), made in America, focuses on Ernest Hemingway's experiences in the First World War. Its doomy romanticism won few friends. *Grey Owl* (1999) fared worse, finding difficulties in obtaining distribution. Pierce Brosnan is uncomfortably cast as a Canadian fur trapper turned conservationist who pretends to be a Native American to further his cause.

Attenborough has been tireless in undertaking official duties to aid his beloved film industry, becoming its ardent public champion. Among his many posts he has been Governor of the National Film School, Vice-President and President of BAFTA and Chairman of the BFI. As a consequence he has been showered with awards – in 1976 he was knighted and was made a lord in 1993.

**British Feature Films:** *Oh! What a Lovely War* (1969); *Young Winston* (1972); *A Bridge Too Far* (1977); *Gandhi* (1982); *Cry Freedom* (1987); *Chaplin* (1992); *Shadowlands* (1993); *Grey Owl* (1999).

**Bibliography:** Andy Dougan, *Actor's Director: Richard Attenborough Behind the Camera* (London: Mainstream, 1994); Jonathan Hacker and David Price (eds), *Take Ten: Contemporary British Film Directors* (Oxford: Oxford University Press, 1991).

$$\boxed{\text{B}}$$

## Roy Ward BAKER

In a long and remarkably varied career, Roy Ward Baker (often credited as Roy Baker in his early films) demonstrated an assured ability to impose a distinctive style on often highly commercial material. Born in London on 19 December 1916, he entered the industry in 1933 with Gainsborough and followed the classic industry career path, working his way up from tea-boy to runner and eventually assistant director. During the Second World War he worked with the Army Kinematograph Unit where he met the writer and producer Eric Ambler who was to give him his first feature credit as director on *The October Man* (1947). This striking debut established many of the qualities which were to distinguish Baker's best work. The film's complex, noirish plot is taughtly controlled, the visual style is lean but atmospheric and there is a detailed sense of both place and time. Baker also draws an unusually ambiguous performance from John Mills as the psychologically troubled central character who is accused of murder.

Much of Baker's work over the next five years was relatively routine, but the success of his Second World War submarine drama *Morning Departure* (1950) was to take him briefly to Hollywood. Traversing familiar territory for the British war film, *Morning Departure* features a cast of stalwart heroic types (John Mills, Richard ATTENBOROUGH, Nigel Patrick) trying to remain calm while faced with the possibility that they won't be rescued from their disabled submarine. Baker intensifies the sense of impending doom with his understated handling, a technique that was to serve him well again on *A Night to Remember* (1958). He returned to Britain in 1955 having made three American films and quickly re-established himself as a consistently reliable director of mainstream fare. *Tiger in the Smoke* (1956) is a thriller marked by the same unnerving mood as *The October Man*, while *The One That Got Away* (1957) presents the real-life story of German POW Franz Von Werra, who repeatedly escaped from British hands, in an exciting and sympathetic manner. Most memorable of his 1950s output is *A Night to Remember*. Overshadowed by James Cameron's Hollywood retelling of the *Titanic* disaster, what Baker's version lacks in CGI effects it more than makes up for in documentary-style realism and strong characterisations. Painstaking authenticity and sober naturalism are the order of the day here.

The influence of the New Wave and the 'social problem' film is apparent in the topical *Flame in the Streets* (1961), centring on a union activist (John Mills again) who has to confront his own prejudices when his daughter wants to marry a black man. The film may look dated now, but was a sincere attempt to address the changing ethnic structures of British society. More fascinating is *The Singer Not the Song* (1960), a project which Baker apparently loathed, but which is startling both for its borrowings from the western genre and for its fairly blatant foregrounding of Dirk Bogarde as an iconic gay figure. His appearance in skintight black leather is more than enough to turn the head of John Mills's repressed Catholic priest.

From the early 1960s Baker began to work on television and directed a number of episodes for some of the most popular and influential adventure series of the period, including *The Avengers*, *The Saint*, *The Champions* and *Randall and Hopkirk (Deceased)*. He also began the forays into the horror genre which were to become the distinctive feature of his later cinema work. His first assignment for Hammer was the third – and most ambitious – in the Quatermass series, *Quatermass and the Pit* (1967). Making full use of its eerie setting in the London underground, the film combines elements of science fiction and the occult, building to a startling conclusion as 'the devil' rises into the sky over London. Further horror films were to follow, making him a key figure in Britain's Gothic film tradition. *The Vampire Lovers* (1970) is one of a number of early 1970s Hammer entries which combine female vampires and lesbianism into a headily decadent brew. *Dr Jekyll and Sister Hyde* (1971) offers a bizarrely original twist on familiar material as the doctor now transforms himself into a young woman who murders prostitutes. For Hammer's rivals Amicus, Baker helmed one of their best portmanteau collections of sting-in-the-tail short stories, *Asylum* (1972). The darkly comic tone typical of Amicus is also apparent in his Hammer production *The Anniversary* (1968), featuring a resplendent Bette Davis sporting an eye-patch and holding dominion over her quivering adult sons with a barrage of one-liners and insults. Grotesque and theatrical as the film is, its unique style set the seal on Baker's ability to bring originality, wit and panache to the genre. The cult status which these films lent him is, however, stretched to breaking point in the cheap opportunism of *The Legend of the Seven Golden Vampires* (1974), which farcically mixes horror with Kung Fu action, and in such low-rent Hammer fillers as *Scars of Dracula* (1970).

Baker returned for the last time to the horror genre with *The Monster Club* (1980) which, like his Amicus films, offers a compendium of three ghoulish short stories and adopts a similarly tongue-in-cheek approach. The last active years of his career were spent in television where he continued to provide a reliable hand with populist dramas such as *The Flame Trees of Thika*, *The Irish R.M.* and *Minder*. Shifts in critical taste have seen Baker's reputation change radically from that of efficient studio craftsman to near cult status as a genre stylist. His best work certainly shows that he was able to lift routine material well beyond its intrinsic merits with economy and style.

**British Feature Films:** *The October Man* (1947); *The Weaker Sex* (1948); *Paper Orchid* (1949); *Highly Dangerous* (1950); *Morning Departure* (1950); *The House in the Square* (1951); *Passage Home* (1955); *Tiger in the Smoke* (1956); *Jacqueline* (1956); *The One That Got Away* (1957); *A Night to Remember* (1958); *The Singer Not the Song* (1960); *Flame in the Streets* (1961); *The Valiant* (1962); *Two Left Feet* (1963); *Quatermass and the Pit* (1967); *The Anniversary* (1968); *Moon Zero Two* (1969); *The Vampire Lovers* (1970); *Scars of Dracula* (1970); *Dr Jekyll and Sister Hyde* (1971); *Asylum* (1972); *Vault of Horror* (1973); *And Now the Screaming Starts!* (1973); *The Legend of the Seven Golden Vampires* (1974); *The Monster Club* (1980).

**Bibliography:** Geoff Mayer, *Roy Ward Baker* (Manchester: Manchester University Press, 2004); Roy Ward Baker, *The Director's Cut* (London: Reynolds & Hearn, 2000).

## For Joy BATCHELOR, see John HALAS

## John BAXTER

John Baxter's reputation as a director rests largely on the films he made during the 1930s and 1940s which, in contrast to much of the mainstream production of the period, show a consistent sympathy with, and understanding for, the economic plight of the working class. It is this theme, whether voiced through the comic traditions of the music hall or in the more sober terms of social realism, which has guaranteed his particular place in the history of British cinema.

Baxter was born in Kent in 1896 and worked initially as an agent and theatre manager before entering the film industry as an assistant director in 1932. His body of work as a director can be usefully divided into distinct groups. Firstly, there are the 'low' comedies which draw on his love of the music hall and which feature some of the key comic talents of the period. He directed Flanagan and Allen in four star vehicles, *We'll Smile Again* (1942), *Theatre Royal* (1943), *Dreaming* (1944) and *Here Comes the Sun* (1945), the much underrated Frank Randle in *When You Come Home* (1947) and Arthur Lucan (in his cross-dressing guise as the grotesque 'Old Mother Riley') in *Old Mother Riley in Society* (1940), *Old Mother Riley in Business* (1940), *Old Mother Riley's Ghosts* (1941) and *Old Mother Riley, Detective* (1943). Through his collaborations with these working-class comedians, Baxter was able to express his empathy with the downtrodden via a defiant good humour and down-to-earth bluntness.

More ambitious and politically direct are his social dramas, which often utilise a semi-documentary style, grounding their realism in sharply observed settings and characters. By common consent, the most memorable of these is *Love on the Dole* (1941). Based on Ronald Gow's stage adaptation of the popular Walter Greenwood novel, the film gets as close to an openly political statement on the human consequences of the 1930s depression as censorship would allow. Despite some naivety, it remained powerful enough to be an influence on the New Wave of the 1960s. His social commitment and strong sense of moral conscience is also apparent in less celebrated films such as *Doss House* (1933), *The Common Touch* (1941) and *The Shipbuilders* (1943).

Baxter was also a prolific producer, having first formed his own production company in 1935 with his colleague from theatre days, John Barter. As well as acting as producer on many of his own films, he also produced several films directed by his former assistant Lance COMFORT. He played a role in founding the National Film Finance Corporation (NFFC) in 1948 and in the 1950s became managing director of Group 3, a government-backed production venture whose first film, *Judgment Deferred* (1951), he produced and directed. His final film as director was the comedy western *Ramsbottom Rides Again* (1956) featuring another music hall stalwart, Arthur Askey. Baxter remains a somewhat unique figure of his time, whose continuing commitment to populist comedy and socially relevant drama made him a champion of working-class culture and a potent voice for the socially deprived. John Baxter died in London in 1975.

**British Feature Films:** *Doss House* (1933); *Song of the Plough* (1933);

*Say It with Flowers* (1934); *Lest We Forget* (1934); *Kentucky Minstrels* (1934); *Flood Tide* (1934); *Music Hall* (1934); *A Real Bloke* (1935); *The Small Man* (1935); *Jimmy Boy* (1935); *Birds of a Feather* (1935); *Men of Yesterday* (1936); *Hearts of Humanity* (1936); *Song of the Road* (1937); *The Academy Decides* (1937); *Talking Feet* (1937); *Stepping Toes* (1938); *Secret Journey* (1939); *What Would You Do, Chums?* (1939); *Laugh It Off* (1940); *Crook's Tour* (1940); *Old Mother Riley in Society* (1940); *Old Mother Riley in Business* (1940); *Old Mother Riley's Ghosts* (1941); *Love on the Dole* (1941); *The Common Touch* (1941); *Let the People Sing* (1942); *We'll Smile Again* (1942); *Theatre Royal* (1943); *Old Mother Riley, Detective* (1943); *Shipbuilders* (1943); *Dreaming* (1944); *Here Comes the Sun* (1945); *The Grand Escapade* (1946); *When You Come Home* (1947); *Fortune Lane* (1947); *Nothing Venture* (1948); *The Last Load* (1948); *Three Bags Full* (1949); *The Second Mate* (1950); *The Dragon of Pendragon Castle* (1950); *Judgment Deferred* (1951); *Ramsbottom Rides Again* (1956).

**Bibliography**: Geoff Brown with Tony Aldgate, *The Common Touch: The Films of John Baxter* (London: BFI, 1989).

## John BOORMAN

Among the first generation of British film directors to emerge from television, John Boorman has become one of the most distinguished and original British film-makers of the last forty years. Although some of his best work belongs to American cinema, his darkly romantic sensibility and fascination with the power of myth can be claimed as distinctly national tendencies. His inclination towards stylistic excess and metaphysical concerns has sometimes put him in conflict with an industry which has often preferred more conventional talents.

Born in Shepperton on 18 January 1933, Boorman moved into television after an early career which included working as a film critic for magazines and radio. He joined the BBC as an assistant editor in 1955, working at their documentary unit in Bristol, and eventually became Head of Documentaries (1960–4), establishing a reputation for innovation. His feature film debut came with *Catch Us If You Can* (1965), released in America as *Having a Wild Weekend*, an attempt to do for the Dave Clark Five what *A Hard Day's Night* (1964) had done for the Beatles. Despite the film's derivative nature, it already possessed a form of quest narrative which Boorman was to return to repeatedly, as well as offering a surprisingly disenchanted view of Swinging Britain. The film was a success in America, taking its young director to Hollywood where he made two striking films with the

American star Lee Marvin: the stylised thriller *Point Blank* (1967) and the anti-war parable *Hell in the Pacific* (1968). Both films show a concern with existential themes of humanity's inner violence, as well as an interest in formal experimentation through fragmented narrative and visual ambiguity.

Boorman returned to Britain for *Leo the Last* (1969), starting a pattern of moving between America and Britain that has continued throughout his career. It stars Marcello Mastroianni as an exiled European aristocrat living in London who is pulled out of his isolation by the plight of the community around him. The film shows Boorman's characteristic concern with outsiders and won him the Best Director award at Cannes. Back again in Hollywood he made his most celebrated film, *Deliverance* (1972), a further treatise on the brutality lying just beneath the civilised veneer of society. Returning to Britain, he made the idiosyncratic science-fantasy *Zardoz* (1973), where Sean Connery finds himself pitted against a coldly repressed, and repressive, social elite of the future. Boorman's highly personal dystopian vision shows the self-belief of a genuine auteur, but the film's quirkiness proved too much for some audiences and critics. Boorman's ability to combine the intellectual with the commercial was some way wide of the mark in his next American film, *Exorcist II: The Heretic* (1977), which pleased neither horror genre fans nor those who valued Boorman as an artistic film-maker.

He was on firmer ground with his next two British ventures, both of which give full expression to his romanticism. *Excalibur* (1981) is a bloody, visually arresting adaptation of the Arthurian legends. It presents a series of beautifully realised tableaux which bring to life an imagined Pre-Raphaelite idyll where characters such as Nicol Williamson's wonderfully eccentric Merlin are mystically attuned to their environment. *Hope and Glory* (1987) evokes another vanished world in its nostalgic vision of Boorman's childhood growing up during the Blitz. The film's tendency towards sentimentality is offset by its warmth and by Boorman's eye for surreal detail. Between these two films he made the big budget international film *The Emerald Forest* (1985) which explores similar themes in its depiction of youthful innocence and the power of environment. Here the Amazonian rain-forest replaces medieval England as a place of mystical enchantment. Boorman's battles with studio executives over the making of the film were chronicled in his 1985 book *Money into Light*.

*Where the Heart Is* (1990), a family drama with strong personal resonances for Boorman, was meant to be set in London, but diffi-culties with financing led to the film being shot in New York with American backing. The following years saw only the release of two short films, the autobiographical *I Dreamt I Woke Up* (1991), originally commissioned by the BBC, and *Two Nudes Bathing* (1995), filmed as one section of the compendium film *Picture Windows* and made for American television. He also contributed to *Lumière et Compagnie* (1996) in which leading international directors were asked to shoot a short sequence using only the kind of early camera operated by the Lumière Brothers. Boorman's next feature was the Hollywood production *Beyond Rangoon* (1995), set amid the political turmoil of contemporary Burma, which again dealt with the role of outsiders faced with a disorienting environment.

Having moved to Ireland in the mid-1970s, Boorman was appointed Chairman of the Board of the National Film Studios of Ireland in 1975 and was a member of the Irish Film Board from 1980 to 1982. He was executive producer on Neil JORDAN's debut *Angel* (1982). *The General* (1998) was shot in Ireland and is the best of Boorman's more recent work. In telling the story of the gangster Martin Cahill (Brendan Gleeson) the film has a similar tone to *Point Blank*, distancing the audience from its erstwhile hero through a fractured narrative and the use of black and white, but still presenting him as something of an outlaw hero. This affection for renegade figures is also apparent in his warmly appreciative documentary about his friend Lee Marvin, *Lee Marvin: A Personal Portrait by John Boorman* (1998). Boorman's most recent work has had a more international flavour, with the American-backed *The Tailor of Panama* (2001) featuring Pierce Brosnan cast against his James Bond persona in a coolly humorous adaptation of John Le Carré's spy novel, and *Country of My Skull* (2004), set in post-apartheid South Africa. Both attest to his liberal political sympathies.

Boorman has been the recipient of innumerable awards, including a British Film Academy Fellowship in 2004, Oscar nominations for *Deliverance* and *Hope and Glory* and a Best Director award at Cannes for *The General*. In a career that has zigzagged between Britain and America, Boorman's consistent fascination with mythic journeys into the dark heart of human experience, along with his willingness to make full use of the formal possibilities of the medium, place him among the most distinctive, creative British directors of his generation.

**British Feature Films:** *Catch Us If You Can* (1965); *Leo the Last* (1969); *Zardoz* (1973); *Excalibur* (1981); *The Emerald Forest* (1985); *Hope and Glory* (1987); *The General* (1998); *Country of My Skull* (2004).

**Bibliography:** John Boorman, *Adventures of a Suburban Boy* (London: Faber, 2003); Michel Ciment (translated by Gilbert Adair), *John*

*Boorman* (London: Faber, 1986); John Boorman, *Money into Light: The Emerald Forest: A Diary* (London: Faber, 1985).

## John and Roy BOULTING

British cinema has produced an unusually high number of writer/director/producer teams. Prominent among them is the thirty-six year partnership of twin brothers John and Roy Boulting. They usually alternated roles, with one brother producing while the other directed, but maintained sufficient consistency across their work together for each release to be recognised as a 'Boulting Brothers' film. A sense of social commitment was frequently the distinguishing feature of their films, whether in the sober realism of their early work or in the broad satire of their popular 1950s comedies.

The brothers were born at Bray in Buckinghamshire on 21 December 1913. Their left-leaning views were quickly apparent when John joined the International Brigade supporting the Republicans in Spain. Always highly independent, they established their own production company, Charter Films, in 1937. After making a number of short supporting features, their breakthrough came with *Pastor Hall* (1940), a powerful drama focusing on a German village pastor who dies resisting the rise of the Nazis. *Thunder Rock* (1942) had a similar political theme. Set in a lighthouse where Michael Redgrave tries unsuccessfully to escape the modern world, it adopted a stylised visual approach perfectly suited to its anti-isolationist allegory.

Both film-makers were enlisted to help the war effort, John joining the RAF Film Unit where he made the drama-documentary *Journey Together* (1945) and Roy working for the Army Film Unit where he made a number of outstanding documentaries, including the Oscar-winning *Desert Victory* (1943). Following the war, they produced a series of striking films dealing with the social unease and dislocation of postwar Britain. Most memorable of these is *Brighton Rock* (1947), adapted from Graham Greene's novel and featuring Richard Attenborough as the young gangster Pinkie. Within a crime genre format, it depicts a seedy Britain of race tracks, public houses and extortion rackets with atmospheric skill. Despite an ending softened from the book, the film is largely faithful to Greene's Catholic sensibility, retaining his concern for the nature of good and evil. Topical issues abound in their films of this period. *Fame is the Spur* (1947) deals evenhandedly with the disillusioning of a working-class Labour politician, again played by Michael Redgrave. *The Guinea Pig* (1948) examines the persistence of class prejudice in postwar Britain with its story of the first working-class boy (Richard Attenborough) to win a scholarship to an elite public school. They were often able to marry popular genre elements with a social message, so that *Seven Days to Noon* (1950) is a taught thriller which deals with the burgeoning anxieties of the nuclear age.

The distinctive engagement with contemporary concerns which marked their work of the late 1940s seemed to dissipate in the mid-1950s as they made a number of rather bland British-based films for Hollywood companies, including the service comedy *Seagulls over Sorrento* (1954), or American films such as *Run for the Sun* (1956). The most interesting film of this period is John's *The Magic Box* (1951), a rare example of the two working apart, which was made for the Festival of Britain. With stars cast in every role, it feels rather like a vaudeville spectacular, but Robert Donat managed to extract considerable pathos from depicting the tragic decline of film pioneer William Friese-Greene.

It is the group of social satires the Boultings made in the late 1950s and early 1960s on which their popular reputation rests. Using a format of broad farce and a plot structure which frequently places an innocent (usually played by Ian Carmichael) into the complexities of an arcane British institution, the films take pretty wide potshots at the more archaic, dated aspects of British life before the revolution of the 1960s arrived. Targets include higher education in *Lucky Jim* (1957), the army in *Private's Progress* (1956), the legal system in *Brothers in Law* (1957), the Foreign Office in *Carlton-Browne of the F.O.* (1958), the Anglican Church in *Heaven's Above!* (1963) and, most famously, trade unions and management in *I'm All Right Jack* (1959). The comic performances from Peter Sellers and Terry-Thomas are immensely appealing, and the films tapped into the mood which led to the 'satire boom' of the early 1960s. Less sympathetic critics have also pointed to the rather conventional soft centre at the heart of these satires, as well as to a surprisingly reactionary streak evident in the anti-union bias of *I'm All Right Jack*.

The Boultings seemed to lose their affinity with the mood of audiences in the 1960s and their later work shows a marked decline. *Rotten to the Core* (1965) was a fairly routine crime comedy and *The Family Way* (1966) an over-blown adaptation of Bill Naughton's play. An increasing heavy-handedness was apparent in the controversial psycho-thriller *Twisted Nerve* (1968), the modish comedy *There's a Girl in My Soup* (1970) and the crude farce *Soft Beds, Hard Battles* (1973). It was an undistinguished end to what had been an often impressive and influential career.

In retrospect, it is the stark, expressionist films of the late 1940s, with their strong political undercurrents, which impress more than the slightly ineffectual satires of the 1950s. The Boultings' reputation suffered considerable neglect, particularly during their declining years, but has recently seen a more sustained attempt to reassess the importance of their work as film-makers who always tried to make socially relevant films. John died of cancer on 17 June 1985 at Sunningdale and was followed by his brother Roy on 5 November 2001 at Oxford, also of cancer.

**British Feature Films:**
**John as director** – *Journey Together* (1945); *Brighton Rock* (1947); *The Magic Box* (1951); *Private's Progress* (1956); *Lucky Jim* (1957); *I'm All Right Jack* (1959); *Rotten to the Core* (1965).

**Roy as director** – *Ripe Earth* (1938); *Consider Your Verdict* (1938); *The Landlady* (1938); *Seeing Stars* (1938); *Inquest* (1939); *Trunk Crime* (1939); *Pastor Hall* (1940); *Thunder Rock* (1942); *Fame Is the Spur* (1947); *The Guinea Pig* (1948); *High Treason* (1951); *Single-Handed* (1953); *Josephine and Men* (1955); *Happy Is the Bride* (1957); *Brothers in Law* (1957); *Carlton-Browne of the F.O.* (1958); *A French Mistress* (1960); *Twisted Nerve* (1968); *There's a Girl in My Soup* (1970); *Soft Beds, Hard Battles* (1973).

**Jointly directed** – *Seven Days to Noon* (1950); *Seagulls over Sorrento* (1954); *Suspect* (1960); *Heaven's Above!* (1963); *The Family Way* (1966).

**Bibliography**: Alan Burton, Tim O'Sullivan and Paul Wells (eds), *The Family Way: The Boulting Brothers and British Film Culture* (Trowbridge: Flicks Books, 2000); Brian McFarlane, *An Autobiography of British Cinema* (London: Methuen, 1977).

## Muriel BOX

In a male-dominated industry, Muriel Box stands out as one of the few women to have sustained a career as a feature film director. Born Muriel Baker in New Malden on the edge of London, 22 September 1905, she entered the industry in 1928 as a typist at British Instructional Films and followed a typical career path for many women in the industry at that time, moving on to work as a continuity girl and then script editor. In 1935 she married the playwright Sydney Box and they became an accomplished professional team, initially writing many short plays together and then making documentary shorts for Sydney's company, Verity Films, during the Second World War. They moved into independent feature production at Riverside Studios in 1943 and scored an enormous commercial success with *The Seventh Veil* (1945) which won them both an Oscar for Best Original Screenplay. When

Sydney took over as head at Gainsborough, with his sister Betty overseeing production at their Islington studio, Muriel ran Gainsborough's script department.

Although she had first directed while at Verity, her feature debut came with *The Happy Family* (1952). Over the next twelve years she directed more than a dozen feature films, making her Britain's most prolific female director. Contemporary (largely male) critics tended to be dismissive and condescending towards her work, but later feminist writers have found much to admire. Although sometimes lacking in obvious visual flair and often reliant on adaptations of stage work, the content of her films was often striking, with a tendency towards foregrounding relationships and viewing the battle between the sexes with an unsentimental, acerbic eye. This is most obvious in the satirical *Simon and Laura* (1955) which dismantles the false notions about marriage perpetrated by early television soap operas. *The Truth About Women* (1957), her own personal favourite among her films, and *Rattle of a Simple Man* (1964) are comedies which address the frustrated ambitions of women protagonists. Strong women are at the centre of both *Street Corner* (1953), which celebrates the achievements of women police officers in a semi-documentary style, and her adaptation of Somerset Maugham's *The Beachcomber* (1954) with Glynis Johns. The courage that she showed in her professional life, where she frequently encountered chauvinist hostility, is also apparent in her willingness to confront controversial issues, such as teenage abortion in *Too Young to Love* (1960).

Following the poor reception for *Rattle of a Simple Man* and her separation from Sydney, she abandoned film-making, although she never ceased to be an active spokesperson for the rights of women working in the industry. She continued to write novels and established the publishing company, Femina Books. She died in London on 18 May 1991. Whatever aesthetic limitations may be apparent in the films she directed, she created a distinctive body of work and provided a model of achievement for future generations of women directors like Sally POTTER and Lynne RAMSEY.

**British Feature Films:** *The Happy Family* (1952); *Street Corner* (1953); *To Dorothy a Son* (1954); *The Beachcomber* (1954); *Simon and Laura* (1955); *Eyewitness* (1956); *A Passionate Stranger* (1957); *The Truth About Women* (1957); *This Other Eden* (1959); *Subway in the Sky* (1959); *Too Young to Love* (1960); *The Piper's Tune* (1962); *Rattle of a Simple Man* (1964).

**Bibliography:** Caroline Merz, 'The Tension of Genre: Wendy Toye and Muriel Box', in Wheeler Winston Dixon (ed.), *Re-Viewing British Cinema, 1900–1992* (Albany, NY: State University of New York Press, 1994); Muriel Box, *Odd Woman Out* (London: Leslie Frewin, 1974).

## Danny BOYLE

Few contemporary British film-makers have made a more dynamic impact on the cultural scene than Danny Boyle did with his second feature, *Trainspotting* (1996). The opening images of Ewan McGregor running full-tilt towards the audience to the pulsating musical accompaniment of Iggy Pop seemed to mirror the energy which Boyle and his team brought to a newly buoyant industry in the mid-1990s. Born in Manchester on 20 October 1956, Boyle moved from the theatre (he was Artistic Director at the Royal Court 1982–7) to television in the late 1980s where he directed a range of projects from the popular *Inspector Morse* to the strikingly original BBC serial *Mr Wroe's Virgins* (1993) with Jonathan Pryce.

Teamed for the first time with producer Andrew Macdonald and writer John Hodge, Boyle made his feature-film debut with the stylish, brutal thriller *Shallow Grave* (1994). Making excellent use of its Edinburgh locations, the film unfolds a classically dark story of cross and double-cross as three yuppyish friends fall out over the suitcase full of cash which a now dead lodger has conveniently left in their flat. Boyle's considerable visual panache is apparent in the opening sequences as his camera takes a dizzying ride round Edinburgh's Georgian streets and there is a real freshness in the acting of his young cast, even if their greed and smugness, neatly caught in a montage where they systematically humiliate applicants for the vacant room in their flat, makes them less than sympathetic.

*Trainspotting* is undoubtedly one of the key British films of the 1990s, helped in no small part by shrewd marketing and an outstanding soundtrack. Adapted from Irvine Welsh's novel, the film is at pains to show both the agony and the ecstasy of the heroin user's lifestyle. The film freely mixes elements of realism with overt fantasy, not least in the sequence when Renton (Ewan McGregor) is forced to dive into a toilet bowl in a filthy public convenience to retrieve his drugs and then finds himself swimming in an imaginary blue sea. Young audiences responded to the film's energy and wit, along with its non-judgmental view of the drug subculture, but some critics found more than a whiff of Thatcherism in its celebration of self-interest, as well as a tendency to evade the genuine realities of its subject matter through humour and visual inventiveness.

The film's success took Boyle to America where he made *A Life Less Ordinary* (1997), a romantic comedy again starring Ewan McGregor, this time opposite Cameron Diaz. Neither this or *The Beach* (2000), an adaptation of Alex Garland's novel turned into a vehicle for heart-throb Leonardo Di Caprio, showed anything like the conviction of their two previous British films. Boyle doesn't appear to have enjoyed the experience of helming a Hollywood blockbuster and his next two projects were small-scale productions for the BBC, *Vacuuming Completely Nude in Paradise* (2001) and *Strumpet* (2001), both written by Jim Cartwright. A pleasing commitment to less ostentatious, home-grown projects is also evident in his taking the role of producer on the Welsh *Trainspotting*, the Swansea-set *Twin Town* (1997) and on Alan Clark's memorable Northern Ireland television film *Elephant* (1989).

*Alien Love Triangle* started life as a thirty-minute episode in a three-part portmanteau film, but in the end John Hodge's script provided enough for a full feature. A modest enough science-fiction comedy featuring Kenneth BRANAGH and Courtenay Cox, the film is a deal better than its production history might suggest. Something nearer to a full return to form is apparent in *28 Days Later* (2002), an angsty horror film in the mode of George A. Romero's zombie shockers, which imagines a Britain decimated by a mystery virus. The opening scenes, reminiscent of *Day of the Triffids*, create real tension in their depiction of an eerily empty London. In complete contrast, *Millions* (2004) is a children's entertainment whose story unfolds like a benign version of *Shallow Grave* as two young boys find themselves with only a week to spend the loot from a robbery which they have discovered, learning some lessons about altruism along the way which wouldn't have gone amiss on *Shallow Grave*'s protagonists. The zest and invention in Boyle's work should mean that he remains a lively talent to watch in the future.

**British Feature Films:** *Shallow Grave* (1994); *Trainspotting* (1996); *Alien Love Triangle* (2002); *28 Days Later* (2002); *Millions* (2004).

## Kenneth BRANAGH

If for nothing else, Kenneth Branagh has a place in British cinema history for his unswerving commitment to reviving Shakespeare on film and in trying to bring his work to a wider audience. Rather in the mould of a traditional actor-manager, Branagh's standing rests equally on his career as an actor as it does as a director, with the two roles frequently dovetailing. He was born to a working-class Belfast family on 10 December 1960 and during his childhood moved with them to Reading. He trained as an actor at RADA where he won the Bancroft Award and was the RSC's youngest ever Henry V at just 23. He had already had West End theatre success acting in *Another Country* (1982) and appeared in a number of television projects, most notably the popular series

*Fortunes of War* (1987). He formed the Renaissance Theatre Company in 1987 bringing together an ensemble including Richard Briers and Derek Jacobi who would go on to appear in his films.

His film version of *Henry V* (1989) established a pattern for much of his subsequent work, with Branagh directing, taking the lead role and adapting the text himself. He succeeded admirably in his objective of broadening the play's popular appeal as evidenced by its comparative box-office success and positive critical reception. Here his strategy takes the form of adopting a semi-realist tone, particularly for the mud-caked battle scenes, and by emphasising the vulnerability of the warrior king as much as his strength. For *Much Ado About Nothing* (1993) he keeps the audience happy with a starry cast, including such Hollywood luminaries as Keanu Reeves and Denzel Washington, and through its sun-drenched Tuscany locations. The play is treated as light romantic comedy, with Branagh playing on the press coverage of his marriage by appearing opposite his then wife, Emma Thompson. Between these films he made a touching short, *Swan Song* (1992), with John Gielgud as an actor recalling a life devoted to the theatre, his American directing debut with *Dead Again* (1991), a noirish pastiche of 1940s Hollywood crime melodramas again featuring himself and Emma Thompson, and *Peter's Friends* (1992), a rather smug ensemble piece about a group of thirty-something friends gathering for a reunion.

Branagh's fondness for rushing camerawork is much in evidence in *Mary Shelley's Frankenstein* (1994), a heavy-handed adaptation of the familiar story which, despite a sympathetic performance from Robert De Niro as the creature, didn't replicate the broad appeal of his earlier Shakespeare films. *In the Bleak Midwinter* (1995) returned Branagh to a theatrical setting with its story of an amateur production of *Hamlet*. The film is untypically low key, but its air of understatement lends it considerable charm. His own version of *Hamlet* (1996), by contrast, is his most ambitious project to date. Eschewing the temptation to soften the play for a more commercial audience, Branagh retains every line of verse in this four-hour version and sets it during the Franco-Prussian War. The film is visually striking, particularly in its set designs and in Branagh's own physical appearance, although consistent to form the cast is littered with Hollywood notables from Charlton Heston to Robin Williams. He took a much freer hand with *Love's Labour's Lost* (2000), imagining the play as a 1930s Hollywood musical complete with song and dance numbers and slapstick humour. His cast copes rather unevenly with the variety of demands the film makes on them, but this doesn't detract from the energy and panache which Branagh brings to his subject.

The inevitable comparisons to Laurence OLIVIER are hard to

avoid and in any case seem justified considering the degree to which Branagh has sometimes wilfully followed in his footsteps. Both have taken a distinctly personal approach to filming Shakespeare and if Olivier's methods were rather more stately and theatrical, then Branagh's has been a more populist line, bringing a muscular brashness to material often treated more reverentially.

**British Feature Films:** *Henry V* (1989); *Peter's Friends* (1992); *Much Ado About Nothing* (1993); *Mary Shelley's Frankenstein* (1994); *In the Bleak Midwinter* (1995); *Hamlet* (1996); *Love's Labour's Lost* (2000).

**Bibliography:** Mark White, *Kenneth Branagh: A Life* (London: Faber, 2005); Kenneth Branagh, *Beginning* (London: Chatto & Windus, 1989).

## Nick BROOMFIELD

Nick Broomfield is one of a new generation of film-makers who have transformed audience expectations of the documentary form. Whereas documentarists once sought objectivity, Broomfield openly takes sides. Rather than remove himself from the picture, he directly intervenes, including himself within the frame virtually as a character in his own films. His confrontational approach often uses humour to engage and entertain the viewer and he is frequently drawn to controversial subject matter. Although his films have been successful, they have also provoked criticism from those who accuse him of being more interested in himself than the subject at hand.

Broomfield was born in London on 30 January 1948. He studied law at Cardiff University and then political science at Essex. His first short documentary, *Who Cares?* (1971), was made while he was still a student. With financial support from the BFI and filming on a wind-up Bolex camera, Broomfield depicts a working-class community in Liverpool threatened by slum clearance. The film's success took him to the National Film School where he made *Proud to Be British* (1973) and *Behind the Rent Strike* (1974), a kind of sequel to *Who Cares?* The latter won him the John Grierson Award, the first of many subsequent international prizes.

From 1976 Broomfield began to work with the American documentarist Joan Churchill. His previous work had been built on his personal affinity for his subjects, portrayed with some sympathy. Working with Churchill, Broomfield moved to a more observational, although no less confrontational, mode. *Juvenile Liaison* (1975) landed him in the first of many controversies. Its shocking depiction of two police officers and their harsh treatment of young offenders led to complaints from the police and the withdrawal of the film by its backers, the BFI. Perhaps as a result, Broomfield and Churchill decamped to America where he has largely worked since. His sympathy for outsiders is apparent again in the depiction of life in a Nevada brothel, *Chicken Ranch* (1983).

After parting from Churchill in the mid-1980s, Broomfield began to develop a more overtly interventionist style. A number of influential documentarist have argued that only by placing the film-maker themselves in front of the camera can a degree of transparency be achieved in the documentary form. Broomfield, like Michael Moore, has taken this to an extreme, creating an on-screen persona as a slightly bemused, naive figure whose apparent innocence is frequently used as a device to lull his subjects into a false sense of security, therefore making them more likely to make some unfortunate gaffe. This is seen to great affect in *The Leader, His Driver and the Driver's Wife* (1991) in which the South African neo-Nazi Eugene Terreblanche is given every opportunity to expose his racist views and duly obliges. He even managed to turn failure into success with *Tracking Down Maggie* (1994) where his inability to get anywhere near the ex-prime minister actually serves to reveal her state of isolation.

Most of his recent work has been American-based. Sex is the theme again in *Heidi Fleiss: Hollywood Madam* (1995) and *Fetishes* (1996), violence is at the centre of *Aileen Wuornos: The Selling of a Serial Killer* (1992) and its sequel *Aileen: Life and Death of a Serial Killer* (2003), the latter made with Joan Churchill, while *Kurt and Courtney* (1998) and *Biggie and Tupac* (2002) focus on celebrity and its darker consequences. Broomfield's films raise questions about the role of the documentary film-maker, bringing into focus debates about objectivity and the status of the film-maker as a celebrity in their own right. Although, his second film about Aileen Wuornos seemed to reveal a greater self-awareness of his own ability to manipulate and be manipulated. His only pure fiction film to date, *Diamond Skulls* (1989), a comedy of misdeeds in high places, was a considerable disappointment.

**British Feature Films:** *Juvenile Liaison* (1975, co-directed with Joan Churchill); *Diamond Skulls* (1989); *Juvenile Liaison 2* (1990, co-directed with Joan Churchill); *The Leader, His Driver and the Driver's Wife* (1991); *Tracking Down Maggie* (1994).

**Bibliography:** Stella Bruzzi, *New Documentary: A Critical Introduction* (London: Routledge, 2000).

## Donald CAMMELL

Few careers in British cinema have promised so much but ended in such tragic disappointment as that of Donald Cammell. Whether through his own intransigence or the shortsightedness of an industry which failed to appreciate his unusual gifts, Cammell's reputation still rests largely on the achievements of just one remarkable film, *Performance* (1970). Cammell was born in Edinburgh, on 17 January 1934, the son of Charles Richard Cammell, heir to a shipbuilding fortune which had been lost in the stock market crash of the 1930s. Prodigiously gifted as a painter, he trained at the Royal Academy and then established himself as a successful portrait painter to fashionable London society in the 1950s. He entered the film industry as a scriptwriter with two unremarkable Swinging London caper films, *The Touchables* (1968) and *Duffy* (1968), both of which deal with the intersection between gangsters and hippie-dom, a theme that was to be central to *Performance*.

Cammell's script for *Performance* drew on his experience of the Chelsea set, a world where gangsters partied alongside pop stars and the aristocracy. The film's experienced cinematographer, Nicolas ROEG, was asked to co-direct with Cammel to reassure its American backers, Warner Brothers. Its story of the encounter between a jaded rock star (Mick Jagger) and a brutal gangster (James Fox) provides the framework for a dazzling examination of the nature of identity, as the repressed Fox gradually unravels under the influence of sex, drugs and rock 'n' roll. Its blurring of the boundaries of sexuality and gender made it the perfect film to express the ethos of Britain's burgeoning counter-culture. The film is also a stylistic tour de force, even if its innovative editing methods were devised principally to get its controversial material past the censor. Its subsequent cult status owes much to the mythology which surrounded the film, with tales of debauchery on set and the consequent breakdown and religious conversion of James Fox.

Basing himself in Hollywood, Cammell was only able to complete a further three feature films over the next twenty-five years. *Demon Seed* (1977) is an inventive, but slightly farcical science fantasy in which a woman (Julie Christie) is impregnated by a computer. *White of the Eye* (1987) is a visually arresting psychological horror exhibiting rather more of the cinematic invention which Cammell had shown on *Performance*. His last feature film, *Wild Side* (1995), was intended as another complex exploration of sexuality and violence, but was so rearranged by its producers that Cammell had his name removed from the credits. He was used to such treatment, having experienced Warner Brothers' attempts to suppress and re-edit *Performance*. *Wild Side* was eventually released in a 'director's cut' version after his collaborator on *Performance*, Frank Mazzola, had re-cut it to more closely reflect Cammell's original intentions. Leaving just these four films as his cinematic legacy, Cammel shot himself and died on 24 April 1996 in Los Angeles. The BBC's superb documentary *Donald Cammell: The Ultimate Performance* provides a vivid portrait of a unique talent unfulfilled.

**British Feature Films**: *Performance* (1970, co-directed with Nicolas Roeg).

**Bibliography**: Jon Savage, '*Performance*: Interview with Donald Cammell', in Steve Chibnall and Robert Murphy (eds), *British Crime Cinema* (London: Routledge, 1999); Colin MacCabe, *Performance* (London: BFI, 1998).

## Alberto CAVALCANTI

If any director's career might serve to prove that there is more to British cinema than gritty realism and cosy comedies, it might be the extraordinarily varied output of Alberto Cavalcanti. Whether making propaganda documentaries or working for mainstream studios handling genre material, Cavalcanti brought a genuinely original sensibility to his work, with an eye (and ear) for unsettling detail. His films have an individuality of expression which marks him out as a unique figure, as well as being a pioneer of art cinema in Britain.

Born in Rio de Janeiro on 6 February 1897, he left Brazil to study architecture and interior design in Geneva. He entered films as a set designer in Paris where he quickly became part of the burgeoning cinematic avant-garde. He had directed more than a dozen films when he was brought to Britain to join the GPO Film Unit by its head, John Grierson, in 1934. Grierson had been particularly impressed by *Rien que les Heures* (1926), an impressionistic 'city symphony' documentary. He worked in a remarkable range of capacities at the GPO including art director, editor and sound supervisor, as well as director, before taking over management of the unit on Grierson's departure in 1937. He produced Humphrey JENNINGS' *Spare Time* (1939) and was the key influence on the groundbreaking *Night Mail* (1936), as well as directing *Pett and Pott* (1934) and *Coal Face* (1935). These short films pushed beyond Grierson's concern with the educational possibilities of documentary, to develop a more fully artistic approach which combined sound (including the reading of poetry and the innovative use of music) with striking imagery. He paved the way for poetic documentary film-makers like JENNINGS and established an approach to the form that was to be influential internationally.

It was logical enough that he should move to Ealing in 1940, a studio which was pioneering the use of documentary techniques to add realism to its wartime propaganda dramas. Nonetheless, Cavalcanti's liking for the surreal is still apparent in *Went the Day Well?* (1942). From a story by Graham Greene, the film successfully conveys its message of the need for vigilance, but the startling violence of the film's final battle between the villagers and the German soldiers who have invaded this peaceful corner of England haunts the mind and suggests a wider concern with the brutality lurking inside everyone. He worked on three further features for Ealing, all of which allowed him to move away from documentary naturalism. The musical *Champagne Charlie* (1944) brought an urbane sophistication and period sense to Ealing's output, while *Nicholas Nickleby* (1947) captured the darkness and grotesquery at the heart of Dickens's vision. Even more startling was his contribution to the port-manteau chiller *Dead of Night* (1945), where the well-worn story of a ventriloquist's dummy coming to life is invested with a disturbing sense of the uncanny. Michael Redgrave's performance convincingly conveys the interior world of man rapidly losing his grasp on reality. Behind the scenes, Cavalcanti was central in assisting Michael Balcon in establishing Ealing's characteristic style. He also helped to foster the roster of young talent which blossomed at the company in the 1940s and 1950s.

Away from Ealing, he made three other British feature films. Although *The First Gentleman* (1948) and *For Them That Trespass* (1948) are relatively unremarkable, *They Made Me a Fugitive* (1947) was a landmark film. It helped to establish the popular, although critically derided, cycle of lurid postwar crime films, but has con-siderable artistic merit too. Although working with fairly routine genre material, Cavalcanti brings to the film his interest in combining surface realism with the evocation of subjective states of mind, so that we increasingly share the central character's skewed view of a Britain lost to black marketeering, violence and corruption.

Cavalcanti returned to Brazil in 1950 to help bolster its developing film industry, but subsequently returned again to Europe where he worked in a number of countries, including a brief return to Britain where he made the animated film *The Monster of Highgate Ponds* (1960). He also spent a period teaching in the States. He died in Paris in 1982. Cavalcanti's British work defied many of the edicts which have dominated British cinema. His work frequently combines a naturalistic depiction of the everyday with a concern for the creative imagination, a combination rare in British cinema of the 1940s. His influence was immense, not just in paving the way for later maverick film-makers, but also in helping to shape the output of the documentary movement and of Ealing Studios. He remains one of the most creative and unsung British film-makers.

**British Feature Films**: *Went the Day Well?* (1942); *Champagne Charlie* (1944); *Dead of Night* (1945, one segment); *Nicholas Nickleby* (1947); *They Made Me a Fugitive* (1947); *The First Gentleman* (1948); *For Them That Trespass* (1948).

**Bibliography**: Ian Aitken, *Alberto Cavalcanti: Realism, Surrealism and National Cinemas* (Trowbridge: Flicks Books, 2000).

## Gurinder CHADHA

Born in Kenya in 1960, Gurinder Chadha moved with her parents to Southall in London in 1961. After studying at the University of East Anglia, she became a broadcast journalist with BBC Radio. Her first film was the remarkable documentary short *I'm British But . . .* (1989), funded under the BFI's New Directors scheme. It captures beautifully the complexities of contemporary multicultural Britain through its interviews with four young British Asians, one each from England, Scotland, Northern Ireland and Wales, who display a dizzying variety of accents and interpretations of their own cultural identity. During the 1990s she continued to make documentaries for television, including *Acting Our Age* (1991) which looked at the experiences of elderly Asians living in Southall, as well as short drama films such as *A Nice Arrangement* (1990) which portrays a British-Asian family on the morning of their daughter's wedding. The latter was selected for Critic's Week at the Cannes Festival.

Her first feature film, co-scripted with Meera Syal, was the engaging *Bhaji on the Beach* (1993). The film contains many of the characteristics typical of her work, focusing on the British-Asian community and in particular the lives of a group of women. It combines serious drama that deals with topical issues (such as interracial relationships and marital violence) with comedy. The sympathetic characterisations and strong performances, along with an acute eye for the hybrid details thrown up by the collision of different ethnic groups in modern Britain (typified by the film's title), make for an original and successful mix. Following a two-part drama for the BBC, *Rich Deceiver* (1995), she made her American debut with *What's Cooking* (2000), a film which demonstrates her continuing fascination for the clash of differing cultures, taking in the Thanksgiving celebrations of four families, one Vietnamese, one

Jewish, one African-American and one Latino. Returning to Britain she scored a major commercial and critical success with *Bend It Like Beckham* (2002). With considerable warmth and good humour, the film charts the aspirations of an Asian girl who wants to be taken seriously as a football player. Along the way, it unfolds the fractured nature of modern British identities, whether in terms of ethnicity, sexuality or gender. The film clearly hit a nerve with British audiences who recognised in it a sharply focused image of their own changing communities.

*Bride and Prejudice* (2004) is a joyful and irreverent retelling of Jane Austen in the form of a Bollywood musical. Handled with a real lightness of touch, and benefiting from a highly effective score, it manages to retain something of Austen's satirical intent alongside the colour and vivacity of Bollywood. In combining gentle humour with contemporary issues, Chadha's films may take the risk of sugaring the pill, but the accurate detail of her observation is sharp enough to convince most audiences that what they are seeing is an astute reflection of an evolving nation.

**British Feature Films:** *Bhaji on the Beach* (1993); *Bend It Like Beckham* (2002); *Bride and Prejudice* (2004).

## Alan CLARKE

British cinema has been distinguished by its long tradition of documentary realism, films that deal with the here and now of British society in a naturalistic manner. Few film-makers have followed this path with such unsparing relentlessness as Alan Clarke. Clarke's films look unblinkingly at the realities of modern British life, revealing uncomfortable areas which many would rather not see, depicting them with a coolness and detachment that never offers easy answers.

Clarke was born in Liverpool on 28 October 1935. Following National Service and a stint as an insurance clerk, he emigrated to Canada at the age of twenty-one and took up gold mining. From 1958 he studied radio and television arts at the Ryerson Institute in Toronto, before returning to England where he entered television as a floor manager at Rediffusion. He graduated to directing short dramas and in 1969 moved to the BBC where he worked for their established contemporary drama slots *The Wednesday Play* and *Play for Today*. In many ways television was Clarke's ideal medium, and much of his subsequent work was for the small screen, as it allowed him to address topical issues while reaching a broad domestic audience.

Clarke's characteristic television work deals with disenfranchised young males, alienated anti-heroes who resort to violence either as an act of rebellion against their environment or simply to survive. More disturbingly, this turn towards aggression is sometimes simply an expression of a more inherent brutality. The shocking revelations of borstal life contained in *Scum* (1977) led to a ban by the BBC. Remade as a cinema film in 1979, the big-screen version retains the powerful performance of a young Ray Winstone, but coarsens the violence to such a degree that the film verges on the exploitative. *Made in Britain* (1983), broadcast by ITV, is a coruscating portrait of casual fascism. Tim Roth brilliantly portrays the intelligent skinhead, Trevor, who is drawn into violent racism by a society that can find little use for him. The programme featured extensive use of steadicam, allowing Clarke to shoot long takes which add to the sense of disorientating intensity. *The Firm* (1989), made back at the BBC, startled audiences by suggesting that football hooligans could be respectable middle-class young men like the character portrayed here by Gary Oldman (another remarkable performance). The drama explicitly links the hooligan's view of violence as entertainment with the Thatcher regime's promotion of self-interest. All three television productions are stark, uncompromising and avoid offering any easy solutions to the social problems they expose.

Clarke's other cinema features are surprisingly tame by comparison. *Billy the Kid and the Green Baize Vampire* (1985) is a quirky musical comedy set in the world of snooker which never really gels and was a box office disaster. *Rita, Sue and Bob Too* (1986), although relatively lightweight, was much more successful. Its story of a council estate lothario and his love affairs adopts a humorous approach, but still conveys both the bleakness of life on the estate and the boisterous energy of characters who survive the best way they can.

Before his premature death from cancer in 1990, he began to move towards an increasingly pared down, minimalist style offering even less in the way of obvious points of sympathy or connection for the audience. This is apparent in the depiction of drug dealing in *Christine* (1987, BBC), but even more striking in *Elephant* (1989, BBC) which was given a limited art house cinema release. It is Clarke's most extreme work: running for thirty-five minutes with barely any dialogue, it presents a series of random assassinations. Although the setting is Northern Ireland, this provides no real context for what we see. Instead we are presented with a savage, surreal meditation on the pointless brutality of human beings – a depressing, but fittingly powerful finish to Clarke's short but invaluable career.

**British Feature Films:** *Scum* (1979); *Billy the Kid and the Green Baize Vampire* (1985); *Rita, Sue and Bob Too* (1986).

**Bibliography:** Richard Kelly (ed.), *Alan Clarke* (London: Faber, 1998).

# Jack CLAYTON

Jack Clayton's eclectic career tends to defy easy categorisation, which may account for the fact that he has rarely been accorded auteur status. However, his dedication to his craft made him a director admired by other film-makers, including John Huston, and the obvious quality of his best work has led to a gradual reassessment of his status as a film-maker of some distinction.

He was born in Brighton on 1 March 1921 and first entered the film industry as a child actor in *Dark Red Roses* (1929). In the 1930s he worked his way up through the ranks of Korda's London Films starting as third assistant director. During the war he worked for the RAF Film Unit, making his directing debut with the short documentary *Naples is a Battlefield* (1944). Returning to the commercial industry, he continued to work in a variety of capacities throughout the 1950s, although increasingly in the role of associate producer. He returned to direction with the short film *The Bespoke Overcoat* (1955), adapted from a Gogol short story, which won a number of international prizes including an Oscar.

Few British directors have made more impact with their feature debut than Clayton did with *Room at the Top* (1959). The film was groundbreaking in its blunt depiction of the British class system and in its sexual frankness, the latter an obvious factor in its enormous commercial success. Adapted from John Braine's novel, the central character, Joe Lampton (Laurence Harvey), became an iconic figure of the time, determinedly fighting his way up the social pecking order at considerable cost to himself and others. In retrospect the film looks decidedly compromised, not least in the uncomfortable casting of Harvey, but nonetheless was key in paving the way for the social realism of the British New Wave.

Clayton clearly had no particular commitment to the 'kitchen sink' ethos and his subsequent films are much more overtly crafted and stylised. *The Innocents* (1961) began a loose trilogy of films concerned with the family. Adapted from Henry James's *The Turn of the Screw*, it is probably Clayton's finest film. With its subtle evocation of period and its claustrophobic interiors, the film treads a fine line between conventional ghost story and a psychological tale of repression; the ghosts seen by the governess (Deborah Kerr) can be explained as a manifestation of her own mental state. The disintegration of a marriage is at the centre of *The Pumpkin Eater* (1964), adapted by Harold Pinter from Penelope Mortimer's novel. The film adopts a fragmented narrative structure, but is still tightly controlled by Clayton and has memorable performances, particularly from Anne Bancroft. The last of the 'trilogy' was the least successful, but is also the most individual.

*Our Mother's House* (1967) adopts a suitably gothic tone for its melodramatic story. The focus here shifts to the children who are determined to keep their household going despite the death of their mother and the return of their errant father (Dirk Bogarde).

Clayton moved to Hollywood in the 1970s where he made two more literary adaptations. He was probably asking for trouble in filming Scott Fitzgerald's much-loved masterpiece *The Great Gatsby* (1974), but he must have been taken aback by the critical mauling it received. Francis Ford Coppola's script is actually meticulously close to the book and Clayton stages the drama with great attention to detail. *Something Wicked This Way Comes* (1983) was adapted from Ray Bradbury's novel and partially succeeds in capturing a teenager's sense of dislocation, but its backers, Disney, prevented the film from being as darkly macabre as it should have been.

Clayton returned to Britain to film Brian Moore's novel *The Lonely Passion of Judith Hearne* (1987), which won considerable plaudits for its central performances from Maggie Smith and Bob Hoskins, and the television film *Memento Mori* (1992) made for the BBC. Both are low-key and melancholy meditations on ageing and isolation. Clayton's output was relatively small, but there is an attention to form and a concern for the destructive nature of relationships which is evident in the visual polish and the seriousness of these films. Clayton died on 25 February 1995.

**British Feature Films:** *Room at the Top* (1959); *The Innocents* (1961); *The Pumpkin Eater* (1964); *Our Mother's House* (1967); *The Lonely Passion of Judith Hearne* (1987).

**Bibliography:** Neil Sinyard, *Jack Clayton* (Manchester: Manchester University Press, 2000).

## Jill CRAIGIE

In a persistently male-dominated industry, Jill Craigie stands out not just as one of the first female directors to work in British cinema, but as that rare thing, an openly politically committed film-maker. Her body of work, mainly in documentaries, is relatively small, but her influence has been considerable.

She was born on 7 March 1914 in London of Scottish-Russian parentage. She worked initially as a journalist, first entering films in the late 1930s as an actress. Increasingly politicised, she began to script documentaries for the British Council in the early 1940s. She moved into commercial cinema when she co-scripted the patriotic *The Flemish Farm* (1943) for her then husband, the director Jeffrey Dell. The film was made for Two Cities who also financed her debut as a director, the short documentary *Out of Chaos* (1944) which looks at the work of war artists such as Henry Moore and Paul Nash. This was followed by another documentary, *The Way We Live* (1946), which portrayed a family in war damaged Plymouth trying, like the city itself, to rebuild their lives. It was while making this film that she met the Labour politician and later leader of the Party, Michael Foot, who was to become her third husband and life partner. The film's theme was continued in *Children of the Ruins* (1948) which follows the work of UNESCO in improving the lives of war-displaced children.

Her most important film is the feature length docu-drama *Blue Scar* (1949), a landmark film in the development of Welsh cinema. In retrospect, the film's depiction of life in a South Wales mining community is compromised by the demands of distributors for audience-pleasing entertainment values. The film is strongest in its location-shot sequences in South Wales which have a feeling of authenticity aided by the non-professional cast, but the romantic narrative and unconvincing London scenes tend to undermine the film's socialist and feminist leanings. To some extent, simply getting the film made at all was the major achievement. Her next film, the documentary short *To Be a Woman* (1951), is in many ways a more trenchant film, making a powerful case for equal opportunities for women.

Worn down by the narrow-minded attitudes of the industry towards women directors, she returned to scriptwriting in the 1950s. Unfortunately, *The Million Pound Note* (1953) and *Windom's Way* (1957), both directed by Ronald NEAME for Rank, have only the faintest hints of Craigie's political commitment within their conventional storylines. Although she then retired from film-making, she was to make a final return with *Two Hours from London* (1995), a self-financed film about the deteriorating situation in Yugoslavia which was screened by the BBC. In her later years she became a renowned expert on the history of the suffragette movement, as well as supporting her husband in his political career. She died in London on 13 December 1999.

**British Feature Films:** *Blue Scar* (1949).

## Charles CRICHTON

Charles Crichton's place in British cinema history is assured on the basis of three films, *Hue and Cry* (1946), *The Lavender Hill Mob* (1951) and *The Titfield Thunderbolt* (1953), which together form a central plank of the well-loved series of Ealing comedies. He may have lacked the individuality and dark edge of Ealing's finest comedy directors such as Alexander MACKENDRICK and Robert HAMER, but he remained the consummate professional, maintaining a solid level of craftsmanship over a career that stretched from the 1930s to the 1990s.

Charles Crichton was born in Wallasey, Cheshire on 6 August 1910. After studying history at Oxford, he joined Alexander Korda's London Films in 1932 where he trained as an editor. He worked on a number of Korda's most prestigious productions including *The Private Life of Henry VIII* (1933), *Sanders of the River* (1935) and *Things to Come* (1936). After a stint with the Crown Film Unit, where he made his debut as a director on the documentary short *The Young Veterans* (1942), he went to Ealing as an editor in the early 1940s. This was to be a crucial move for Crichton as he remained at the studio until 1957 and directed thirteen of his first fourteen films for them.

He fell in comfortably with Ealing's dominant mode of documentary-realism, making *For Those in Peril* (1944) about the Air-Sea Rescue Service and *Painted Boats* (1945) depicting life on the English canals. His contribution to the classic portmanteau chiller *Dead of Night* (1945) was, prophetically enough, its solitary comic episode intended as light relief. *Hue and Cry* was intrinsically a film of modest ambitions, but Crichton showed an ability to combine Ealing's characteristic surface realism with broad comedy, creating a winning format. The film is particularly memorable for its finale in which hordes of schoolboys swarm across London's bombsites to capture the villains who have been using the boys' favourite comic to pass coded messages. The film established a formula that became the basis for the Ealing comedies, perhaps the most enduringly popular and critically well-regarded comedies in British film history. *The Lavender Hill Mob* is quintessential Ealing comedy in its gently anarchic story of a shy bank clerk (Alec Guinness) who turns against the conventions of mundane English life by pulling off a gold bullion robbery. Despite the moral ending imposed by censorship, the film is a joyful celebration of mild-mannered subversion, handled with a loving attention to detail. Crichton's other comedies for Ealing, *Another Shore* (1948), *The Love Lottery* (1954) and particularly *The Titfield Thunderbolt*, typify the soft underbelly of Ealing where the love of whimsy easily drifts into cosy conformity.

Crichton's other work for Ealing is mainly routine, ranging across a variety of genres in a proficient but unremarkable manner. *Against the Wind* (1947) is an interestingly anti-heroic Second World War drama and *Dance Hall* (1950) has some vigour in its realism. The problem of war-displaced children is handled with sympathy in *The Divided Heart* (1954) and *Hunted* (1952), made for Rank, is a fairly tense thriller, but none of these films ranks with his best work. After Ealing's demise in 1959, his output was uneven with just a few hints of better days in the occasionally acid humour of *The Battle of the Sexes* (1959) and the sub-Ealing charm of *Law and Disorder* (1958). Sadly, he departed from *The Birdman of Alcatraz* (1961) after disagreements with its star/producer Burt Lancaster.

Most of Crichton's later work was done for television, including popular adventure series such as *The Avengers*, *Danger Man*, *Space 1999* and *The Professionals*. He finally ended up making corporate training videos which bizarrely led to his final flourish as a feature film director at the age of 78. His employer on these videos was Video Arts, a company owned by John Cleese, who subsequently invited Crichton to direct a script Cleese had written. *A Fish Called Wanda* (1988) was an enormous commercial and critical success, winning Crichton an Oscar nomination. It neatly combines Ealing-style warmth with a more Pythonesque black comedy. Crichton's skill with actors is evident in the skilful deployment of such varied performers as Kevin Kline, Michael Palin and Cleese himself, all of whom have rarely been better on film than they are here. It was a remarkably happy ending to Crichton's cinema career, although he continued to work in television into the 1990s. He died in London on 14 September 1999.

**British Feature Films:** *For Those in Peril* (1944); *Dead of Night* (1945, one segment); *Painted Boats* (1945); *Hue and Cry* (1946); *Against the Wind* (1947); *Another Shore* (1948); *Train of Events* (1949, one segment); *Dance Hall* (1950); *The Lavender Hill Mob* (1951); *Hunted* (1952); *The Titfield Thunderbolt* (1953); *The Love Lottery* (1954); *The Divided Heart* (1954); *The Man in the Sky* (1956); *Law and Disorder* (1958); *Floods of Fear* (1958); *The Battle of the Sexes* (1959); *The Boy Who Stole a Million* (1960); *The Third Secret* (1964); *He Who Rides a Tiger* (1965); *A Fish Called Wanda* (1988).

**Bibliography:** Charles Barr, *Ealing Studios* (London: David & Charles, 1977).

## Terence DAVIES

Terence Davies is one of the most distinctive talents to have emerged from British cinema in the last thirty years. His approach to film-making is the cinematic equivalent of literature's magic realism, in which a vivid recreation of the everyday world is fused with dreams and memories to produce a form of hyper-realism, reflecting both the external world and inner world of the film-maker. Along with directors like Bill DOUGLAS and Lynne RAMSEY, he has pushed the British tradition of social realism into whole new areas.

Born in Liverpool on 10 November 1945, Davies was the youngest of ten children (three of whom did not survive into adulthood) in a working-class, Catholic family. Leaving school at fifteen, he spent the next twelve years as a clerk in a shipping office and then in a firm of accountants. He took up amateur dramatics and joined Coventry Drama School in 1971. His first short film, *Children* (1976), was made with £8,500 from the BFI Production Board and on the strength of it he gained a place at the National Film School where he completed *Madonna and Child* (1980). After leaving film school, he made *Death and Transfiguration* (1983) with funding from the BFI and the Greater London Arts Association. Together these three short films form *The Terence Davies Trilogy* and were released as a feature under this name in 1984. The trilogy follows the life of the fictional Robert Tucker, although aspects of the films are clearly autobiographical. Many of Davies' characteristic themes are here: the legacy of an unhappy childhood and painful family life dominated by an oppressive, violent father and an intensely close relationship with the mother; the misery of being forced to cover-up homosexuality in a community living in fear of a stifling Catholicism which encourages feelings of guilt; sympathy for a central character who remains an outsider, ostracised at school and work. These themes are handled in a striking cinematic manner, with haunting black and white imagery and fluid, elliptical editing, the narrative moving backwards and forwards in time, capturing significant memory-moments like snapshots in a family album.

Similar themes and techniques run through his first two feature films, *Distant Voices, Still Lives* (1988) and *The Long Day Closes* (1992). The former again examines a family damaged by an unpredictable and brutal father, but also celebrates the warmth and vitality of working-class life, often expressed through song. The latter is a happier film, although the shadow of church and school still loom large. Escape is offered through the loving presence of Mam and through the magic of cinema. Although we never see the films which young Bud watches at the cinema, we hear them on the soundtrack which provides a collage of filmic references. In typical Davies manner, many shots are framed like tableaux and he uses extremely long takes to capture the beauty of the mundane, such as light passing through curtains, casting patterns on a carpet.

Davies' two most recent films have been made in America. *The Neon Bible* (1995), although set in the Deep South, has many familiar elements in its depiction of a lonely childhood. *The House of Mirth* (2000) is something of a departure in depicting an adult central character. Adapted from Edith Wharton's novel, it still focuses on an outsider, Lily Bart (Gillian Anderson), who has difficulty finding her place in the shallow world of American high society in the early years of the twentieth century. Although more conventional in technique, these films still make expressive use of colour, framing and camera movement to capture the protagonist's subjective viewpoint.

Although Davies' output over thirty years has been relatively small (obtaining funding has been a constant battle), he has created a highly personal body of work which combines consistent thematic concerns with a strikingly formalised visual vocabulary. The results have placed him at the forefront of British art cinema.

**British Feature Films:** *The Terence Davies Trilogy* (1984); *Distant Voices, Still Lives* (1988); *The Long Day Closes* (1992).

**Bibliography:** Wendy Everett, *Terence Davies* (Manchester: Manchester University Press, 2004).

## Basil DEAN

Basil Dean is a major figure in British film production of the 1930s. At least as important as a producer and studio executive, his output as a director only partially indicates his centrality to British cinema in that period. His career is one of the clearest examples of the influence of the theatre in the formation of British cinema, although his lasting reputation is more likely to be as the film-maker who most helped to bring the 'low' traditions of the music hall to the screen.

He was born in Croydon on 27 September 1888 and entered the theatre in 1906 as an actor, joining Manchester repertory company in 1907. He was appointed as the first director of Liverpool Repertory Theatre in 1911 and by the 1920s had established himself as one of the most successful producers in British theatre. It was the introduction of sound which first alerted Dean to the possibilities which cinema offered, although he seems to have viewed film as an adjunct to his theatrical projects. He founded Associated Talking Pictures (ATP) in 1929 to bring contemporary plays to a wider audience, effectively making him a founding father of the literary tradition in British cinema. He subsequently developed Ealing Studios as the first in Britain specifically designed for sound production.

The majority of the films Dean directed himself in the 1930s (as well as those he produced) tend to betray their theatrical origins. Both *The*

*Constant Nymph*, which he filmed twice (1928 and 1933), and *Autumn Crocus* (1934) had been earlier theatrical hits for him. His first film as director for ATP, *Escape* (1930), was based on a John Galsworthy play and his other work of the 1930s includes an adaptation of *Lorna Doone* (1934). Critics, and even some of his colleagues, have tended to be unflattering about his limitations as a film director, seeing him as too rooted in theatrical traditions to fully exploit the possibilities of the new medium, and this despite some striking use of location sequences in his films. Nonetheless, as a producer he had a good eye for future directorial talent, with Carol REED, David LEAN and Michael POWELL all getting a start with him.

His really lasting achievement of the 1930s was in finding a suitable format for bringing stars of the music hall, such as Gracie Fields and George Formby, to the screen. These stars proved immensely popular with audiences, offering them a slice of genuinely working-class humour and irreverence not seen previously in British cinema. Although he was more often producer, Dean himself directed Fields' most appealing vehicle, *Sing As We Go!* (1934). Set against a backdrop of social deprivation and industrial unrest, our Gracie manages to unite workers and management (albeit slightly unconvincingly), marching them off to a brighter future together with a jaunty song in their hearts. It's easy to be cynical about the political naivety of the film, but at the time it offered a reasonably authentic portrait of northern working-class life, as well as a good deal of heartfelt optimism. In the process he established an approach to production which combined entertainment values with a broadly realistic visual style, and which addressed the concerns of a specifically British audience, an ethos which was to be central to Ealing's future output.

By the end of the 1930s Dean had returned to his first love, the theatre, leaving Ealing in the capable hands of Michael Balcon. During the Second World War he became the founding director of ENSA which provided entertainment for servicemen and women throughout the War. He continued his theatre career into the 1970s. He was awarded the MBE in 1918 for his services to national entertainment in the First World War and in 1947 he received the CBE. He died of a heart attack on 22 April 1978.

**British Feature Films:** *The Constant Nymph* (1928, co-directed with Adrian Brunel); *Escape* (1930); *Birds of Prey* (1930); *The Impassive Footman* (1932); *Nine Till Six* (1932); *Looking on the Brightside* (1932); *The Constant Nymph* (1933); *Loyalties* (1933); *Autumn Crocus* (1934); *Sing As We Go!* (1934); *Lorna Doone* (1934); *Look Up and Laugh*

(1935); *Whom the God's Love* (1936); *The Show Goes On* (1937); *21 Days* (1937).

**Bibliography:** Rachel Low, *Film Making in 1930s Britain* (London: Allen & Unwin, 1985); Basil Dean, *Mind's Eye: An Autobiography* (London: Hutchinson, 1973).

### Basil DEARDEN

Basil Dearden was born on 1 January 1911 in Westcliffe-on-Sea as Basil Dear. His youthful interest in amateur dramatics led to him entering the theatre as an actor, but he quickly moved behind the curtain to become a stage manager. In 1931 he went to work for theatre producer Basil DEAN as his general stage manager, subsequently making the same shift into films that DEAN had, joining him at Associated Talking Pictures (ATP) where Dean was studio head. He changed his name to Dearden to avoid any confusion with his boss. When Michael Balcon took over the ATP studios at Ealing, Dearden remained. During the late 1930s he worked on a number of Ealing films, including five George Formby vehicles, usually as writer or associate producer. His directing career began on three comedies featuring another of Ealing's music hall stars, Will Hay, with Dearden co-directing with Hay.

His first solo effort was *The Bells Go Down* (1943), which paid tribute to the wartime heroism of the Auxiliary Fire Service. The film's art director was Michael Relph and his meeting with Dearden marked the beginning of a remarkable collaboration which was to last nearly thirty years. As a director-producer-writer team they became the most prolific film-makers working at Ealing. It was, perhaps, their role as studio workhorses that led to a rather poor critical reputation, with commentators dismissing their work as routine, well-meaning but dull. In retrospect, this assessment of their Ealing output seems inadequate. There are films which certainly fit the 1940s Ealing ethos in terms of adopting a realist style and dealing with contemporary issues, but Dearden and Relph frequently showed a preference for subjects which raised wider moral issues. *The Captive Heart* (1946) is a moving POW film, whilst *Frieda* (1947) deals sympathetically with the prejudice facing a German woman who, through marriage, finds herself living in postwar England. *The Blue Lamp* (1949) tackles juvenile crime within an exciting thriller format (a technique that was to become a trademark), but is best remembered for Dirk Bogarde's intense performance as a young tearaway. A number of their films deal with the difficulties of postwar readjustment, from the melodramatic *The Ship that Died of Shame* (1955), through the documentary approach of *Out of the Clouds*

(1955), to the crime caper *The League of Gentlemen* (1960). The latter was made after the demise of Ealing, but within its genre narrative offers a remarkably cynical depiction of a group of ex-soldiers who find themselves discarded in postwar Britain.

However, the sober realism that predominates in these films doesn't tell the full story of Dearden's output in this period. Notable among his other films are the gloriously melancholy costume piece *Saraband for Dead Lovers* (1948), with its sumptuous colour cinematography and rich production design, and the whimsical comedy *The Smallest Show on Earth* (1957), which pays nostalgic tribute to the magic of film-going in a style close to the tradition of the Ealing comedies. Dearden also provided a section for Ealing's macabre portmanteau film *Dead of Night* (1945). Another reason for Dearden and Relph's poor standing may have been this eclecticism, which didn't sit comfortably with the strictures of the auteur theory.

In the late 1950s Dearden and Relph embarked on a series of 'social problem' films which explicitly tackled topical themes within a deliberately audience-pleasing entertainment format, often using the crime genre. *Sapphire* (1959) was among the first British films to deal with racial tensions, while *Victim* (1961) was groundbreaking in depicting the way that homosexuals were subject to blackmail under contemporary laws. The film was credited with being central to the subsequent decriminalisation, and eventual legalisation, of homosexuality. *Violent Playground* (1958) again dealt with juvenile delinquency and *Life for Ruth* (1962) focused on an ethical clash between religious fundamentalism and modern medicine. These films, which have become intrinsically associated with Dearden and Relph, drew a good deal of criticism on the grounds that their timid liberalism failed to fully address the complexity of the issues involved, and that the attempt to frame the topics within fairly conventional storylines drained them of any sense of conflict. The recent, and more sympathetic, reassessment of their work has tended to place the films in context, showing the risks they took in making a film like *Victim*, as evidenced by the fact that it effectively ended Dirk Bogarde's Rank contract.

Their later films shifted on to safer ground, but still threw up a number of interesting items including the spectacular epic *Khartoum* (1965) and the modest, but neatly executed, supernatural thriller *The Man Who Haunted Himself* (1970), with Roger Moore as a dull man whose exciting alter ego is released in a car crash. In a ghastly irony, Dearden's career was brought to a premature end when he died as the result of a car accident on 23 March 1971. Dearden's considerable output is certainly uneven, particularly in the early 1950s, so it's unsurprising that some critics dismissed him as all too typical of the restraint and mediocrity which has sometimes beset British cinema. However, his work has gradually been given more of the due it deserves. The sheer variety of his output shouldn't obscure the consistency of his concern with moral issues tackled within clear social settings.

**British Feature Films:** *The Black Sheep of Whitehall* (1941, co-directed with Will Hay); *The Goose Steps Out* (1942, co-directed with Will Hay); *My Learned Friend* (1943, co-directed with Will Hay); *The Bells Go Down* (1943); *The Halfway House* (1944); *They Came to a City* (1944); *Dead of Night* (1945, one segment); *The Captive Heart* (1946); *Frieda* (1947); *Saraband for Dead Lovers* (1948); *The Blue Lamp* (1949); *Train of Events* (1949, one segment); *Cage of Gold* (1950); *Pool of London* (1950); *The Gentle Gunman* (1952); *I Believe in You* (1952); *The Square Ring* (1953); *The Rainbow Jacket* (1954); *Out of the Clouds* (1955); *The Ship that Died of Shame* (1955); *Who Done It?* (1956); *The Smallest Show on Earth* (1957); *Violent Playground* (1958); *Sapphire* (1959); *The League of Gentlemen* (1960); *Man in the Moon* (1960); *All Night Long* (1961); *The Secret Partner* (1961); *Victim* (1961); *Life for Ruth* (1962); *The Mind Benders* (1963); *A Place to Go* (1963); *Woman of Straw* (1964); *Masquerade* (1965); *Khartoum* (1966); *Only When I Larf* (1968); *The Assassination Bureau Limited* (1968); *The Man Who Haunted Himself* (1970).

**Bibliography:** Alan Burton, Tim O'Sullivan and Paul Wells (eds), *Liberal Directions: Basil Dearden and Postwar British Film Culture* (Trowbridge: Flicks Books, 1997).

## Thorold DICKINSON

Despite a relatively small output of feature films, Thorold Dickinson managed to have a considerable impact on British cinema. His interest in film aesthetics, as well as his sense of political commitment, tended to separate him from the conformist mainstream, but he was still able to take a very active public role in promoting his concerns and raising the profile of cinema as an art form in Britain.

Dickinson was born in Bristol on 16 November 1903, son of the city's Archdeacon. He was sent down from Keble College, Oxford (where he was studying history) for neglecting his studies in favour of cinema and theatre. He entered the industry in 1925 as an assistant director and then editor for the pioneering film-maker George PEARSON. He then established himself as chief editor at ATP (later to become Ealing) during the 1930s. His credits as editor include Basil DEAN's *Sing As We Go!* (1934) and Carol REED's *Midshipman Easy*

(1935). It was during this period that his anger at working conditions in the industry led to his involvement in the main industry union, ACT, of which he was to be Vice-President from 1936 to 1953.

Unusually for a British director, Dickinson was fascinated by the artistic and intellectual possibilities of the medium. He was a central figure in the London Film Society throughout the 1930s, serving on its Council and acting as Programme Controller until the Society's last screenings in 1939. Here he came into contact with the masterpieces of European art cinema, including the work of Eisenstein which was to have a profound influence on him. His independent streak became apparent when he formed his own production company, Fanfare Pictures, in order to make his debut as a director. *High Command* (1937) is a melodramatic yarn set in West Africa and distinguished only by the inventiveness of Dickinson's direction. With the rapid demise of Fanfare, his political commitment again came to the fore when he went to Civil War Spain to make two documentary shorts, *Spanish ABC* and *Behind the Enemy Lines* (both 1938 and co-directed with Sidney Cole), for Ivor Montague's Progressive Film Institute.

Back in Britain, Dickinson made the entertaining second feature *The Arsenal Stadium Mystery* (1939), which won plaudits from Graham Greene. His first major film was *Gaslight* (1940), an adaptation of Patrick Hamilton's popular stage play which helped to send Gainsborough on its successful path into period melodramas. Dickinson brilliantly evokes the Victorian atmosphere of cluttered domestic tension, as Anton Walbrook's charmingly evil husband sets about driving his mentally fragile wife (Diana Wynyard) insane. It is considerably more subtle than the Hollywood remake, a fact that its makers, MGM, acknowledged by trying to suppress Dickinson's version.

With the Second World War, Dickinson made a number of cinematic contributions to the war effort. His biopic of Disraeli, *The Prime Minister* (1941), was tailored to emphasise its patriotic elements, but this pales beside the effectiveness of *The Next of Kin* (1942). The film is an object lesson in how to get a propaganda message across in an entertaining format, its tragic narrative spelling out how careless talk can cost lives with the exciting grip of a classic thriller. Dickinson also made the short *Yesterday Is Over Your Shoulder* (1940) and was central to establishing and managing the Army Kinematograph Service's film unit. He spent three years working on *Men of Two Worlds* (1946), made by Two Cities for the Colonial Office, a project designed to show how a more enlightened approach might bring about fruitful collaboration in Britain's rapidly diminishing Empire. For all Dickinson's socially progressive attitudes, the film can't survive its own worthiness or a tendency to patronise.

*The Next of Kin* had shown that Dickinson could master the realist mode, but he was clearly more in his métier with subjects that allowed full range to his expressive tendencies. This is nowhere clearer than with *Queen of Spades* (1948), a magnificently stylised adaptation of Pushkin's ghost story with Anton Walbrook as the Russian officer who makes a Faustian pact with the devil. Set designs, cinematography and performances all combine to maximise the mood of fatalistic gloom. It was another four years before Dickinson was finally able to bring his most personal project to the screen. *Secret People* (1952) is set in the 1930s and tells of political exiles in Britain fighting against fascism in their unnamed home country. Perhaps the film had been nurtured too long, as critics were divided and audiences indifferent to its obvious sincerity.

*Secret People* proved to be Dickinson's last British film. He went to work in Israel in the early 1950s as a film adviser and made *Hill 24 Doesn't Answer* (1955), a propagandist film with realistically staged battle scenes. From 1956 to 1960 he headed up film services at the United Nations and then in 1960 he became a lecturer at the Slade School of Fine Art, helping to establish film studies as an academic discipline. He became Britain's first professor of film studies in 1967, finally retiring in 1971. Throughout his career he had shown a belief in the power of cinema as a means of conveying a positive, liberal message to a wide audience, as well as a concern for the expressive potential of the medium as art. His individualism and personal vision puts him in that select band of maverick British film-makers who include Michael POWELL and Alberto CAVALCANTI, exulted company indeed. He died in Oxford on 14 April 1984.

**British Feature Films:** *High Command* (1937); *The Arsenal Stadium Mystery* (1939); *Gaslight* (1940); *The Prime Minister* (1941); *The Next of Kin* (1942); *Men of Two Worlds* (1946); *Queen of Spades* (1948); *Secret People* (1952).

**Bibliography:** Jeffrey Richards, *Thorold Dickinson and the British Cinema* (Lanham, MD and London: Scarecrow Press, 1997); Thorold Dickinson, *A Discovery of Cinema* (Oxford: Oxford University Press, 1971); Lindsay Anderson, *Making a Film: The Story of 'Secret People'* (London: Allen & Unwin, 1952).

## Bill DOUGLAS

Bill Douglas has a special place in British cinema history as one of its most unique, uncompromising talents. His career was cut short by illness and his legacy is a scant handful of films, but there are moments in his work that haunt the memory in a manner that few British film-makers have matched. He was born at Newcraighall, a mining community near Edinburgh, on 17 April 1937. His childhood was marked by poverty, but also by a love of the cinema as a magically transformative medium. During National Service in Egypt he met Peter Jewell who became his long-time companion. Back in London, he took up acting with Joan Littlewood's Theatre Workshop and then studied at the London Film School where he made a number of shorts.

Douglas's reputation is based on the trilogy of films he produced with (limited) financial support from the BFI: *My Childhood* (1972), *My Ain Folk* (1973) and *My Way Home* (1978). Based on his own experiences, the films are ostensibly realist depictions of an impoverished, painful childhood and adolescence as we follow young Jamie (Stephen Archibald) towards adulthood. However, Douglas does not follow the usual linear narrative structures of realism, preferring an elliptical editing style in which key plot information is frequently withheld, forcing the audience to engage actively with the films to fill in the missing pieces. Sequences unfold like fragmentary memories, full of unforgettably vivid images. The darkness of Jamie's upbringing is broken by moments of sustaining warmth which build towards the intimations of a possible new life which he finds during National Service. The final image of a tree in bud is a movingly optimistic one.

It took eight years to bring his final film, *Comrades* (1987), to the screen, during which time he taught at the National Film and Television School and Strathclyde University while trying to raise sufficient funds to complete the film. Again he moves beyond the easy naturalism that might have been expected for retelling the story of the Tolpuddle Martyrs – six farm labourers deported for forming a trade union in 1834. By introducing the figure of an itinerant magic lanternist into the narrative, Douglas widens the film into a meditation on the process of recording history as well as a celebration of the pioneers of cinema. His fascination with the latter led to he and Peter Jewell amassing an extraordinary collection of film ephemera and books, including many early optical instruments and amusements which are now housed in the Bill Douglas Centre at the University of Exeter. Douglas was diagnosed with cancer and died on 18 June 1991 at the age of 54. He left a number of unrealised scripts, including an adaptation of James Hogg's *Confessions of a Justified Sinner*.

During his lifetime Douglas's work was little appreciated, or even seen, by critics and audiences. Thanks to the enthusiasm of writers like Derek Malcolm of *The Guardian* and the re-evaluation by scholars of Scottish film culture, his status has been subject to a complete overhaul, although he still remains a little known figure to the wider film-going public. The unsentimental rigour and poetic immediacy of the *Trilogy* indicated a way out of the cul-de-sac which had been reached by the realist tradition in British cinema, one which has subsequently been taken up by the likes of Terence DAVIES and Lynne RAMSEY. It remains required viewing for those who love the medium of film.

**British Feature Films**: *My Childhood* (1972); *My Ain Folk* (1973); *My Way Home* (1978); *Comrades* (1987).

**Bibliography**: Eddie Dick, Andrew Noble and Duncan Petrie (eds), *Bill Douglas: A Lanternist's Account* (London: BFI, 1993).

## E

## Cy ENDFIELD

Born in Scranton, Pennsylvania on 10 November 1914, Cyril Raker Endfield studied at Yale before working with a number of liberal theatre projects of the kind which developed under Roosevelt's depression-era New Deal policies. At university Endfield's political interests had developed and he became involved with the Young Communist League. Another passion was for magic, particularly card tricks. It was the latter which was to gain him entry to Orson Welles' Mercury production company in Hollywood in the early 1940s, Welles being another devotee of magic.

For the next ten years he was in regular employment as a director, usually credited at this time as Cyril Endfield. He made eight short films and seven features in Hollywood. The bulk of his feature films are routine 'B' movies and low budget fillers like *Gentleman Joe Palooka* (1946) and *Tarzan's Savage Fury* (1952), but his political leanings are apparent in the powerful lynch mob drama *The Sound of Fury* (1950) and the taughtly directed crime thriller *The Underworld Story* (1950). His first short film, *Inflation* (1942), a wartime propaganda parable about the dangers of conspicuous consumption, was shelved after complaints from the Chamber of Commerce that it was anti-capitalist. In 1951 he fled the United States after being named a Communist by the House Un-American Activities Committee (HUAC); he resettled in Britain.

In Britain he worked initially in television for ITV before graduating to a number of 'B' movies, writing and directing under a series of pseudonyms (C. Raker Endfield, Hugh Raker, Charles De Latour) to avoid distribution difficulties in America. On *Child in the House* (1956) he first met Welsh actor Stanley Baker who was to become his friend and collaborator on six British films which include Endfield's best work. *Sea Fury* (1958) and *Jet Storm* (1959) are unremarkable action dramas, but *Hell Drivers* (1957) has achieved cult status. It is a rugged, gritty depiction of the world of lorry drivers who take huge risks competing with each other over who can make faster deliveries of ballast. The faintly ludicrous plot is disguised by the punchy economy of Endfield's handling and the energy of the film's driving sequences, as well as by a remarkable cast of British heavies including Patrick McGoohan, Sidney James and (briefly) a very young Sean Connery. Endfield's finest moment came with the military epic *Zulu* (1964), which he co-produced with Baker. The film manages to combine the excitement and spectacle of its tightly coordinated battle scenes with a genuine thoughtfulness which acknowledges the sacrifices on both sides and questions the legitimacy of British imperialism.

Endfield's final film with Baker was the disappointing *Sands of the Kalahari* (1965). Beset with casting difficulties, it looks flabby in comparison with the sharpness of their best work together. *De Sade* (1969) was another ill-fated project financed by Roger Corman's American International Pictures and completed by Corman after Endfield had become ill. His final film was *Universal Soldier* (1971), a well intentioned but desultory anti-war film. He became involved in the creation of a sequel to *Zulu*, eventually released as *Zulu Dawn* (1979), but withdrew from the project after Stanley Baker's premature death from cancer. In later years he turned his constantly inventive mind towards the invention of such gadgets as the Microwriter, a sort of electronic pocket notebook. He died in Shipston-on-Stour, Warwickshire on 16 April 1995.

**British Feature Films**: *Colonel March Investigates* (1953); *The Limping Man* (1953); *The Master Plan* (1954); *The Secret* (1955); *Impulse* (1955); *Child in the House* (1956); *Hell Drivers* (1957); *Sea Fury* (1958); *Jet Storm* (1959); *Mysterious Island* (1961); *Hide and Seek* (1963); *Zulu* (1964); *Sands of the Kalahari* (1965); *Universal Soldier* (1971).

**Bibliography**: Sheldon Hall, *Zulu – With Some Guts Behind It: The Making of the Epic Movie* (Sheffield: Tomahawk Press, 2005).

## Mike FIGGIS

Mike Figgis is something of a renaissance figure whose work spreads across theatre, television, film and music. As well as directing, he frequently writes the scripts for his films as well as the music score. His career also belongs as much to American cinema as it does British. He was born in Carlisle on 28 February 1948, raised in Nairobi until he was eight and then returned with his family to Newcastle. His career started in pop music with the band Gas Board (whose singer was a young Bryan Ferry), followed by a period studying music in London. He joined the avant-garde theatre group The People Show before going on to form his own theatrical company, The Mike Figgis Group, in 1980. He started to experiment with the use of film in his theatre work, which led to a commission from Channel 4 for a television film, *The House* (1984).

His love of music is apparent in his feature film debut, *Stormy Monday* (1988), set among the jazz clubs of his native Newcastle. The film has a strong sense of place and evokes the clichés of film noir with considerable visual panache, but is let down by a forgettable storyline and lack of emotional depth. The film was a decent success and took him to Hollywood where he made two further stylish thrillers, the slickly efficient *Internal Affairs* (1990) and the rather more cerebral, dream-like *Liebestraum* (1991). His Hollywood career temporarily stalled with the misjudged romance *Mr Jones* (1993), which sank without trace.

Figgis returned to Britain with a rather surprising choice of subject, an adaptation of Terence Rattigan's play *The Browning Version* (1994), which had previously been successfully filmed by Anthony AS-QUITH. Figgis's version is more overtly pessimistic and downbeat than ASQUITH's and gains from Albert Finney's strong central performance, but somehow it never catches the sensitive, poignant understatement of the earlier version. Returning to America Figgis made his most successful film to date, the independently produced *Leaving Las Vegas* (1995). A dark portrait of alcoholic self-destruction, it crossed over to the mainstream and won a barrage of awards including an Oscar for its star Nicholas Cage.

Figgis's progress has been erratic and unpredictable. The success of *Leaving Las Vegas* was followed by another commercial failure with the American drama *One Night Stand* (1997). He then took a radical turn towards a more experimental cinema with *The Loss of Sexual Innocence* (1999), a film set in Africa, England and Italy which combines elements of autobiography with an interracial retelling of the story of Adam and

Eve. His increasing concern with formal experimentation, along with an obvious interest in the shifting tensions within sexual relationships, informs his adaptation of Strindberg's *Miss Julie* (1999), which makes use of fluid hand-held camerawork and split-screens. The film was shot within one set using digital cameras in a series of long takes which add to the intensity and claustrophobia of the piece. He took these techniques further again with the American-based *Timecode* (2000) where four interlocking stories are depicted on a split-screen, with the drama unfolding in real time and shot as one continuous take. The results offer a considerable challenge to our normal expectations of film narrative, but also raise questions over how meaningful the manipulation of technique here actually is. *Hotel* (2001) offers more radical departures. A British-Italian co-production, it is set in a Venetian hotel where a Dogme-style version of *The Duchess of Malfi* is being shot while a television crew makes a documentary about the filming. The fragmentary structure and obtuse layering proved too alienating for most audiences and critics.

His recent work has been almost wilfully eclectic, from the television documentary reconstruction *The Battle of Orgreave* (2001) about the 1984–5 miners' strike, to the incomprehensibly awful creepy-house thriller, *Cold Creek Manor* (2003). He returned to the use of split-screens and multiple perspectives in his short contribution to the portmanteau film *Ten Minutes Older: The Cello* (2002) and filmed a masterclass he held for film students in Slovenia as *Co/Ma* (2004). These films veer from the blatantly commercial to the idiosyncratic and personal, qualities which have been apparent throughout Figgis's work. He remains one of the most unclassifiable contemporary British directors.

**British Feature Films:** *Stormy Monday* (1988); *The Browning Version* (1994); *The Loss of Sexual Innocence* (1999); *Miss Julie* (1999); *Hotel* (2001).

## Terence FISHER

In his book *A Heritage of Horror* (1973), David Pirie claims the Gothic tradition as British cinema's equivalent to the American western, a kind of national cinematic myth. If this is the case then Terence Fisher might be regarded within British film history in the same light that John Ford is in American cinema. Fisher is unquestionably the master of the British horror film and his work with Hammer forms the cornerstone of the gothic tradition which Pirie sought to celebrate.

Terence Fisher was born in London on 23 February 1904 and joined the industry in 1933 after drifting through a variety of jobs, including a spell in the Merchant Navy. He worked his way up from clapperboy, establishing himself as a reliable editor with credits including Gainsborough's classic bodice ripper *The Wicked Lady* (1945). He started directing in 1948 with three short films made at Rank's Highbury studio before graduating to Gainsborough where he made four features, two of them co-directed with Anthony Darnborough. The second of these, *So Long at the Fair* (1950), is an atmospheric suspense story which can now be seen as a precursor for his later horror films. After Gainsborough's demise in the early 1950s, Fisher became a jobbing director making mainly low-budget 'B' movies, churning out nearly twenty of them over the next six years. Eleven of these were made for Hammer in the years before they established themselves as Britain's premier maker of horror films. These films range across a variety of genres, but feature a number of crime subjects, as well as two interesting SF thrillers, *Four Sided Triangle* (1953) and *Spaceways* (1953).

Fisher directed the first of Hammer's period horrors, *The Curse of Frankenstein* (1957), an enormous box office success that set director and studio on a lucrative path for the next twenty years. The film features many of the elements that were to become the basis of Hammer's house style. Produced cheaply and quickly, the film nonetheless makes the most of its striking sets and vivid colour cinematography. The memorable score and an archetypal role for Peter Cushing as the Baron established the tone, although contemporary critics were more concerned by what they saw as the shocking level of violence than by the film's visual grace. Nearly twenty gothic horrors followed from Fisher until his last gasp, *Frankenstein and the Monster from Hell*, in 1974, with only the briefest falling out with Hammer after the comparative commercial failure of *The Phantom of the Opera* (1962). Roy Armes' assessment in his *A Critical History of British Cinema*, published in the late 1970s, that Fisher was little more than a journeyman director who made tasteless genre films, remained fairly typical of the critical consensus regarding Fisher's work, but that view has been largely revised following an extensive critical re-evaluation of Hammer over the last thirty years. Although a good deal of Fisher's work conforms to the formula which he helped to establish, there is much to admire in his restrained use of editing, camera position and *mise en scène* which create tension with more subtlety than might be expected.

Among his most striking features for Hammer are the first, and best, of the Dracula series, *Dracula* (1958), with iconic performances from Cushing as Van Helsing and Christopher Lee as the Count. The film uncovers all of the narrative's latent sexual tensions, turning Dracula into a seductively attractive figure. He brings considerable visual panache to *The Brides of Dracula* (1960) and a real inventiveness, along with a little gender politics, to the bizarre revenge plot of *Frankenstein Created Woman* (1967). A potentially routine series entry like *Frankenstein Must Be Destroyed* (1969) is lifted out the rut by the unexpected pathos of Freddie Jones's performance, while the tightly directed supernatural chiller *The Devil Rides Out* (1968) indicated a fruitful direction for Hammer's future progress if they had only had the nerve to follow it up. His other Hammer horrors include the effective reworking of familiar material in both *The Mummy* (1959) and *The Curse of the Werewolf* (1961), the latter with Oliver Reed in the sympathetic title role. As well as gothic horrors, Cushing made a number of SF films in the 1960s which form part of a small sub-genre of paranoid invasion fantasies typical of the period. These include *The Earth Dies Screaming* (1964) and *Night of the Big Heat* (1967). There was also an intelligent and restrained Sherlock Holmes adventure, *The Hound of the Baskervilles* (1959).

It is easy enough to dismiss these films for their cheap sensationalism or to suggest that Fisher's undemonstrative directorial style indicates a lack of imagination, but at the very least Fisher was able to unerringly keep his audience coming back for more. Young British filmgoers ignored the dire warnings from critics and found themselves entering a surprisingly moral fairytale world where scientific rationality struggles to come to terms with the violently disruptive, erotic forces that seem to lie just beneath the straight-laced surface of British society. With the benefit of hindsight, Fisher handles these excesses with a remarkable sense of cinematic control, creating a body of work which seems quintessentially British in both its content and style. Fisher died on 18 June 1980 in Twickenham.

**British Feature Films:** *Portrait from Life* (1948); *Marry Me* (1949); *The Astonished Heart* (1950, co-directed with Anthony Darnborough); *So Long at the Fair* (1950, co-directed with Anthony Darnborough); *Home to Danger* (1951); *Wings of Danger* (1952); *Distant Trumpet* (1952); *The Last Page* (1952); *Stolen Face* (1952); *Four Sided Triangle* (1953); *Mantrap* (1953); *Spaceways* (1953); *Blood Orange* (1953); *Mask of Dust* (1954); *Children Galore* (1954); *Face the Music* (1954); *Final Appointment* (1954); *The Stranger Came Home* (1954); *Murder by Proxy* (1955); *Stolen Assignment* (1955); *The Flaw* (1955); *The Last Man to Hang?* (1956); *Kill Me Tomorrow* (1957); *The Curse of Frankenstein* (1957); *Dracula* (1958); *The Revenge of Frankenstein* (1958); *The Hound of the Baskervilles* (1959); *The Man Who Could Cheat Death* (1959); *The Mummy* (1959); *The Stranglers of Bombay* (1959); *The Brides of Dracula*

(1960); *Sword of Sherwood Forest* (1960); *The Two Faces of Dr Jekyll* (1960); *The Curse of the Werewolf* (1961); *The Phantom of the Opera* (1962); *The Earth Dies Screaming* (1964); *The Gorgon* (1964); *The Horror of It All* (1964); *Dracula Prince of Darkness* (1965); *Island of Terror* (1966); *Frankenstein Created Woman* (1967); *Night of the Big Heat* (1967); *The Devil Rides Out* (1968); *Frankenstein Must Be Destroyed* (1969); *Frankenstein and the Monster From Hell* (1974).

**Bibliography:** Peter Hutchings, *Terence Fisher* (Manchester: Manchester University Press, 2001); Wheeler Winston Dixon, *The Charm of Evil: The Life and Films of Terence Fisher* (London: Scarecrow Press, 1991); David Pirie, *A Heritage of Horror: The English Gothic Cinema 1946–1972* (London: Gordon Fraser, 1973).

## Bryan FORBES

Bryan Forbes' career must rank as one of the most varied in British cinema history, ranging from acting to writing and directing, producing and even a period as head of one of Britain's major production companies. It's easy for his achievements as a director to be overlooked among the wide range of his work, but particularly in the 1960s he carved out a distinctive niche for himself as a director of understated and often sensitive dramas.

Born as John Clarke in Stratford, London on 22 July 1926, he started his career as an actor, joining RADA at seventeen. His military service included a spell with the Intelligence Corps and with the Combined Forces Entertainment Unit. He began acting in films from 1948 under his stage name of Bryan Forbes and for the next ten years appeared regularly, establishing himself as a reliable supporting player without ever making it to the front ranks of British stardom. Among his more memorable roles are two Second World War dramas, *The Wooden Horse* (1950) and *The Colditz Story* (1955). From the mid-1950s he began to switch his attention to screenwriting where he proved more immediately successful. An acid wit is apparent in his adaptation of the Kingsley Amis novel *Only Two Can Play* (1962) for director Sidney GILLIAT and he brings a similarly cynical tone to Basil DEARDEN's entertaining caper film *The League of Gentlemen* (1960) which he also acted in. He continued to write the scripts for most of his later films as director.

In 1959 his career took another turn when he founded Beaver Films with Richard ATTENBOROUGH. For Beaver he produced and wrote *The Angry Silence* (1960) with ATTENBOROUGH starring as the factory worker persecuted for not taking part in an unofficial strike. Forbes' instinctive conservatism is apparent here and the film was vehemently attacked by critics on the Left. There is a clear allegory at the centre of his directorial debut, the still popular *Whistle Down the Wind* (1961). The young Hayley Mills stars as one of three Yorkshire children who mistake the escaped criminal in their barn (Alan Bates) for the second coming of Jesus Christ. The film portrays the children with unpatronising warmth and captures their innocent faith with visual lyricism. The naturalism of both these films is repeated in *The L-Shaped Room* (1962), with its rather contrived cross-section of British life represented by the tenants of a suburban London house. These films are close enough in style to nominate them as an adjunct to the realism of the British New Wave, but they are more conventional and sentimental in approach.

Forbes' other films of the 1960s are uneven and increasingly stylised. *Séance on a Wet Afternoon* (1964) is an odd mixture of psychological study and Hitchcockian suspense with Kim Stanley as the medium involved in a kidnapping case, while *The Whisperers* (1966) offers a coldly restrained study of old age bolstered by a touching central performance from Edith Evans. *The Wrong Box* (1966) is a frenetic Swinging Sixties black comedy with a neatly evoked Victorian setting and an all-star cast, adopting a much lighter approach than the rather self-important character-driven thriller *Deadfall* (1968). Things reached a low ebb with the highly theatrical and unconvincing *The Madwoman of Chaillot* (1969) which boasts one of the strangest cast lists ever assembled. In 1969 he changed direction once again, this time to become Head of Production at EMI where he was brave enough to instigate a policy of making family-oriented films. The delightful and much-loved *The Railway Children* (1970, Lionel Jeffries) was an indication of what might have been. He also achieved international art house success with Joseph Losey's *The Go-Between* (1970), but after barely eighteen months of wrangling and in-fighting Forbes had had enough and resigned.

Forbes' interest in family entertainment resurfaces in *The Slipper and the Rose* (1976), a saccharin reworking of the Cinderella story, and with *International Velvet* (1978), a thoroughly unsympathetic sequel to the 1944 children's classic *National Velvet* with Tatum O'Neal in the Elizabeth Taylor role. Forbes showed a surer touch with *The Raging Moon* (1971) about the romance between two paraplegics played by Malcolm McDowell and Forbes' wife of many years Nanette Newman. Newman has appeared regularly in Forbes' films. Two of Forbes' strongest feature films were made in America, the hard-edged POW drama *King Rat* (1965) and *The Stepford Wives* (1975), a suitably acerbic adaptation of Ira Levin's story of a group of suburban men who replace their wives with obedient, domesticated robots. In the 1980s he directed a segment in the internationally produced portmanteau film *Sunday Lovers* (1980) and two bland features, *Better Late than Never* (1982) and *The Naked Face* (1984), neither of which really registered with critics or audiences. In later years Forbes turned to writing novels, as well as two enjoyable volumes of memoirs.

Despite, or perhaps because of, the diversity of Forbes' interests, his career as a director seems strangely unfulfilled. There is a clear dedication to reaching family audiences, a liking for well-crafted scripts and an obvious affinity for actors in his work. His best films combine a sensitive depiction of innocence with a more world weary cynicism, but somehow there is the feeling that such an engaging talent should have produced a filmography with rather more lasting substance in it. He was awarded a CBE in 2004.

**British Feature Films:** *Whistle Down the Wind* (1961); *The L-Shaped Room* (1962); *Séance on a Wet Afternoon* (1964); *The Whisperers* (1966); *The Wrong Box* (1966); *Deadfall* (1968); *The Madwoman of Chaillot* (1969); *The Raging Moon* (1971); *The Slipper and the Rose* (1976); *International Velvet* (1978); *Better Late than Never* (1982); *The Naked Face* (1984).

**Bibliography:** Bryan Forbes, *A Divided Life* (London: Heinemann, 1992); Bryan Forbes, *Notes for a Life* (London: Collins, 1974).

## Bill FORSYTH

With just eight feature films in twenty-five years, Bill Forsyth has nonetheless created a thoroughly distinctive cinematic world, one full of warmth and humour, but also with a hint of something more mournful or elegiac. This world is peopled with everyday eccentrics, celebrated by Forsyth for their uniqueness. He was born on 29 July 1946 in Glasgow and started in films at the age of seventeen working on commercial documentary shorts, frequently with Scottish subjects. He continued with this for fifteen years, interrupted only by brief spells with the BBC and at the National Film School. He struggled to find the funding for his first low-budget feature, *That Sinking Feeling* (1980), but managed to scrimp together £6,000 to make it. Created with actors from the Glasgow Youth Theatre, it has the air of being semi-improvised. Forsyth treats its story, of a group of unemployed youngsters who steal a consignment of stainless steel kitchen sinks from a warehouse, with enormous sympathy as well as a good deal of irreverent wit.

Much of the same cast took part in *Gregory's Girl* (1981), including John Gordon Sinclair appearing here as the bewildered Gregory. The film's slender plot is just a frame on which to hang a series of beautifully observed comic vignettes of life in a Scottish new town, the episodic structure adding to the charm. Few British films have captured the pangs of adolescent first love with such tenderness. The film was a surprise box office success and took the eye of producer David Puttnam who financed Forsyth's next feature, *Local Hero* (1983). Comparisons with Ealing have apparently annoyed Forsyth and yet the plot of *Local Hero*, with its Scottish villagers saved from the prospect of an American business man (Burt Lancaster) building an oil refinery on their beautiful coastland, bears obvious comparisons with *Whiskey Galore* (1949). The bigger budget and glossier production values don't detract from Forsyth's heartfelt hymn to a rural community and any sentimentality is undercut by his taste for surreal detail. This period of his career was brought to a close by *Comfort and Joy* (1984) in which the humour is offset by an undercurrent of melancholy. Bill Paterson plays the DJ whose partner has left him and who becomes embroiled in Glasgow's ice cream wars. This comic backdrop doesn't disguise the fact that this is a moving film about loneliness.

Forsyth followed Puttnam to America, where the producer was now head of Columbia, to make *Housekeeping* (1987), another low-key plea for individualism that is full of wistful charm. His second American film, *Breaking In* (1989), featured Burt Reynolds as an ineffectual burglar and again shows Forsyth's characteristic appreciation for the underdog. Production difficulties beset both these films, but were nothing compared to the run-in he had with studio executives on the big-budget *Being Human* (1993) starring Robin Williams, a film which seemingly ended Forsyth's American career. Returning to Scotland he directed a sequel to his first major success with *Gregory's Two Girls* (1999), in which we now find Gregory working as a teacher at his old school and still as confused by the opposite sex as before. It has much of the appeal of his earlier work, but found precious little favour with British critics.

Forsyth's is a precious talent. The delicacy of his character observation and the quirkiness of his humour may have been out of place in Hollywood, but they fit perfectly into the traditions of British cinema. It can only be a source of regret that nothing has been seen from him on the big screen since 1999.

**British Feature Films:** *That Sinking Feeling* (1980); *Gregory's Girl* (1981); *Local Hero* (1983); *Comfort and Joy* (1984); *Gregory's Two Girls* (1999).

**Bibliography:** Jonathan Hacker and David Price, *Take Ten: Con-*

*temporary British Film Directors* (Oxford: Clarendon Press, 1991); Alan Hunter, 'Bill Forsyth: The Imperfect Anarchist', in Eddie Dick (ed.), *From Limelight to Satellite: A Scottish Film Book* (Edinburgh: Scottish Film Council/BFI, 1990).

## Freddie FRANCIS

Freddie Francis occupies an oddly schizophrenic position in British cinema. In a national cinema which has produced a remarkable roster of talented cinematographers, Francis is one of the most distinguished with an impressive list of credits and international awards to his name. But Francis is also a director of gothic horror films and, perhaps to his own irritation, has developed something of a cult following for his work with Hammer and Amicus, two of the key producers of British horror.

Born in Islington, London on 22 December 1917, he trained as a stills photographer at Shepherd's Bush Studios before becoming a clapper-loader at Gaumont-British from 1936. He worked with the Army Kinematographic Unit during the Second World War and then rejoined the industry as a camera operator, where his credits include three films with POWELL AND PRESSBURGER. He undertook the same role on several films made in Britain by the American director John Huston and was his second unit cinematographer on *Moby Dick* (1956). His first full credit as cinematographer was on *A Hill in Korea* (1956) and he quickly made a name for himself with work on black-and-white realist films such as *Room at the Top* (1959, Jack CLAYTON) and *Saturday Night and Sunday Morning* (1960, Karel REISZ), winning his first Oscar for *Sons and Lovers* (1960, Jack Cardiff).

His debut as a director came with the effective romantic comedy *Two and Two Make Six* (1962), but it was his third film, *Paranoiac* (1963), made for Hammer, which really set him on a path as a horror specialist. The film is unusual for Hammer in having a contemporary setting and combines some psychological depth in its characterisations with a suspense story about something, or someone, nasty lurking in the woodshed. The film was a considerable box office hit and Francis repeated the formula on two further atmospheric Hammer psycho-thrillers, *Nightmare* (1963) and *Hysteria* (1964). He also made his own contribution to two of Hammer's established monster cycles with *The Evil of Frankenstein* (1964) and *Dracula has Risen from the Grave* (1968), although neither adds anything particularly new to the house style.

Rather more individual are the low-budget horrors he made for Milton Subotsky's Amicus, one of Hammer's few rivals in the genre during the 1960s. A certain mordant wit is apparent in *The Skull* (1965) in which the Marquis de Sade's decapitated remains menace the central characters, but Amicus's greatest successes came with the series of portmanteau films they made in which sting-in-the-tale short stories are linked together by a narrative device, such as the various characters visiting a bookshop. Francis was responsible for the first of these with *Dr Terror's House of Horrors* (1965), and went on to make *Torture Garden* (1967), *Tales from the Crypt* (1972) and *Tales that Witness Madness* (1973) in the same vein. Francis also worked for a number of other poverty-row horror producers, making the rather stylish *The Creeping Flesh* (1972) with Peter Cushing for Tigon, along with some quite embarrassingly bad genre items including *Craze* (1973) and the wretched *Trog* (1970), the latter featuring an elderly Joan Crawford in her last screen role. Francis also worked on several undistinguished German co-productions including *Vengeance* (1962) and *Traitor's Gate* (1964). His prolific output as a director during this period also encompassed work in British television for series like *The Saint*.

His final forays into big screen horror came with *Legend of the Werewolf* (1974) and *The Ghoul* (1975), both rather crude efforts made for Tyburn, the company established by his son, Kevin. With odd exceptions, such as his adaptation of Dylan Thomas's screenplay *The Doctor and the Devils* (1985) and some further work for television, Francis effectively abandoned directing to return to cinematography in the 1980s. His subsequent credits have included the stunning black-and-white evocation of Victorian London in David Lynch's *The Elephant Man* (1980) and another Oscar for the American Civil War drama *Glory* (1989). His work as a director has inevitably been overshadowed by his success as a cinematographer and his reputation hasn't been helped by the bottom-of-the-barrel nature of some of his weaker horror films, but his best efforts in the genre have a dark humour, macabre inventiveness and visual flair that are more than worthy of the cult status they have achieved for him.

**British Feature Films:** *Two and Two Make Six* (1962); *Vengeance* (1962); *Paranoiac* (1963); *Nightmare* (1963); *Hysteria* (1964); *Evil of Frankenstein* (1964); *Traitor's Gate* (1964); *Dr Terror's House of Horror* (1965); *The Skull* (1965); *The Deadly Bees* (1966); *The Psychopath* (1966); *They Came from Beyond Space* (1967); *Torture Garden* (1967); *Dracula has Risen from the Grave* (1968); *Mumsy, Nanny, Sonny and Girly* (1969); *Trog* (1970); *Vampire Happening* (1971); *The Creeping Flesh* (1972); *Tales from the Crypt* (1972); *Craze* (1973); *Tales that Witness Madness* (1973); *Son of Dracula* (1974); *Legend of the Werewolf* (1974); *The Ghoul* (1975); *The Doctor and the Devils* (1985).

**Bibliography**: Wheeler Winston Dixon, *The Films of Freddie Francis* (London: Scarecrow Press, 1991).

## Stephen FREARS

Chief among Stephen Frears' attributes are his sensitive handling of actors, as evidenced in the succession of fine performances that grace his films, and his obvious rapport with writers (he has worked successfully with Alan Bennett, Christopher Hampton and Hanif Kureishi). Oddly, these qualities have sometimes worked against him as critics have unfairly seen him as a craftsman rather than an auteur. However, strong themes do emerge in his work, particularly a concern for the down-trodden and marginalised, and in his best work there is frequently an acerbic view of the condition of contemporary Britain.

Frears was born on 20 June 1941 in Leicester. After studying law at Trinity College, Cambridge, he joined the Royal Court Theatre in 1964 where he met Karel REISZ and Lindsay ANDERSON. Moving into films, he was assistant director to REISZ on *Morgan: A Suitable Case for Treatment* (1966) and for ANDERSON on *If . . .* (1968). His first directing credit came with the short film *The Burning* (1967), set in apartheid South Africa. He made his feature debut with *Gumshoe* (1971), a wry, whimsical portrait of a bingo caller (Albert Finney) whose dreams of becoming a private detective come all too true. The film already shows Frears' understated skill with actors and his liking for restrained humour. The film proved to be a false start to his cinema career as he spent the next twelve years working in television drama and occasionally in advertising. This included a number of distinguished productions such as the politically motivated *Bloody Kids* (1979), *Saigon: Year of the Cat* (1983), David Hare's depiction of the last days of American involvement in Vietnam, and *Walter* (1982) with Ian McKellan, the first in Channel 4's *Film on Four* franchise.

He finally returned to the big screen in 1984 with *The Hit*, a darkly comic thriller set in Spain with neatly etched performances from Terence Stamp, John Hurt and Tim Roth. It garnered some excellent reviews from the British press. Frears' real breakthrough came with the Channel 4 financed *My Beautiful Laundrette* (1985). Brilliantly scripted by Hanif Kureishi, the film is a landmark for British cinema both in its almost casual portrayal of homosexuality and in the realistic depiction of the British Asian community. With warmth and considerable humour, the film is a remarkably astute depiction of the complexities and inequities of Thatcher's Britain. It remains one of the best documents of the period. Working again with Kureishi, Frears made *Sammy and Rosie Get Laid* (1987), a much more self-conscious attempt to depict the state of the nation, which lacks the razor sharp observation of their previous collaboration and seems overburdened by good intentions. More relaxed and successful was *Prick Up Your Ears* (1987), scripted by Alan Bennett. This reconstruction of the life of the playwright Joe Orton and his lover Kenneth Halliwell is beautifully played by Gary Oldman and Alfred Molina, depicting the closeted world of gay men in the Britain of the 1960s with sympathy and dry wit. Frears clearly had an affinity for Bennett's vision of Englishness as they had collaborated on six television plays in the run up to *Prick Up Your Ears*.

Frears' success took him to America where he started confidently with *Dangerous Liaisons* (1988). Written by Christopher Hampton, it is a compelling depiction of the game of seduction as played out by jaded eighteenth-century aristocrats. He followed it with *The Grifters* (1990), perhaps his best American film, an edgy depiction of the underworld of con artists which won him an Oscar nomination as best director. Unfortunately the big budget *Accidental Hero* (1992), with Dustin Hoffman, failed at the box office and returned Frears to the UK where he made two films based on Roddy Doyle novels. *The Snapper* (1993), originally made for the BBC for television broadcast but given a theatrical release, and *The Van* (1996) are both set in working-class Dublin and portray stunted lives on depressing housing estates without a hint of condescension. The former crackles with authentic dialogue and has a tough humanity whereas the latter seems to strive a little too much for sentimental effect.

Frears has continued to work intermittently in the United States, despite the critical roasting and commercial failure of *Mary Reilly* (1996). This unusual version of the story of Dr Jekyll and Mr Hyde, with Julia Roberts in the title role and again scripted by Christopher Hampton, is rather more interesting than its reputation allows. He achieved a stronger critical response with the offbeat contemporary western *The Hi-Lo Country* (1998) and better commercial results with *High Fidelity* (2000), which successfully transfers Nick Hornby's London-set novel to America. He was back on familiar British territory with the social realism of *Liam* (2000) written by Jimmy McGovern and set in depression-era Liverpool. The film tackles such familiar themes as unemployment, racism and religious prejudice with Frears' usual eye for gritty detail. *Dirty Pretty Things* (2002) was extremely well received. Its story of illegal immigrants in London and the international trade in body parts for surgery feels literally torn from the headlines. Its willingness to tackle contemporary issues through a sympathetically human drama is very typical of Frears' approach. Reviews were more uneven for the relatively lightweight *Mrs Henderson Presents* (2005). It tells the story of the Windmill Theatre which never missed a show throughout the Second World War and became famous for flouting censorship laws with its nude tableaux. His latest film is *The Queen* (2006), which, like his early television film about Tony Blair, *The Deal* (2003), takes its story right out of the headlines.

Frears' career has switched backwards and forwards between Britain and America, film and television, commercialism and more socially conscious projects. His lack of an overtly recognisable visual signature may not please some critics, but his films have showcased an exceptional gallery of performances, contained some of the best writing in recent British cinema and often shown a willingness to reflect the nature of contemporary British society. These qualities have made him an indispensable talent.

**British Feature Films:** *Gumshoe* (1971); *The Hit* (1984); *My Beautiful Laundrette* (1985); *Sammy and Rosie Get Laid* (1987); *Prick Up Your Ears* (1987); *The Snapper* (1993); *The Van* (1996); *Liam* (2000); *Dirty Pretty Things* (2002); *Mrs Henderson Presents* (2005); *The Queen* (2006).

**Bibliography:** Charles Barr and Stephen Frears, *Typically British* (London: BFI, 1995); Jonathan Hacker and David Price, *Take 10: Contemporary British Film Directors* (Oxford: Oxford University Press, 1991).

## Charles FREND

Born in Pulborough, Sussex on 21 November 1909, Charles Frend was educated at Kings School, Canterbury and then at Oxford, where he was film reviewer for the student magazine *Isis*. He entered the industry as an assistant editor at British International Pictures in 1931, moving on to Gaumont-British in 1933. During the 1930s he became one of British cinema's most respected editors, working with Alfred Hitchcock on four films including *Sabotage* (1936) and with the American director Sam Wood on the populist *Goodbye Mr Chips* (1939), one of four glossy productions by MGM-British. He made his directorial debut at Ealing with *The Big Blockade* (1942). The film is a fairly typical Ealing wartime propaganda piece in their familiar semi-documentary style, but features the only straight performance by the great comedian Will Hay. Frend had found his spiritual home at Ealing where he remained for the next fifteen years, directing a further twelve films for the studio.

He made four further films during the war, all of them following Ealing's pattern of combining propaganda content with social realism. *The Foreman Went to France* (1942) is thoroughly engaging in its mix of drama (the air attack on a group of fleeing refugees is genuinely gripping) and cheerful good humour, the latter provided by the likeable Tommy Trinder. *San Demetrio London* (1943) is a similarly understated and powerful tribute to the heroism of the Merchant Navy. In comparison, *Johnny Frenchman* (1945) is a rather heavy-handed, unconvincing attempt to emphasise the need for postwar friendship between Britain and France. The documentary *The Return of the Vikings* (1944) was made for the exiled Norwegian government which subsequently rewarded Frend with the Order of St Olav for his services to their cause.

Frend's characteristic work frequently celebrates traditional aspects of British life. This is certainly apparent in the romantic period drama *The Loves of Joanna Godden* (1947) where the director seems as interested in the detail of farming life on Romney Marshes as he is by the central love story. The film benefits considerably from Vaughan Williams's score. This quality is also there in the modest *Lease of Life* (1954) which depicts the last year in the life of a dying vicar (Robert Donat), but where the focus is really on the everyday life of the village which he serves. The heart of Frend's work can be found in *Scott of the Antarctic* (1949) with its low-key heroism and self-sacrifice. John Mills is the epitome of a certain kind of British hero, tight-lipped and undemonstrative but resolutely assured in his moral certainty, who appears frequently in Frend's films. Perhaps more surprising is the visual beauty of the film, with its snowscapes reflecting the characters' emotional isolation. Many of the same qualities are also evident in *The*

*Cruel Sea* (1952) where the narrative centres on the camaraderie of the male crew of a warship and on the human cost of conflict. Jack Hawkins plays another of Frend's stoic leaders who must face the sometimes tragic consequences of his decisions. Like *Scott of the Antarctic*, the film rises above the predictable plotting to be genuinely moving.

Frend also made three comedies for Ealing: *A Run for Your Money* (1949), *The Magnet* (1950) and *Barnacle Bill* (1957). In comparison with the finest of Ealing's comedies these are relatively minor pieces that tend towards the whimsical end of the studio's output rather than their more acerbic black farces, but they still possess their fair share of charm and *A Run for Your Money* gets a decent amount of fun out of its story of two Welsh innocents up in London for a rugby international. With the demise of Ealing, Frend moved into television working on such popular 1960s adventure series as *Danger Man* and *Man in a Suitcase*. He also made two further feature films, *Cone of Silence* (1960) and *Girl on Approval* (1961), which have his familiar clear sense of morality but which added little to his reputation. His final film as director, *The Sky Bike* (1967), was made for the Children's Film Foundation, although he subsequently worked as a second unit direc-tor, including on David LEAN's *Ryan's Daughter* (1970).

It's easy enough to mock Frend's work, with its stiff upper-lipped heroes who remain assured and quietly heroic even when the ship is going down, but there is much that is quintessentially British here. Even the understated simplicity of his direction seems to mirror national characteristics and easily can obscure the fact that his films are always crisply edited and frequently have an eye for visual spectacle. Few directors have been as consistent in their appreciation for a modest integrity and sense of honour seen as intrinsic parts of a national cultural identity. He died on 8 January 1977.

**British Feature Films:** *The Big Blockade* (1942); *The Foreman Went to France* (1942); *San Demetrio London* (1943); *Return of the Vikings* (1944); *Johnny Frenchman* (1945); *The Loves of Joanna Godden* (1947); *Scott of the Antarctic* (1948); *A Run for Your Money* (1949); *The Magnet* (1950); *The Cruel Sea* (1952); *Lease of Life* (1954); *The Long Arm* (1956); *Barnacle Bill* (1957); *Cone of Silence* (1960); *Girl on Approval* (1961): *The Sky Bike* (1967).

## Sidney J. FURIE

Sidney Furie was born in Toronto, Canada on 28 February 1933. After studying at the Carnegie Institute of Theatre, he worked in Canadian television and then made two minor teen movies, the self-financed *A*

*Dangerous Age* (1958) and the beat movie *A Cool Sound from Hell* (1959). Furie moved to the UK in 1960 and became a reliable and prolific director of low-budget exploitation fare, including the ludicrous horror films *Dr Blood's Coffin* (1960) and *The Snake Woman* (1961). He hit box office success with two vehicles for Britain's premier pop star of the moment, Cliff Richard. Richard's film debut, *The Young Ones* (1961), combines a conventional putting-on-a-show narrative with a plea for greater understanding of the lives of young people, but unfortunately drains Richard of any connotations of youth rebellion or sexuality which his following might have implied. *Wonderful Life* (1964) is cheerful and zany, but thoroughly routine – a sort of tame British equivalent to the already limp Elvis Presley vehicles coming from America.

Furie cashed in on the popularity of the 'social problem' films of the period with *The Boys* (1962) and the unfortunately titled *The Leather Boys* (1963). He had already touched on the genre with *During One Night* (1961), the odd story of an impotent Second World War American airman. *The Boys* includes another statement on behalf of misunderstood youth via a contrived courtroom drama about four lads accused of murder. The film's rather showy use of flashback was an indication of the kind of directorial flourishes with which Furie was later to become heavily associated. *The Leather Boys* is rather more interesting as an attempt to deal sympathetically with the then topical and controversial issue of homosexuality. Its clichés are certainly dated now, but there is a frankness and lack of condescension in its handling of the subject. Furie's films of the early 1960s, for all their showiness and commerciality, are at least an interesting reflection of public concerns of the time, particularly about young people.

Furie gained his first international success with *The Ipcress File* (1965), adapted from Len Deighton's spy thriller, which won a BAFTA as Best British Film. The film is a fascinating mixture of contradictory elements. One part offers a downbeat, realistic antidote to the fantasies of the Bond films, with the world of secret agents depicted as largely dreary routine. On the other hand, the film develops the fashionable stylisation of his earlier comedy *Three on a Spree* (1961) and features many examples of Furie's fetish for placing the camera behind various objects which partially obscure the view. Michael Caine's Harry Palmer, with his NHS spectacles and penchant for supermarket shopping, became an iconic working-class hero appearing in two sequels.

The deserved success of the film took Furie to Hollywood where he has largely remained since. His American output was initially uneven, ranging from the thoughtful, if over-directed western *The Appaloosa* (1966) with Marlon Brando, to the blaxploitation-style violence of *Hit!* (1973) and the crude gung-ho heroics of *The Boys in Company C* (1978). His two biopics, *Lady Sings the Blues* (1972), with Diana Ross as Billie Holiday, and *Gable and Lombard* (1976), are by turns luridly sensationalist and sentimentally old fashioned. His only British film of the period, the meretricious spy thriller *The Naked Runner* (1967) with Frank Sinatra, is distinguished only by a barrage of Furie's manic directorial mannerisms. Subsequently, what personality Furie had brought to his films evaporated in a series of strictly routine studio products including three entries in the series of aerial action films *Iron Eagle* (1986–95) and the fourth in the *Superman* franchise. He has continued to work in television, as well as to make straight-to-video features and a number of films in Canada. His recent work is strictly that of a jobbing director and has little hint of the talent he showed in his British work when, for a time in the 1960s, he seemed to have a remarkably astute eye for contemporary trends in youth culture and an exuberant style to match.

**British Feature Films:** *Dr Blood's Coffin* (1960); *During One Night* (1961); *Three on a Spree* (1961); *The Young Ones* (1961); *The Snake Woman* (1961); *The Boys* (1962); *The Leather Boys* (1963); *Wonderful Life* (1964); *The Ipcress File* (1965); *The Naked Runner* (1967).

# G

## Lewis GILBERT

Born in Hackney, London on 6 March 1920, Lewis Gilbert has had a long and varied career in British cinema. Coming from two generations of music hall performers, Gilbert came into cinema as a child actor and had appeared in more than seventy films by 1938. He moved behind the camera to become an assistant director in the late 1930s and then during the Second World War was seconded from the RAF Film Unit to the US Air Corps Film Unit. After being invalided out of the services in 1944, he joined Gaumont-British Instructional Films where he made short documentaries. His feature film debut came with the modest children's film *The Little Ballerina* (1947). Half a dozen poverty-row 'B' movies followed before he moved towards mainstream respectability with the entertaining POW drama *Albert RN* (1953).

During the 1950s Gilbert steadily built his commercial reputation by specialising in two popular genres, the crime film and the nostalgic Second World War drama. In the crime genre he produced the first British 'X' film with the joyfully lurid *Cosh Boy* (1953), a downbeat caper movie *The Good Die Young* (1954) with Laurence Harvey and *Cast a Dark Shadow* (1955), an atmospheric suspenser with Dirk Bogarde cast against type as a wife-murderer. However, his greatest success came with his war films and particularly the phenomenally popular *Reach for the Sky* (1956) which tells the moving story of the pilot Douglas Bader (Kenneth More) who lost both legs in a flying accident but managed to return to active duty in the war. Seen now, the relentless stoicism and cheeriness of More is inadvertently annoying and not entirely convincing, but no one could refute the film's ability to hit a nerve with audiences. More appears again in the neatly effective *Sink the Bismark!* (1960) which emphasises character as strongly as patriotic action. Similar qualities are to be found in *Carve Her Name with Pride* (1958) which made Virginia McKenna a star in the role of the wartime spy Violette Szabo and which provides another understated celebration of British courage.

Gilbert's films of the late 1950s and early 1960s are much less cohesive and veer around in tone and content. *Ferry to Hong Kong* (1959) and *The Seventh Dawn* (1964) are poorly acted blockbusters aimed at an international market, while *HMS Defiant* (1962) is a rather wooden variation on *Mutiny on the Bounty*. *The Greengage Summer* (1961) offers a coming-of-age drama with the young Susannah York which must have seemed dated even on its release. His most interesting film of this period is *The Admirable Crichton* (1957) based on J. M. Barrie's play and again featuring Kenneth More, this time as the manservant who turns the tables on his employer when they are stranded on a desert island. Although sentimental and slightly overwhelmed by the photogenic backgrounds, the film retains enough of the play's commentary on class to be effective and Moore is unusually acerbic.

Gilbert's biggest hit came with *Alfie* (1966), adapted from Bill Naughton's play. Its tale of a cockney Lothario, memorably played by Michael Caine complete with direct address to the camera, is undeniably an iconic movie of the Swinging Sixties. It's a film of two distinct halves, the first an amusing account of Alfie's hedonistic, misogynist lifestyle and the second a sort of moral comeuppance in which he finds that one of his 'birds' has replaced him with a younger model. The abortion scene, as well as being a landmark for frankness in British cinema, is still powerfully moving. Further commercial success followed with the first of Gilbert's three Bond outings, *You Only Live Twice* (1967). Despite the impressive set used for the finale and the Japanese locations, this is a formulaic addition to the series, as are Gilbert's later Bond entries, the turgid *The Spy Who Loved Me* (1977) and the more tongue-in-cheek, *Star Wars*-influenced *Moonraker* (1979).

The international impact of *Alfie* took Gilbert to America for the glossy excesses of *The Adventurers* (1970), a Harold Robbins adaptation. If Gilbert has sometimes seemed the proficient craftsman turning out solid mainstream films rather than an auteur pursuing his personal vision, then this is especially true of his 1970s output. Other than his two Bond movies, the decade saw him make the sentimental teenage romance *Friends* (1971) and its sequel *Paul and Michelle* (1974), as well as the preposterous *Seven Nights in Japan* (1976) and the downbeat American-made war drama *Operation Daybreak* (1975). He showed a much surer touch in the 1980s returning to intrinsically British subjects. Both *Educating Rita* (1983) and *Shirley Valentine* (1989) are based on Willy Russell plays and benefit from his witty one-liners, as well as from striking performances by Michael Caine, Julie Walters and Pauline Collins. The frustrations of the two female leads, trying to find a way out of the narrow confines placed on them by a male-dominated society, are captured with affection and empathy.

Gilbert's recent work continues to be eclectic, from the American-made *Stepping Out* (1991), a putting-on-a-show, feelgood movie with Liza Minnelli and Julie Walters, to *Haunted* (1995), a rather old fashioned creepy-house ghost story from a James Herbert novel. The solid professionalism which has distinguished Gilbert's long career has been acknowledged by a number of prizes including BAFTA's Michael Balcon Award in 1990 and a BFI Fellowship in 2001. This can be seen as recognition by his peers for a lifetime's work which, if not always marked by high artistic individualism, has often shown a concern for a characteristically British kind of bravery.

**British Feature Films:** *Little Ballerina* (1947); *Once a Sinner* (1950); *The Scarlet Thread* (1951); *There is Another Sun* (1951); *Time Gentleman Please!* (1952); *Emergency Call* (1952); *Cosh Boy* (1953); *Albert RN* (1953); *Johnny on the Run* (1953); *The Good Die Young* (1954); *The Sea Shall Not Have Them* (1954); *Cast a Dark Shadow* (1955); *Reach for the Sky* (1956); *The Admirable Crichton* (1957); *Carve Her Name With Pride* (1958); *A Cry from the Streets* (1958); *Ferry to Hong Kong* (1959); *Light Up the Sky!* (1960); *Sink the Bismarck!* (1960); *The Greengage Summer* (1961); *HMS Defiant* (1962); *The Seventh Dawn* (1964); *Alfie* (1966); *You Only Live Twice* (1967); *Friends* (1971); *Paul and Michelle* (1974); *Seven Nights in Japan* (1976); *The Spy Who Loved Me* (1977); *Moonraker* (1979); *Educating Rita* (1983); *Not Quite Jerusalem* (1984); *Shirley Valentine* (1989); *Haunted* (1995); *Before You Go* (2002).

**Bibliography:** Brian McFarlane, *An Autobiography of British Cinema* (London: Methuen, 1997).

# Terry GILLIAM

British cinema can only make a partial claim to Terry Gilliam as he was born in the United States and has made a number of his feature films there. Nonetheless, his quirky individualism, offbeat humour and fascination with the surreal have often found a safer home in British cinema and television than in Hollywood. Gilliam is an unapologetic maverick, frequently at odds with producers and executives. Even so, he has still managed to carve out a body of work which bares his unmistakable signature. His is a unique cinematic vision, anarchic and dreamlike, with something of the child's unfettered wonder at the strangeness of the world.

Gilliam was born in Minneapolis on 22 November 1940 and moved with his family to Los Angeles in 1951. He studied physics at Occidental College, where he also founded and edited the satirical student magazine *Fang*. After graduation he moved to New York where he had a job as assistant editor for the humorous magazine *Help*. He then worked in advertising and as a freelance illustrator before moving to London in 1967. Here he established himself in television working on a number of comedy shows before becoming part of the team behind *Monty Python's Flying Circus*. Gilliam's principle contributions to the groundbreaking comedy series were the bizarre cut-out animations which were frequently one of the most memorable features of the programmes. It was through Python that Gilliam made his directorial debut as co-director with Terry Jones of the team's second feature film, *Monty Python and the Holy Grail* (1975). Along with the familiar absurdist humour, the film offers a knowing satire of the Arthurian legends and of popular images of the medieval era, both elements that were to reappear in Gilliam's later films. Although he contributed animation sequences to the other Python films he left the directorial reigns to Terry Jones.

His solo career as a director was launched by *Jabberwocky* (1977), adapted very loosely from Lewis Carroll's poem. The film bares the marks of *Python* in its surreal visual comedy and echoes *Holy Grail* in its debunking of romantic images of medieval England, but adds an additional level of crude slapstick which proved off-putting for audiences. Much more appealing was *Time Bandits* (1981), the charming story of a boy travelling through time with a band of mischievous dwarfs. The film is full of memorable imagery such as a giant emerging from under the sea and managing to get a sailing ship lodged on the top of his head. Amid the chaos is something more poignant as well, in the figure of the lonely child, ignored by his overly conventional parents, who finds a temporary surrogate father in the part of Agamemnon (Sean Connery).

Escape into the imagination takes on a wholly different and more disturbing aspect in Gilliam's most impressive film, *Brazil* (1985). Bearing more than a passing resemblance to Orwell's *1984*, the film paints a dismal image of a future dystopia where a totalitarian state and rampant bureaucracy have sapped its citizens of their spirit. Gilliam's everyman (Jonathan Pryce) in his fight against the system mirrors the struggles that Gilliam had to maintain control over the film. He was vindicated by the positive reception and awards heaped on the film, which included two Oscar nominations. Clashes with producers were to undermine his last British film to date, *The Adventures of Baron Munchausen* (1988). Its central character, a teller of tall tales, seems to stand in for Gilliam's view of the world as a dark place requiring the transformative power of the imagination. The film's ambitious visual design and special effects ran up its budget to an astronomical degree and the costs were not recovered by its disappointing box office returns.

*The Fisher King* (1991) was Gilliam's first mainstream American film and appears to have been made under much tighter studio control. Nonetheless, it contains many of Gilliam's favourite themes in the clash between materialism and the pursuit of a more spiritual way of life, and it has one magical set-piece when travellers in Grand Central Station are suddenly transformed into dancers in an Astaire and Rogers production number. *Twelve Monkeys* (1995) is another ambitious dystopian fable which managed, like *The Fisher King*, to balance the director's personal obsessions with a more accessible, glossy approach. His adaptation of Hunter S. Thompson's *Fear and Loathing in Las Vegas* (1998) was probably a case of taking on the impossible, but the film does capture something of the manic, surreal nightmare of the book.

Gilliam returned to Europe to make *The Man Who Killed Don Quixote*, but after a catalogue of serious production problems led the budget to spiral, the film's financiers pulled out and it was not completed. The documentary *Lost in La Mancha* (2002, Keith Fulton and Lou Pepe) gives some indication of what might have been. The American-backed *The Brothers Grimm* (2005), although providing what would seem to be ideal Gilliam material, was a disappointment and took a critical hammering. Gilliam's difficulty has frequently been that the epic productions he plans require the backing of major Hollywood producers, which then lead to inevitable compromises which have diluted the distinctive flavour of his work. The sheer idiosyncrasy of his films tends to invite interference from anxious producers while offering considerable pleasure to his legions of fans who long for the unadulterated subversiveness of the real thing. Unfortunately, the dark fantasy of his most recent film, *Tideland* (2006), seems to have proved too much even for them.

**British Feature Films**: *Monty Python and the Holy Grail* (1975, co-directed with Terry Jones); *Jabberwocky* (1977); *Time Bandits* (1981); *Brazil* (1985); *The Adventures of Baron Munchausen* (1988).

**Bibliography**: Bob McCabe, *Dark Knights and Holy Fools* (London: Orion, 1999); Ian Christie (ed.), *Gilliam on Gilliam* (London: Faber & Faber, 1999).

**For Sidney GILLIAT, see Frank LAUNDER**

## Jack GOLD

Jack Gold was born on 28 June 1930 in London. After graduating from the University of London with a degree in law and economics, he joined the BBC where he became an editor on the influential news programme *Tonight*. Moving into directing and producing, he made a large number of documentaries and fictional pieces for television during the 1960s, frequently with a strongly political angle. He had made a short cinema film called *The Visit* for the BFI in 1959, but he didn't direct his first feature film until *The Bofors Gun* in 1968. An expansion of John McGrath's television play, it has something of the same anti-establishment tone as his best television work in its depiction of the largely futile activities of an army unit guarding an unused heavy gun in peacetime. The film benefits greatly from the intense perfor-mances of David Warner as the well-meaning but ineffectual officer and Nicol Williamson as a rebellious but increasingly violent enlisted man. Williamson is also highly impressive in *The Reckoning* (1969), again scripted by McGrath, a tough portrait of the brutalities of the corporate business world which is handled with an economy and sense of purpose which testify to Gold's training in actuality television.

Gold's left-wing sympathies are apparent in much of his 1970s output. *The National Health* (1973) is a bleak comedy adapted from Peter Nichols' stage play. It contrasts the chronic underfunding of an NHS ward with imagined scenes from a glamorous hospital soap opera. The casting of Jim Dale, and the film's mordant humour, led to it being dubbed by critics as 'Carry On Death'. *Man Friday* (1975) re-examines Daniel Defoe's classic novel from the viewpoint of Robinson Crusoe's manservant and offers a critique of imperialist attitudes. *Aces High* (1976) successfully transfers R. C. Sherriff's anti-war play from the trenches to the aerial dogfights of the First World War. In contrast, *The Medusa Touch* (1978) is a much more commercial project, with Richard Burton's charismatic presence adding some gravitas to its supernatural plot about a man who seems to have the mental capacity to cause disasters wherever he travels. *The Sailor's Return* (1978) centres on more familiar social themes in its depiction of the discrimination experienced by a Victorian sailor who returns to Britain with a black wife. The film did not receive a theatrical release and first came to light on television in 1980.

Most of Gold's work since the beginning of the 1980s has been for television. A good deal of this has been considerably more routine than his earlier work (Shakespeare for the BBC, the courtroom drama series *Kavanagh QC* for independent television), but it does include the immensely popular, albeit blatantly sentimental, *Goodnight Mister Tom* (1998) featuring one of his favourite actors, John Thaw. He also directed Thaw in the final episode of *Inspector Morse* in which the much-loved character was finally laid to rest. Nothing in his more recent television work quite matches up to the memory of *The Naked Civil Servant* (1975), a wonderfully funny, sympathetic portrait of Quentin Crisp with a superbly camp central performance from John Hurt. His only feature film since the 1970s is the slight house-moving comedy *The Chain* (1984) which is engaging enough, but certainly looks more like another expanded television play than a really cinematic project.

Gold's immersion in television has been both to the benefit and detriment of his cinema work. On the negative side is the lack of visual flair exhibited by films which often seem small on the big screen. On the positive side, there is the sensitive handling of loyal actors, the realism and the sense of political commitment which was fostered in the public service ethos of British television in the 1960s and 1970s.

**British Feature Films:** *The Bofors Gun* (1968); *The Reckoning* (1969); *The National Health* (1973); *Who?* (1974); *Man Friday* (1975); *Aces High* (1976); *The Sailor's Return* (1978); *The Medusa Touch* (1978); *The Chain* (1984).

## Peter GREENAWAY

Peter Greenaway has cut a very particular pathway through British cinema. Adamantly opposed to conventional narrative and entertainment values, his films explore the formal possibilities of the medium often utilising the latest technology to push at existing boundaries. His subjects are also frequently controversial and have sometimes outraged, but throughout his work there is a single-minded dedication to the cinema as an intellectual and aesthetic medium.

Born in Newport, Wales on 5 April 1942, he studied painting at Walthamstow College of Art before joining the Central Office of Information in 1965. Here he worked as an editor on public information films. With regular support from the BFI he produced a large number of short films during the 1960s and the first half of the 1970s. These films, such as *Dear Phone* (1977), *Water Wrackets* (1978) and *A Walk Through H* (1978), resemble documentaries, but Greenaway subverts their apparent realism, highlighting the artifice behind their construction. Frequently using a voice-over, they offer narratives that go nowhere and construct endless lists of seemingly random information. The results have an almost hypnotic fascination, full of baffling detail and mordant humour; they seem to suggest the futility of trying to make sense of the world through narrative structures. His one feature film of this period is *The Falls* (1980), an experimental three-hour work which provides biographies of ninety-two people whose names start with the word 'Fall'.

Greenaway's first mainstream feature, *The Draughtsman's Contract* (1982), was part financed by Channel 4 and achieved a degree of art house success. Set in the seventeenth century, it is a visually ravishing film depicting the relationship between an artist and his aristocratic employer. Full of narrative ambiguities and playful stylisation, it offers a puzzle without solution while raising questions about power and the social role of the artist. It also benefits greatly from Michael Nyman's score; Greenaway's other regular collaborators have included cinematographer Sacha Vierny and the Dutch producer Kees Kesander who has consistently supported/indulged him. *A Zed and Two Noughts* (1985) didn't generate the same appeal. It returns to the style of his short films in its near abstract fascination with mirror images and duality (the central characters are twins), as well as with attempts to catalogue the world. *The Belly of an Architect* (1987) is more accessible, with a fine central performance from Brian Dennehy as the American architect organising an exhibition in Rome. Familiar themes reappear, such as the relationship between artists and their patrons, but are given greater warmth by Dennehy's characteristion. *Drowning by Numbers* (1988) tells of three women who murder their husbands by drowning them. Themes of mortality and the power of nature are placed against Greenaway's continuing fascination with human efforts to order reality, expressed here in the use of numbers. The film itself unreels to a numerical count to one hundred on screen. The film's striking visuals and black humour won it a wider art house audience.

Greenaway's greatest commercial success came with *The Cook, The Thief, His Wife and Her Lover* (1989) which was widely interpreted as a political commentary on the materialism and greed engendered by the Thatcher administration. This is conveyed in the character of the ignorant, brutal 'thief' brilliantly played by Michael Gambon. The film offers plenty to engage the eye and mind, with its startling use of colour to mark the different areas of the restaurant, its theatrical sets, striking costumes by Jean-Paul Gaultier and near operatic score by Michael Nyman. The ugliness of its most violent sequences shocked some, but with hindsight the more troubling aspect is the film's snobbery; Greenaway's objection to Thatcherism appears to be that it enabled uneducated plebs to get rich quick and gain entry to the halls of culture only previously open to those with the 'good taste' to appreciate it. He achieved further art house success with the highly referential *Prospero's Books* (1991), his free adaptation of Shakespeare's *The Tempest* featuring John Gielgud. Greenaway is less interested in the play than in the figure of Prospero, the artist as magician, and his attempts to capture the world by recording its contents in his books. The books themselves are rendered with the aid of computer technology, an area of increasing interest to Greenaway.

By this time he had firmly established himself as a leading figure in British art cinema, but that pre-eminence has diminished with much of his subsequent work. *The Baby of Macon* (1993), a satire on organised religion which also takes in an examination of the nature of audiences, alienated many with its repellent multiple rape sequence and gave fresh fuel to critics who accuse him of pretentiousness and obfuscation. *The Pillow Book* (1996) returns to *Prospero's Books* in its attempts to use new technology to reinvent the visual space of cinema through split-screen images, calligraphy and superimposition. The meditation on language and meaning is seductive, but the film is open to criticisms of orientalism in its depictions of the sensuous East. Accusations of misogyny resurfaced with *8½ Women* (1999), a film which found very few supporters. Perhaps because of commercial disinterest in his work or through a desire for greater freedom, Greenaway's most recent work has moved outside of conventional cinema into utilising DVD and CD-ROM technology to produce interactive, collaborative work. *The Tulse Luper Suitcases* (2003–4) is an ongoing project with many individual sections which can be accessed in a variety of formats. Its full version currently runs to nine hours, but could be expanded with more additions.

Greenaway has often divided critical opinion. For his critics there is more than a whiff of the emperor's new clothes about him, compounded by what they see as his obsession with nudity and violence. For supporters, he is a rare voice in British cinema, closer to traditions in European art cinema and the avant-garde; his films combine a concern for film aesthetics (that owes little to realism or narrative cinema) with self-reflexive meditations on the nature of art (and cinema) itself.

**British Feature Films:** *The Draughtsman's Contract* (1982); *A Zed and Two Noughts* (1985); *The Belly of an Architect* (1987); *Drowning by Numbers* (1988); *The Cook, The Thief, His Wife and Her Lover* (1989); *Prospero's Books* (1991); *The Baby of Macon* (1993); *The Pillow Book* (1996); *8½ Women* (1999); *The Tulse Luper Suitcases* (2003–04).

**Bibliography:** Vernon Gras and Marguerite Gras (eds), *Peter Greenaway Interviews* (Jackson, MS: University of Mississippi, 2000); Amy Lawrence, *The Films of Peter Greenaway* (Cambridge: Cambridge University Press, 1997); Alan Woods, *Being Naked Playing Dead: The Art of Peter Greenaway* (Manchester: Manchester University Press, 1996).

## Val GUEST

Few British directors can boast a longer or more prolific career than Val Guest. His fifty years in the industry saw him take part in over eighty films including credits as director, writer, producer and composer. Born on 11 December 1911 in London as Valmond Guest, he spent part of his childhood in India and began his career as an actor on stage as well as in films. After a period working as a journalist, he returned to cinema in 1935 as a scriptwriter at Gainsborough. Over the next seven years he built a reputation as an outstanding writer of music hall-style comedies, including some of the best vehicles for Will Hay. His feature debut as director was with an Arthur Askey comedy *Miss London Ltd* (1943). For the next ten years he was a jobbing director churning out fairly undistinguished genre fare for a variety of British studios. Among his more interesting efforts are the satirical comedy *Mr Drake's Duck* (1950), featuring the American actress Yolande Donlan who was to become his second wife, and *The Runaway Bus* (1954), an amiable farce with Frankie Howerd.

*Life with the Lyons* (1954), the first of two routine spin-offs from the popular television comedy series, started Guest's association with Hammer which eventually led to *The Quatermass Experiment* (1955). The film was a landmark for the studio, its popularity convincing them to shift into the horror genre. Another television adaptation, this time from Nigel Kneale's science fiction serial, the film overcomes its low budget to produce a genuinely tense, and even touching, variation on the Frankenstein theme. The sequel, *Quatermass II* (1957), is equally taughtly handled and ranks among the best British examples of the Cold War paranoia genre. Along with *The Abominable Snowman* (1957), another surprisingly thoughtful monster film with a fine performance from Peter Cushing and eerily atmospheric snowscapes, these films show Guest's real strengths. His neat, economic direction maximises tension while providing plenty of room for character development and the use of allegory.

Despite such aberrations as Hammer's crudely exploitative *The Camp on Blood Island* (1958) and formulaic comedies like *Up the Creek* (1958), Guest entered his best period as a film-maker in the late 1950s and early 1960s. Cold War anxieties surface again in the compelling *The Day the Earth Caught Fire* (1961), in which the earth is thrown off its axis by the testing of nuclear weapons. Unusually, the narrative unfolds as it is reported by the journalists of a London newspaper office. *Expresso Bongo* (1959) is an acerbic, amusing critique of Britain's developing pop music scene which makes remarkably good use of Laurence Harvey and Cliff Richard, as well as providing a vivid impression of contemporary Soho. In a series of memorable films, Guest combined populist genre elements with social commentary and low-key realism. The crime dramas *Hell Is a City* (1959) and *Jigsaw* (1962) set their police investigations against the backdrop of a drab, decaying urban Britain, while *Yesterday's Enemy* (1959) is an effective anti-war film. In *The Beauty Jungle* (1964) the seamy world of beauty pageants and glamour modelling is uncovered, whereas contemporary angst is again the subtext of *80,000 Suspects* (1963) with its story of the hunt for a deadly virus. Guest exhibits his characteristic ability to bring out the tensions just under the mundane surface of everyday British life in these films.

His later work unfortunately shows a clear decline. He was one of many directors on the James Bond spoof *Casino Royale* (1967) which, like *Where the Spies Are* (1965), epitomises all that was superficial and self-indulgent in Swinging London pop culture. He made a belated return to Hammer for the silly but likeable fantasy of *When Dinosaurs Ruled the Earth* (1969), but nothing can really redeem the depressing inanities of the sexploitation comedies *Au Pair Girls* (1972) and *Confessions of a Window Cleaner* (1974). His subsequent output until the mid-1980s is mainly routine television work, with the exception of a few middling comedies including *The Boys in Blue* (1983), a vehicle for the bland comedians Cannon and Ball which looked dated even on its release. It was a tame end to Guest's career, but one that still reflected his extraordinary work ethic. In his best films he surpassed the limitations of genre formula and restricted budgets to produce work of real interest. In these films a lean, purposeful directorial style is combined with intelligent scripting to produce work with higher ambitions. In particular, at the end of the 1950s he managed to capture a vivid impression of a dreary, anxious postwar Britain on the cusp of radical change. He died on 10 May 2006.

**British Feature Films:** *Miss London Ltd* (1943); *Give Us the Moon* (1944); *Bees in Paradise* (1944); *I'll Be Your Sweetheart* (1945); *Just William's Luck* (1947); *William Comes to Town* (1948); *Murder at the Windmill* (1949); *Miss Pilgrim's Progress* (1949); *The Body Said No!* (1950); *Mr Drake's Duck* (1950); *Penny Princess* (1952); *The Runaway Bus* (1954); *Life with the Lyons* (1954); *The Men of Sherwood Forest* (1954); *Dance Little Lady* (1954); *The Lyons in Paris* (1955); *Break in the Circle* (1955); *The Quatermass Experiment* (1955); *They Can't Hang Me* (1955); *It's a Wonderful World* (1956); *The Weapon* (1956); *Carry on Admiral* (1957); *Quatermass II* (1957); *The Abominable Snowman* (1957); *The Camp on Blood Island* (1958); *Up the Creek* (1958); *Further Up the Creek* (1958); *Life Is a Circus* (1958); *Yesterday's Enemy* (1959); *Expresso Bongo* (1959); *Hell Is a City* (1959); *The Full Treatment* (1960); *The Day the Earth Caught Fire* (1961); *Jigsaw* (1962); *80,000 Suspects* (1963); *The Beauty Jungle* (1964); *Where the Spies Are* (1965); *Casino Royale* (1967, co-directed with John Huston, Ken Hughes, Robert Parrish and Joe McGrath); *Assignment K* (1968); *When Dinosaurs Ruled the Earth* (1969); *Toomorrow* (1970); *Au Pair Girls* (1972); *Confessions of a Window Cleaner* (1974); *The Diamond Mercenaries* (1975); *The Shillingbury Blowers* (1980); *Dangerous Davies – The Last Detective* (1981); *The Boys in Blue* (1983).

**Bibliography:** Val Guest, *So You Want To Be In Pictures?* (London: Reynolds & Hearn, 2001).

# H

## John HALAS and Joy BATCHELOR

British cinema has had more than its fair share of directorial duos, but this is probably the only one where the partners were married to each other. British cinema has also secured an international reputation for animation; the foundations of that tradition lie in the work of this husband and wife team. John Halas, birth name János Hálász, was born in Budapest, Hungary on 16 April 1912. He began his career there working with the future Hollywood special effects wizard George Pal. When he came to Britain in 1936, Joy Batchelor (born in Watford on 22 May 1914) answered his advertisement for an assistant. They initially worked together in graphic design, but soon began making animated shorts together and in 1940 founded their own animation company, Halas-Batchelor Cartoon Films. They were married the same year.

The company began by making commercials for clients like Kelloggs but was quickly recruited by the Ministry of Information to make propaganda shorts for the war effort. They produced over seventy of these engaging films, including *Filling the Gap* (1941) which encouraged the public to make better use of their gardens by growing vegetables.

After the war they continued to take commissions from government departments for public education films. Among these were the series featuring 'Charley', a curmudgeon who needs to have the advantages of the welfare state explained to him. They made similar films for the American government to promote their postwar policies for European cooperation and economic recovery. As the largest animation unit working in Britain, they began to branch out in the 1950s employing a variety of techniques, from puppets in *The Figurehead* (1953) to 3D effects in *The Owl and the Pussycat* (1952). By far their most ambitious work was an adaptation of George Orwell's allegory of communist Russia, *Animal Farm* (1954). It took three years to make and was the first feature-length cartoon made in Britain. Employing a visual style that is clearly influenced by Disney, but which dispenses with their reliance on sentiment and knockabout humour, the film tackles its very adult themes head on, even if the ending offers a much more affirmative message about revolution than Orwell's sombre warning of the dangers of totalitarianism.

Two interesting series for television followed in the 1960s. *Tales of Hoffnung* (1964), made for the BBC and adapted from Gerald Hoffnung's caricatures, has a whimsical charm, whereas the *Foo-Foo* (1960) cartoons for the American broadcaster ABC have the naive quality of early animation in their simplified figures. These shorts show Halas and Batchelor moving away from the fully realised, smoothly pictorial style of *Animal Farm* into something rather leaner and more experimental. This is particularly apparent in two satirical animations about the impact of the automobile, *Automania 2000* (1963), which was nominated for an Oscar, and *Cars of the Future* (1969), both of which betray the influence of the American studio UPA in their pared-down style.

In the 1970s the studio was sold to Tyne Tees Television and made a series of popular, undemanding cartoon series for children including *The Jackson Five* (1971) and *The Osmonds* (1972), although *The Count of Monte Cristo* (1973) managed a good deal of romantic panache. Towards the end of their career together they moved back into more adventurous work using computer technology and engaged in a number of European co-productions. John Halas became something of a public champion for animation, initially as the first Chairman of the British Animation Group and then as President of the International Animated Film Association (ASIFA). Joy Batchelor died in London on 14 May 1991 and her husband followed her four years later on 21 January 1995. Their work together bridged the accessibility of Disney's populism with the quirky individualism of European traditions in animation and frequently gave expression to their liberal, humanistic outlook. Notwithstanding Aardman, they are still the most important animators that Britain has produced.

**British Feature Films**: *Animal Farm* (1954); *Ruddigore* (1966).

**Bibliography**: John Halas, *Masters of Animation* (London: BBC Books, 1987); Roger Manvell, *Art and Animation: The Story of Halas and Batchelor Animation Studio 1940–1980* (Keynsham: Clive Farrow, 1980).

## Robert HAMER

The output of Ealing Studios tended to be dominated by the house style imposed by its head, Michael Balcon. Occasionally, one or two of its directors broke away from Balcon's ethos to produce work with a more personal, individual quality. This is certainly true of Robert Hamer, a tragic figure in the history of British cinema whose career ended early due to alcoholism, but who left a small, deeply impressive body of work behind him.

Hamer was born on 31 March 1911 in Kidderminster, son of the actor Gerald Hamer. He was sent down from Cambridge, but subsequently went into the film industry as an assistant editor with Gaumont-British in 1934. From there he moved to KORDA's London Films and then on to Mayflower, the company formed by German producer Erich Pommer and British actor Charles Laughton, where he edited *Jamaica Inn* (1939), Alfred HITCHCOCK's last British picture before departing for Hollywood. After a brief stint with the GPO Film Unit, he was recruited by Ealing where he was employed initially as an editor and then as an associate producer. He made his debut as a director with the 'Haunted Mirror' section for the portmanteau horror film *Dead of Night* (1945). It is one of the most disturbing stories in the film, taking a well-worn theme and investing it with a sense of the danger lying underneath the surface of bourgeois life. His first feature, *Pink String and Sealing Wax* (1946), again featured Googie Withers as the barmaid trying to lead poor Gordon Jackson astray. The film manages a similar atmosphere to 'The Haunted Mirror', portraying a claustrophobic world of Victorian conformity almost undone by unbridled desire.

Set in London's working-class East End and centring on the story of a bored wife who gives shelter to her former lover (now an escaped convict), *It Always Rains on Sunday* (1947) might be expected to be a standard piece of Ealing social realism, but Hamer takes it in a different direction. With Googie Withers again in the lead, the film is visually striking with more attention paid to creating a gloomy mood than in naturalistic observation. It scored a considerable commercial and critical success. Hamer's undisputed masterpiece, voted sixth in a BFI poll of the best British films, is *Kind Hearts and Coronets* (1949). With its witty, literate script and suitably disdainful performance from Dennis Price as Louis, the poor relation of the grand D'Ascoyne family who murders his way towards the family inheritance, the film adopts a uniquely taciturn attitude towards its dark subject matter. Alec Guinness is suitably outlandish playing all eight victims (one of them female) and the film still seems remarkably modern in both its critique of class and its liberated attitude towards sex.

After a number of possible projects had been rejected by Balcon, he made *The Spider and the Fly* (1950) back at the revamped Mayflower. The pessimistic undercurrent in Hamer's work is most obvious here, with its story of a three-sided relationship (often a feature of his films) set against the backdrop of France just before the outbreak of the First World War. He returned to Ealing for one final film, the disappointingly stagey comedy *His Excellency* (1951) which, as with his previous film, stars Eric Portman. Unable to gain Balcon's approval for any further projects, he made *The Long Memory* (1952) for producer Hugh Stewart. John Mills is slightly unlikely as the ex-convict seeking revenge after serving time for a crime he didn't commit, but Hamer invests the film with his now familiar fatalism and makes striking use of the setting on a barge and of the dreary mudflats at Gravesend for the final chase. Hamer's melancholy is even apparent in the understated *Father Brown* (1954), adapted from G. K. Chesterton's short stories. Alec Guinness is the priest turned detective, but the film is as concerned with the moral salvation of his arch-enemy, played sympathetically by Peter Finch, as it is in Chesterton's hero.

Struggling to find suitable film projects in the mid-1950s – *To Paris with Love* (1955) is an insubstantial comedy again with Alec Guinness – he turned instead to television making *A Month in the Country* (1955), a touching adaptation of Turgenev for the independent company Rediffusion. The last cinema film he completed was *The Scapegoat* (1958), an intermittently fascinating adaptation from Daphne du Maurier with Guinness this time playing a holidaymaker tricked into taking on another's man's identity. The film's potential was certainly hampered by post-production cutting by its American backers, as well as by disputes Hamer had with the author and his star. The break-up of his second marriage and his own confused sexuality may have contributed to his descent into chronic alcoholism; he had to be replaced while shooting *School for Scoundrels* (1959). There is still much to admire in the film's comic take on the cruelties of the British class system and the performances by Ian Carmichael, Alastair Sim and Terry-Thomas are perfectly judged. He didn't direct again, although he completed a couple of assignments as a scriptwriter before succumbing to his addiction. He died on 4 December 1963 at St Thomas's Hospital in London.

It was a tragic end to a career that should have delivered so much more. Nonetheless, the small group of films he directed indicates a film-maker of real substance, typified by his visual panache as well as by a mordantly humorous view of British manners and methods. Even without knowing his life story, there is a detectable strain of melancholy in his work which invests even his comedies with an underlying depth of emotion and pathos.

**British Feature Films:** *Dead of Night* (1945, one segment); *Pink String and Sealing Wax* (1945); *It Always Rains on Sunday* (1947); *Kind Hearts and Coronets* (1949); *The Spider and the Fly* (1949); *His Excellency* (1951); *The Long Memory* (1952); *Father Brown* (1954); *To Paris with Love* (1955); *The Scapegoat* (1958); *School for Scoundrels* (1959, completed by Cyril Frankel).

**Bibliography:** Philip Kemp, 'The Long Shadow: Robert Hamer after Ealing', in Ian MacKillop and Neil Sinyard (eds), *British Cinema of the 1950s: A Celebration* (Manchester: Manchester University Press, 2003); Charles Drazin, *The Finest Years: British Cinema of the 1940s* (London: André Deutsch, 1998).

## Guy HAMILTON

Born on 16 September 1922 in Paris but educated in England, Guy Hamilton's long cinema career began modestly as a clapperboy at the Victorine Studios in France in 1938. With the outbreak of war he returned to Britain where he worked briefly at Paramount's film library before joining the Royal Navy. After the war, he went back into the industry, rising to first assistant director, working on such notable projects as *The Third Man* (1949) for Carol REED, where he occasionally doubled for Orson Welles in long shots, and *The African Queen* (1951) with the American director John Huston. He made his

directorial debut with *The Ringer* (1952), a successful adaptation of a
thriller by Edgar Wallace, starring Donald Wolfit. His reputation as a
solidly efficient film-maker grew with *The Intruder* (1953), which
depicts some of the problems facing postwar Britain, and in *An
Inspector Calls* (1954), an effective version of J. B. Priestley's vaguely
supernatural morality play about a bourgeois family who must face
their culpability in the death of a young girl. He reached an early high
point with *The Colditz Story* (1955), a characteristically understated
Second World War drama which excitingly portrays the attempts of a
group of British POWs to escape from a German high-security prison.
The film's strengths lie in its authentic detail and its willingness not to
water down the more tragic elements in its story.

Hamilton's work over the next nine years is uneven and frequently
unremarkable. The best of an indifferent bunch include *Charley Moon*
(1956), a passable musical vehicle for Max Bygraves, *The Devil's
Disciple* (1959), a star-studded adaptation of a minor Shaw play
produced by Burt Lancaster's company, and *A Touch of Larceny*
(1959), an urbane comedy with James Mason. A low point was reached
with *The Party's Over* (1963, released 1965), a rather hysterical attack
on the immorality of Swinging London disowned by its producer,
Rank, and much cut about by the British censor. He had already
handled large-scale action sequences on the American-backed war film
*The Best of Enemies* (1961), but the decisive moment in Hamilton's
career, which promoted him into the arena of big-budget international
movies, took place when he had the chance to replace Terence
YOUNG on the third of the phenomenally successful James Bond
films, *Goldfinger* (1964). It is, perhaps, the best of the Bonds and
certainly the most memorable of Sean Connery's 1960s outings in the
role. As well as the usual exotic locations, beautiful girls and spectacular stunts, star and director bring a nonchalant humour to proceedings which neatly undercut the increasing level of fantasy. He was to
return to Bond three more times. *Diamonds Are Forever* (1971) marks
the slightly desultory final appearance of Connery in the role, whereas
*Live and Let Die* (1973) successfully introduced his new, lightweight
replacement, Roger Moore. Moore brought broader humour to his first
Bond, but *The Man with the Golden Gun* (1974) was the weakest entry
in the series to date, with its threadbare attempt to cash in on the
contemporary audience taste for martial arts.

Outside of the Bond movies, Hamilton also made the second in the
Harry Palmer spy series, *Funeral in Berlin* (1966). Here a bespectacled
Michael Caine returns as the poor man's Bond, providing a downbeat,
grittier take on 1960s Cold War anxieties. *Battle of Britain* (1969) again

assembled a starry cast for its depiction of Britain's 'finest hour', but the romantic sub-plots, poor characterisation and slow pace drained the spectacular action sequences of much of their power. By the 1970s Hamilton's work had diminished to strictly routine, commercial chores. *Force Ten from Navarone* (1978) is a belated sequel to *The Guns of Navarone* (1961, J. Lee THOMPSON) which bears little connection to its predecessor and presents some fairly predictable wartime action adventures. He followed this with two glossy Agatha Christie adaptations, *The Mirror Crack'd* (1980) and *Evil Under the Sun* (1981), whose main virtues lie in their professionalism. His final films before retiring, *Remo Williams: The Adventure Begins* (1985) and *Try This One for Size* (1989), were made in America and France respectively and added little to his reputation.

Although few would attempt to make the case for Hamilton as an auteur film-maker, his is a more typical workman-like career in what is, after all, a highly commercial industry. His best work handles popular genre material with considerable vigour and not a little humour, bringing a polished technique to sometimes routine subjects and frequently making of it superior entertainment.

**British Feature Films:** *The Ringer* (1952); *The Intruder* (1953); *An Inspector Calls* (1954); *The Colditz Story* (1955); *Charley Moon* (1956); *Manuela* (1957); *A Touch of Larceny* (1959); *The Devil's Disciple* (1959); *The Party's Over* (1963); *Man in the Middle* (1963); *Goldfinger* (1964); *Funeral in Berlin* (1966); *Battle of Britain* (1969); *Diamonds Are Forever* (1971); *Live and Let Die* (1973); *The Man with the Golden Gun* (1974); *Force Ten From Navarone* (1978); *The Mirror Crack'd* (1980); *Evil Under the Sun* (1981).

## Cecil HEPWORTH

Cecil M. Hepworth was one of the key pioneers in the development of narrative cinema in Britain and became one of its most prominent film-makers throughout the silent period. He was born on 19 March 1874 in London. Following the example of his father, the renowned magic lanternist T. C. Hepworth, he entered the burgeoning film industry when it was in its initial artisan phase. He briefly assisted another important pioneer, Birt ACRES, worked for Charles Urban's film company, patented an electric arc lamp (1896) and wrote the first book on cinema technique, *The ABC of the Cinematograph*, in 1897. In 1899 he built a studio in a small converted house in Walton-on-Thames and set up Hepworth and Co. with his cousin Monty Wicks. They made a range of short actuality subjects (including a very popular film of

Queen Victoria's funeral in 1901) and scenic films, with Hepworth usually acting as director and cameraman. They also produced charming trick films like *The Bathers* (1900) where the audience was offered the amazing sight of two men diving into a river and then, in reverse motion, apparently rising back out.

In 1904 the firm became the Hepworth Manufacturing Company and Hepworth moved from directing to overseeing the company's output. They poured out large numbers of tiny films covering a wide variety of genres from travelogues to slapstick comedy. In 1905 Hepworth released *Rescued by Rover* (Lewin Fitzhamon) which has come to be seen as a landmark in British cinema, occupying something like the same position that Edwin S. Porter's *The Great Train Robbery* (1903) has in relation to American cinema. Its sophisticated (for the time) storytelling, with editing which progressed the narrative, set new standards in professionalism, as well as introducing cinema's first canine star. Hepworth recognised the potential draw of stars and made a sequence of films featuring a roster of contracted performers such as Alma Taylor, Stewart Rome and Chrissie White. His liking for innovations found expression in the Vivaphone, an early attempt at producing synchronised sound using recorded discs which ultimately failed. He returned to directing in 1911, instigating a sequence of prestigious literary adaptations including an ambitious hour-long version of *Hamlet* (1913, Hay Plumb).

Hepworth continued to work successfully into the 1920s with his company renamed as Hepworth Picture Plays. He made melodramas, including a remake of *Comin' Thro' the Rye* (1923) which he had previously filmed in 1916 and which remained his favourite among his own work, and comedies such as *Alf's Button* (1920), a considerable commercial success. Hepworth's ambitions eventually got the better of him when his attempts to establish a large integrated studio at a country estate he had purchased led in 1924 to the receiver being called in. Catastrophically, all of his negatives were melted down for their silver content to help repay his debts. He maintained his connections with the industry making trailers for the National Screen Service in the 1930s and working for the Ministry of Information in the Second World War. Later he chaired the History Research Committee at the BFI.

Hepworth developed a style of film-making which was highly theatrical in mode, using simple stories which unfold on a flat plane in front of a static camera in mid-shot and using actors whose methods frequently tend towards exaggerated gesticulating. This approach quickly dated and Hepworth's unwillingness to take on board contemporary developments in Hollywood and other European cinemas proved fatal for the audience appeal of his films. Now his work seems to have a peculiarly British quality which gives it a warmer appeal, whether through the pictorial values of *Comin' Thro' the Rye* with its feeling for landscape or in the eccentric humour of irresistible early films like *How it Feels to be Run Over* (1900). In later years he undertook lecture tours to talk about what had been a central role in the pioneering of cinema. He died at Greenford, Middlesex on 9 February 1953.

**Selected British Feature Films:** *The Basilisk* (1914); *The Baby on the Barge* (1915); *Trelawney of the Wells* (1916); *Comin' Thro' the Rye* (1916); *Annie Laurie* (1916); *Nearer My God to Thee* (1917); *Sheba* (1919); *Alf's Button* (1920); *Anna the Adventuress* (1920); *Tansy* (1921); *Wild Heather* (1921); *Mist in the Valley* (1923); *Comin' Thro' the Rye* (1923); *The House of Marney* (1926).

**Bibliography:** Cecil M. Hepworth, *Came the Dawn: Memories of a Film Pioneer* (London: Phoenix House, 1951).

## Mark HERMAN

Mark Herman was born in Bridlington, East Yorkshire in 1954. After art college he attended the National Film School at Beaconsfield where he specialised in animation. Here he made the short film *See You at Wembley, Frankie Walsh* (1987) which went on to win Best Foreign Film at the Student Oscars. This auspicious start was not repeated with his debut feature, the sadly inept farce *Blame It on the Bellboy* (1992). Following a period working on a television sitcom and writing pop songs, he made *Brassed Off* (1996), perhaps the best of the new breed of popular British comedies which combined realism with elements of the American 'feelgood' tradition. The film manages a darker, grittier quality than the likes of *The Full Monty* (1997) and is more overt in its denunciation of Thatcherism, with its devastating impact on working-class communities such as the mining village depicted here. The film was well received, picking up a plethora of international awards including a French 'Oscar' (the César for Best Foreign Film) and the Peter Sellers Award for Comedy at the London *Evening Standard* Awards.

Herman's subsequent films have strived for the same qualities, but have been only partially successful in achieving this. *Little Voice* (1998) also concerns itself with the frustrated ambitions of working-class characters and adopts a style that mixes naturalism with stylised fantasy. The unevenness of effect is typified in the variety of performance styles, ranging from the theatrical tour-de-force offered by Jane Horrocks and the genuine emotional power generated by Michael

Caine (who won a Golden Globe), to the unrestrained pantomime of Brenda Blethyn's role. A degree of toughness usually undercuts any tendency towards sentimentality in Herman's work, as is apparent in *Purely Belter* (2000), the story of two teenage lads and their fraught attempts to raise the money for a season ticket at their football club, Newcastle United. The film has enough grit to depict their lives without condescension or recourse to easy solutions and the performances are fresh and likeable.

His most recent film was *Hope Springs* (2002), a charming American-set romantic comedy with Colin Firth and Heather Graham. Herman wrote the screenplay for this, as he has with all of his work to date. Over this small group of films, Herman has established his credentials as a writer and director of populist comedy films which successfully combine humour with social commentary, an approach which has frequently been a feature of British film production. He promises to be a talent to watch for the future.

**British Feature Films:** *Blame It on the Bellboy* (1992); *Brassed Off* (1996); *Little Voice* (1998); *Purely Belter* (2000).

## (Sir) Alfred HITCHCOCK

Often considered the most important film-maker, with Charles Chaplin, to have been born in the UK, Alfred Hitchcock's British films have been overshadowed by his more famous work in Hollywood. There is obviously some justification for this, but it gives a false impression by underestimating the quality of the work he produced in his early years in England. Here he explored many of the techniques and themes which were to make his films so distinctive throughout this career.

Alfred Hitchcock was born on 13 August 1899 at Leytonstone on the outskirts of London. He later moved with his parents to London's East End where they again lived over the family business, a greengrocer's shop. Educated at a Jesuit school, the devout Catholicism of his family upbringing was to leave a considerable imprint on his outlook and his films. Leaving school at fourteen, he worked initially as a clerk in a telegraph company. Using drawing skills he had developed at evening classes with the University of London, he obtained a job designing title cards for the American company Famous Players-Lasky who had opened a studio in Islington in 1919. He joined Gainsborough when they took over the studio in 1924 and served his apprenticeship as scriptwriter, assistant director and set designer for their leading director Graham Cutts. His first two films as director, *The Pleasure Garden* (1925) and *The Mountain Eagle* (1926), were made in Germany

as co-productions. His exposure to the sophisticated cinematic methods of German film-makers were to have a major influence on his later
work, as did his membership of the London Film Society where he saw
the work of the most exciting contemporary European film-makers.
This is already apparent in his first significant film, *The Lodger* (1926),
with its expressionist lighting effects and startling camera tricks. Ivor
Novello is the mysterious figure who is almost martyred by the crowd
when the police suspect him of being a murderer in the mould of Jack

the Ripper. With its themes of guilt and persecution it prefigures Hitchcock's later preoccupations.

Hitchcock made a further six silent films which range across a variety of genres with the emphasis on melodrama, comedy and adaptations of successful West End plays. Although this material is relatively unremarkable, his fluent handling of it established him as the best director working in Britain. Critics hailed the 'Hitchcock touch', his ability to convey the narrative in purely visual terms, which was often apparent in striking set-pieces. Moving to British International Pictures in 1927 he completed the first British sound film, *Blackmail* (1929). Hitchcock made typically imaginative use of the new technology, particularly in the justly famous sequence in which the repeated word 'knife' leaps out of the soundtrack to mirror the heroine's sense of guilt. For the first half of the 1930s he continued to work in the standard generic forms of the period, making stage adaptations like *Juno and the Paycock* (1930) and *The Skin Game* (1931) and even a filmed operetta, *Waltzes from Vienna* (1933). The most memorable of these is the intriguing *Rich and Strange* (1932) which tells the ironic story of a married couple whose happiness is almost destroyed when they come into money and go on a cruise. The penny plain story provides a framework for Hitchcock to explore the possibilities of cinematic technique, as well as indulge his liking for cynical humour.

Joining Michael Balcon at Gaumont-British he was given virtually free reign and, with *The Man Who Knew Too Much* (1934), he embarked on a series of six thrillers which were to create his reputation as the 'master of suspense.' These films contain virtually all of the characteristics which we might expect from a later Hitchcock film. There is the innocent hero accused of a crime he didn't commit, who is then chased across country by a dimwitted police force as he in turn tries to catch the real villains. Along the way he encounters an icy blonde and they enter into a bickering, flirtatious relationship which eventually blossoms into romance. Deadpan humour is alternated with thrill sequences which show a remarkable visual ingenuity. Memorable set-pieces abound: in *The 39 Steps* (1935) there is the sudden cut from a woman's scream to the whistle of a steam engine; in *Sabotage* (1936) there is the heroine who has just learned of her young brother's death but who can't prevent herself laughing at the film cartoon she is watching; or in *Young and Innocent* (1937) the extraordinary crane shot as the camera swoops over the dancers to discover that the criminal who can only be identified by his twitching eyelids is actually the band's drummer. These films may seem lighter and more humorous than many of his later American films, but they frequently deal with similar themes of suppressed violence, desire and obsession which threaten to overwhelm the forces of order and restraint. As contemporary espionage thrillers, the stories frequently suggest that the threat comes from abroad, but more often it really comes from within the characters themselves.

Hitchcock's last British film before heading for Hollywood to join producer David O. Selznick was *Jamaica Inn* (1939), an adaptation of Daphne du Maurier's romantic yarn about Cornish smugglers. Leaving Britain on the eve of war seems to have pricked his conscience and as a result a number of his early American films contain pleas for America to join the war. He also returned home to make two French language short propaganda pieces for the Ministry of Information, *Bon Voyage* and *Aventure Malgache* (both 1944). A number of his American films of the 1940s are distinctly British in tone, often featuring English actors and settings, such as *Suspicion* (1941) with Cary Grant and *Rebecca* (1940), again adapted from Daphne du Maurier. In the late 1940s he formed Transatlantic Pictures with British exhibitor Sidney Bernstein in an attempt to alternate between Hollywood and domestic projects, but only one British film came of this, *Under Capricorn* (1949), an uncharacteristically stodgy period drama set in Australia and partially made using the 'ten minute take' method he had experimented with in Hollywood on *Rope* (1948). He returned to make two more films in Britain: *Stage Fright* (1950) is a rather heavy-handed thriller set in the theatre world, but *Frenzy* (1972), regarded by many as a late masterpiece, returned him to the familiar territory of a man wrongly accused of being a sex murderer. Unfortunately, the film's production methods are frequently dated and whereas his great films force the audience to face their own identification with the morally dubious behaviour of the central character, this one seems uncomfortably to offer up sadism for their entertainment.

It is easy enough to see Hitchcock's British period as a kind of youthful apprenticeship for his mature American work, as François Truffaut certainly did. But this is to overlook what is by any estimation a remarkable body of work. He had no real rival in British cinema of the 1920s and 1930s, either for command of the medium or the ability to examine complex themes within a commercial context. His British films are witty, elegant, cinematically adventurous and even surprisingly sexy. They can also be unnerving, disturbing and formally experimental. In later life he was showered with awards and received an honorary knighthood in 1980; a full knighthood was prohibited as he had by then become an American citizen. He married the scriptwriter Alma Reville in 1926 (she worked on some of his early films) and they were together until his death in Los Angeles on 29 April 1980.

**British Feature Films:** *The Pleasure Garden* (1925); *The Mountain Eagle* (1926); *The Lodger: A Story of the London Fog* (1926); *Downhill* (1927); *Easy Virtue* (1927); *The Ring* (1927); *The Farmer's Wife* (1928); *Champagne* (1928); *The Manxman* (1929); *Blackmail* (1929); *Juno and the Paycock* (1930); *Murder* (1930); *The Skin Game* (1931); *Rich and Strange* (1932); *Number Seventeen* (1932); *Waltzes from Vienna* (1933); *The Man Who Knew Too Much* (1934); *The 39 Steps* (1935); *Secret Agent* (1936); *Sabotage* (1936); *Young and Innocent* (1937); *The Lady Vanishes* (1938); *Jamaica Inn* (1939); *Under Capricorn* (1949); *Stage Fright* (1950); *Frenzy* (1972).

**Bibliography:** Mark Glancy, *The 39 Steps: A British Film Guide* (London: I. B. Tauris, 2002); Charles Barr, *English Hitchcock* (Moffat: Cameron & Hollis, 1999); Tom Ryall, *Blackmail* (London: BFI, 1993); Tom Ryall, *Alfred Hitchcock and the British Cinema* (London: Croom Helm, 1986); François Truffaut (with Helen G. Scott), *Hitchcock* (London: Secker & Warburg, 1969).

## Mike HODGES

Mike Hodges was born in Bristol on 29 July 1932. After training as a chartered accountant and completing two years' National Service, he moved into television in the late 1950s. Working in independent television, he rapidly moved up the ranks to become a scriptwriter, then as director and producer he made topical documentaries for the cutting-edge investigative series *World in Action*, as well as entries for the arts slot *Tempo*. Moving into fictional drama, he wrote and directed two thrillers for Thames Television, *Suspect* (1969) and *Rumour* (1970), which paved the way for his cinema debut with the gangster film *Get Carter* (1971). Poorly received at the time, it is now considered one of the cornerstones of British crime cinema. The film skilfully combines classic genre elements reminiscent of Raymond Chandler's novels (its story tells of a man visiting retribution on those responsible for his brother's death), with a gritty realism which took British crime films into previously uncharted areas of then explicit sex and violence. With its vivid setting in a dismal-looking Newcastle and an unexpectedly steely performance from Michael Caine, the film seemed to capture the cheerless mood of a nation rapidly descending from the brightly coloured exuberance of the 1960s into the fragmentation of the 1970s.

Subsequently Hodges struggled to match the prescience of his first film, although there is plenty to admire in *Pulp* (1972) in which Michael Caine plays a writer of trashy novels whose real life starts to resemble one of his books. The film's playful pastiche of genre conventions and guest star cameos might be called postmodern now but at the time proved difficult to sell to distributors. He spent a difficult few years in Hollywood where he made the gloomy science fiction film *The Terminal Man* (1974) before returning to Britain for *Flash Gordon* (1980), an enjoyably camp space adventure based on the 1920s comic strip character but owing rather more to Universal's unintentionally funny low-budget serials of the 1930s. Remaining in Britain he made an even broader sci-fi spoof, *Morons from Outer Space* (1985), scripted by and starring the television comedians Griff Rhys Jones and Mel Smith. The film misfires badly, playing like a weak relation to the Carry On series.

Hodges career has been severely marred by clashes with producers and difficulties with distribution. He was so incensed by the corporate re-cutting of his IRA drama *A Prayer for the Dying* (1987) that he publicly disowned it. The film as it stands is turgid and self-pitying, hampered by the mannered performance of Mickey Rourke. The American-made supernatural chiller *Black Rainbow* (1989) is intelligent and atmospheric but was barely released. He didn't make another film for nearly ten years and even then *Croupier* (1998) was only widely seen in Britain in 2000 after it had been an unexpected success in America and on the back of a wave of public interest generated by a re-release of *Get Carter*. There are echoes of *Get Carter* in its stylised depiction of the seedy world of casinos, their false glamour masking moral degeneration. There is a striking central performance from Clive Owen as another of Hodge's troubled, loner heroes. He also appears in *I'll Sleep When I'm Dead* (2003), a revenge thriller which bears more than a passing resemblance to *Get Carter* with its story of a gangster coming out of 'retirement' to avenge his brother's death. Typically, Hodges interest is drawn more to the psychological aspects of the narrative and its opportunities to explore issues around masculinity. Hodges' output has clearly been truncated by his disputes with production companies, but when he has worked unhindered he has made highly individual films which exemplify how genre formats can be the vehicle for powerful explorations of serious themes.

**British Feature Films**: *Get Carter* (1971); *Pulp* (1972); *Flash Gordon* (1980); *Morons from Outer Space* (1985); *A Prayer for the Dying* (1987); *Croupier* (1998); *I'll Sleep When I'm Dead* (2003).

**Bibliography**: Steven Davies, *Get Carter and Beyond: The Cinema of Mike Hodges* (London: Batsford, 2002); Robert Murphy, 'The Revenger's Tragedy – *Get Carter*', in Steve Chibnall and Robert Murphy (eds), *British Crime Cinema* (London: Routledge, 1999).

# Hugh HUDSON

Hugh Hudson, along with fellow directors Alan PARKER and Ridley Scott and the producer David Puttnam, forms part of a new strain in British cinema which emerged in the 1970s and which owes much to their shared background in advertising. For critics, their films suffered from the same deficiencies as the commercials they had trained on: they were glossy, empty and materialistic. For more sympathetic commentators, they brought a renewed sense of cinematic style and commercial acumen to an industry sorely in need of both.

Hudson was born in London on 25 August 1936 and educated at Eton. He went into advertising in the 1960s and made a considerable name for himself in the next decade with a series of visually arresting television commercials which won a number of international awards. Appropriately enough, it was Puttnam who gave him a chance to move into feature films with *Chariots of Fire* (1981), a nostalgic celebration of British sprinting success at the 1924 Olympics in Paris. The film was an enormous critical and commercial success, winning the Oscar for Best Film. It exemplifies the two contrasting viewpoints which have emerged about Hudson's work. Hudson, Puttnam and the film's writer Colin Welland have all been publicly open about their left-wing leanings, which for some are apparent in the film's critique of the British ruling class and their bigotry. Others argued that the film was the epitome of Thatcherism, a jingoistic endorsement of wealth and advantage. No one could dispute its place as a key British film of the period. It was a hard act to follow, but *Greystoke: The Legend of Tarzan, Lord of the Apes* (1984) proved at least partially successful. This handsome retelling of a familiar story focused on its more serious undercurrents, offering a commentary on the double standards of the Victorian class system, as well as an environmentalist message, contrasting the corruption of 'civilised' society with the more natural life of the jungle.

Few directors have suffered such a heavy fall from grace as Hudson did with his next film, *Revolution* (1985). It was a notorious critical and commercial disaster which played a part in bringing down Puttnam's production company, Goldcrest. This expensive, ambitious portrayal of the divided loyalties engendered by the American War of Independence was hampered by some eccentric casting but in retrospect is rather undeserving of its dire reputation. The film is surprisingly even-handed in its portrayal of the conflict and unsparing in depicting the chaos of war, but nothing could save it from economic oblivion. The American-made *Lost Angels* (1989), a pleasing, small-scale youth drama, did little to restore his reputation but at least slipped more quietly from view. It was ten years before his next feature film, *My Life So Far* (1999), a modest portrait of the early life of Denis Forman (film and TV executive) focusing on the relationship between father and son which failed to gain much attention. His last release was the American *I Dreamed of Africa* (2000) which was praised for its sumptuous photography but little else.

Tellingly, his most interesting work following the *Revolution* debacle was his 1987 Party Political Broadcast for the Labour Party which, in a glossy, cinematic style, presented its leader, Neil Kinnock, in the guise of an American presidential figure. It proved both controversial and remarkably influential. Hudson remains something of a lost talent for British cinema, his output following the boom and bust pattern of the Thatcher era. Few directors have started in a more dramatic fashion or had a subsequent career quite as frustratingly unfulfilled.

**British Feature Films:** *Chariots of Fire* (1981); *Greystoke: The Legend of Tarzan, Lord of the Apes* (1984); *Revolution* (1985); *My Life so Far* (1999).

**Bibliography:** Jake Eberts and Terry Ilott, *My Indecision Is Final: The Rise and Fall of Goldcrest Films* (London: Faber & Faber, 1990).

## James IVORY

James Ivory's name immediately conjures up glowing images of Edwardian England, where elegant figures in beautiful costumes move through cluttered drawing rooms or picturesque landscapes and, as the narrative unfolds, the hypocrisies underlying Britain's class system are gradually revealed. Few directors have become quite as synonymous with one particular style of film-making as Ivory, so that his name is a byword for tasteful period literary adaptations.

Ironically, for a director associated with as British a genre as the so-called 'heritage film', Ivory was born in Berkeley, California on 7 June 1928. After graduating from the University of Oregon, he attended film school at USC and then began his career making short documentaries in the late 1950s. He met the Indian producer Ismail Merchant and in 1961 they formed the production company Merchant-Ivory with the intention of making English language films in India which would play to an international market. Their first project together was *The Householder* (1963) based on a novel by Ruth Prawer Jhabvala (born in Germany of Polish parents, educated in England and Indian by marriage) who became the crucial third partner in their team, going on to script most of Ivory's subsequent films. They made three further films in India during the 1960s: *Shakespeare Wallah* (1965) is an affectionate story of the misadventures of an English theatre troupe on tour; *The Guru* (1969) is a slightly clumsy critique of the then fashionable western interest in Eastern mysticism with Michael York as an unlikely pop star; and *Bombay Talkie* (1970) tries to satirise Hindi cinema while itself teetering close to melodrama. In these films we see the emergence of Ivory's characteristic fascination for the confusions that occur when different cultures interact or where someone finds themselves an outsider in an alien environment.

Ivory made three uneven films in America during the 1970s including *The Wild Party* (1975), a bungled depiction of decadent Hollywood in the silent era (although studio re-editing took its toll), and *Roseland* (1977), a subtly affecting collection of short stories centred on the famous New York ballroom. Ivory's first British ventures were for television, where he made *Autobiography of a Princess* (1975) and *Jane Austen in Manhattan* (1980). These projects continued to deal with issues of cultural displacement. The real turning point in his career came with *The Europeans* (1979), an adaptation of Henry James set in New England, but British financed and made with a largely British crew. The film has a peculiarly distanced approach to its subject. It set Ivory on a path of literary adaptations from which he has rarely strayed since. Further films drawn from Henry James followed with *The Bostonians* (1984) and *The Golden Bowl* (2000), but he had his greatest success with E. M. Forster, particularly the sumptuously romantic *A Room with a View* (1985) and the coolly restrained *Howard's End* (1992). These films were well received critically, with Ivory nominated three times for the Best Director Oscar and four times for the equivalent BAFTA, and proved a solid box-office draw on art house circuits in both Britain and America. Other films taken from literary sources include Jean Rhys's *Quartet* (1981) and Kazuo Ishiguro's *The Remains of the Day* (1993).

These films became the subject of a wider debate about the nature of 'heritage cinema'. At a straightforward level, the films were accused of simply being twee and formulaic, but the criticisms also had a political dimension, with the suggestion that they were inherently conservative, looking back nostalgically to a time of class privilege and clear gender divides. The rather patronising depiction of the working-class characters in *Howards End* and the overly decorated *mise en scène* throughout these films might be used to support the case. However, this critique tends to underestimate the real variety and achievement of these films. The theme of lives thwarted by repressive social conventions is at the heart of *The Remains of the Day*, while there is a clear undercurrent of eroticism, and homoeroticism, in *A Room with View*. Homosexuality is dealt with more explicitly and sympathetically in *Maurice* (1987), from another Forster novel. Whatever political deficiencies the films might possess, they are usually beautiful to look at and have provided many memorable performances such as those of Anthony Hopkins and Emma Thompson in *The Remains of the Day* and *Howards End*. It might be fairly suggested, however, that there was a feeling of ennui when Ivory returned yet again to Henry James in 2000 with *The Golden Bowl* and went for a period setting in the Hanif Kureishi-scripted *The White Countess* (2006).

Among his other British films, *Heat and Dust* (1982) stands out for its performances and the subtle restraint of its direction (often a feature of Ivory's work), as well as for the complex depiction of Anglo-Indian relations. He has continued to work in America where he made *Slaves of New York* (1989), *Jefferson in Paris* (1995) and *Le Divorce* (2003), none of which were very successful. In contrast, the beguiling and wistful *Mr and Mrs Bridge* (1990), with Paul Newman and Joanne Woodward appropriately playing a long married couple, is among Ivory's finest, treating his favourite subjects of emotional repression and social conformism with a characteristic lightness of touch. It is these qualities which may well allow the best work of Merchant-Ivory to outlive contemporary political debates about 'heritage cinema'. Sadly, the death of Ismail Merchant in 2005 brought to an end one of the longest creative collaborations in recent cinema.

**British Feature Films:** *The Europeans* (1979); *Quartet* (1981); *Heat and Dust* (1982); *The Bostonians* (1984); *A Room With a View* (1985); *Maurice* (1987); *Howards End* (1992); *The Remains of the Day* (1993); *Surviving Picasso* (1996); *A Soldier's Daughter Never Cries* (1998); *The Golden Bowl* (2000); *The White Countess* (2006).

**Bibliography:** Robert Emmet Long, *The Films of Merchant Ivory* (New York: Harry M. Abrams, 1997); John Pym, *The Wandering Company: Twenty-one Years of Merchant Ivory Films* (London and New York: BFI/MOMA, 1983).

### Derek JARMAN

The emergence in the 1970s of a publicly recognised British art cinema is often attributed to the impact of two directors, Peter GREENAWAY and Derek Jarman. Both have flitted between the avant-garde and more

mainstream projects, and there were other similarities in their concern with the formal possibilities of the medium and in their rejection of conventional narrative. However, if GREENAWAY has sometimes been cerebral and cold, Jarman's films are more often warm and instinctive. Despite a career cut tragically short, his life and work constitute a unique, influential legacy.

Born in Northwood, Middlesex on 31 January 1942, Derek Jarman attended Kings College and the University of London, then from 1963 studied painting at the Slade School of Art. After working as a set designer at the Royal Opera House, Covent Garden, he moved into cinema as art director on two Ken RUSSELL films, *The Devils* (1971) and *Savage Messiah* (1972). On the former he created the memorable, gleamingly white interiors. His directorial debut, *Sebastiane* (1976), established a number of his recurrent themes. Its depiction of the martyrdom of St Sebastian allows Jarman to consider the figure of the outsider, as well as giving him considerably free reign for homoerotic imagery and his painterly instincts. The film gathered some notoriety for its male nudity and deserves a special footnote in film history as the first, and perhaps last, film in which the dialogue is spoken in Latin. His position as rebel was one he felt was forced upon him by circumstances as he saw himself more as a traditionalist, with his love of renaissance art, Elizabethan literature and Englishness. Rebellion is certainly an element in *Jubilee* (1978), the first film to really tap into Britain's punk scene, but Jarman's principle concern is with depicting a Britain that has fallen into near terminal decline. When Elizabeth I travels forward in time to witness the jubilee celebrations of Elizabeth II, she finds a country on the brink of social disintegration and anarchy. The film was remarkably prescient in predicting what would happen in the Thatcherite Britain of the 1980s.

Like GREENAWAY, Jarman took a fairly free hand in his adaptation of Shakespeare's *The Tempest* (1979), adopting a wittily irreverent approach best seen in the sequence where Elizabeth Welch sings 'Stormy Weather' with a chorus of sailors dancing the hornpipe. With *The Angelic Conversation* (1985) Jarman begins to experiment more radically with the juxtaposition of sound and image, as he had been doing for some time in his short films. Judi Dench reads Shakespeare's sonnets and Jarman re-imagines the love affair they describe as one between two men through montages of striking imagery. Something of the same approach was seen in his setting of Wilfred Owen's poetry and Benjamin Britten's music in *War Requiem* (1989), a restrained, moving elegy for the grief and loss of war. Art and the role of the artist are at the heart of *Caravaggio* (1986). On a tiny budget, Jarman creates a sumptuously beautiful film which visually echoes the master's paintings, but he successfully resists the temptation to film a straightforward biopic, interrupting the film's narrative with deliberately disruptive modern anachronisms such as someone using a typewriter.

Jarman always said he would have worked in the commercial mainstream if he had been allowed to, but increasingly he found himself marginalised, struggling to obtain financial support for his films. Channel 4 and the BFI frequently came to the rescue and he made a living directing pop music videos, some of which were works of art in themselves. Particularly striking are 'The Queen is Dead' for The

Smiths and the Pet Shop Boys' 'It's a Sin'. Jarman seemed to find a considerable affinity with the youthful rebels of pop music. He also continued to make short films using a variety of formats including Super-8, 16 mm and video. These elements are incorporated into both *The Last of England* (1987), perhaps his masterpiece, and *The Garden* (1990). These highly personal films adopt a collage structure in which we are presented with a series of seemingly random images and sounds which explore a central theme. In the latter, the remarkable garden which Jarman created at his house near Dungeness provides links to the Garden of Eden and awakens religious themes of guilt, persecution and redemption. In *The Last of England* we are presented with another nightmare vision of contemporary Britain, a place where military police violently maintain order across shattered cityscapes while a mock royal wedding takes place. Incorporating elements from the camp underground films of Kenneth Anger and references to art history, Jarman mourns for the loss of an older, kinder, more civilised England.

His version of Marlowe's *Edward II* (1991) focuses on a gay reading of the play and offers another bleak commentary on the homophobia and intolerance of the Thatcher years. His final film was in many ways his most radical. Mirroring his gradual descent into blindness (one of the effects of his infection with HIV), *Blue* (1993) presents the viewer with an unchanging blue screen, forcing you to focus on the soundtrack where we hear voices, sounds and music which evoke the interior world of the dying artist. The film was a moving elegy for one of the most original, inspirational figures in recent British cinema. Jarman's legacy goes beyond his films and is there in his work as a campaigner for gay rights and AIDS awareness, as well as in his books, paintings, music videos and photographs. He died on 19 February 1994.

**British Feature Films:** *Sebastiane* (1976); *Jubilee* (1978); *The Tempest* (1979); *The Angelic Conversation* (1985); *Caravaggio* (1986); *The Last of England* (1987); *War Requiem* (1989); *The Garden* (1990); *Edward II* (1991); *Wittgenstein* (1993); *Blue* (1993).

**Bibliography:** Michael O'Pray, *Derek Jarman: Dreams of England* (London: BFI, 1996); Chris Leppard (ed.), *By Angels Driven: The Films of Derek Jarman* (Trowbridge: Flicks Books, 1996).

## Humphrey JENNINGS

Humphrey Jennings is the most creative and celebrated film-maker of the British documentary movement, but for some he is more than this; he is, as Lindsay ANDERSON famously put it, the only real poet of British cinema. Born in Walberswick, Suffolk on 19 August 1907, he studied

English at Cambridge and while a student became active in Britain's burgeoning avant-garde. At Cambridge he founded and edited the literary journal *Experiment* with William Empson and Jacob Bronowski, as well as designing the first British production of Stravinsky's *A Soldier's Tale*. He became a central figure in British surrealism helping to organise the 1936 International Surrealist Exhibition in London along with Herbert Read and Roland Penrose. He was also a painter and poet in his own right. In 1934 he was recruited to the GPO Film Unit where he first worked on short documentaries. Other than a brief spell with the Shell Film Unit where he assisted the animator Len LYE, he was to remain with the GPO as it transformed during wartime into the Crown Film Unit until his departure in 1949. In 1936 he helped to found Mass Observation with the poet and sociologist Charles Madge and the anthropologist Tom Harrison, which attempted to record the everyday experiences and views of the British people.

The two dominant strains of the British documentary movement were the desire to record actuality (as part of a broadly humanist endeavour to better understand our world) and to do this in a manner which recognised the creative possibilities of the form. Jennings' preference was to overlay the former with the latter, leaning towards a formalism which apparently caused disquiet to the movement's founder John Grierson. Jennings' films offer a montage of carefully selected images juxtaposed with music and diegetic sound which form a cohesive whole. These elements are linked by underlying themes which only emerge through the associations created by the editing; he always acknowledged the contribution made to his work by editors like Stewart McAllister. The subject, particularly in wartime, is often a meditation on traditional aspects of the British way of life, celebrated through public symbols (Nelson's column, the royal family, Kipling's poetry) and more everyday imagery (children in a playground, dancers in a ballroom, an English landscape). These combinations produce results that are both cinematically poetic and deeply affecting, especially in the context of a nation fighting for its survival.

The beginnings of this technique are already apparent in the prewar *Spare Time* (1939), which was accused by some of patronising the working-class people whose leisure pursuits it recorded. He achieved a greater focus and sense of urgency in wartime shorts like *Words For Battle* (1941) and *The Heart of Britain* (1941), reaching a peak in the sublime *Listen to Britain* (1942), which is composed like a piece of classical music with movements in different moods. Without recourse to explanatory voice-over, it presents an enduring image of the British spirit of resistance, as well as celebrating beauty in the everyday, whether through a rippling field of corn or factory workers singing along to the radio. It was a method more suited to the compactness of the short film. His first feature length documentary, *Fires Were Started/I Was a Fireman* (1943) introduces narrative elements and the restaging of actuality scenes using the real people involved but with scripted dialogue. The results are sometimes a little awkward, but the film is still powerfully dramatic in its vivid scenes of firefighting, as well as moving in its tribute to the bravery of the fire service during the London blitz. *Silent Village* (1943) is also an ambitious project, commemorating the brutal Nazi annihilation of the Czech village of Lidice. The events are restaged as if they had actually happened in a Welsh mining village, using actual miners and their families from a village in West Wales. Despite some stiffness in the presentation, the film is not only emotionally engaging but suggests a link between the miners in Wales and those in Czechoslovakia which has clear political under-currents.

Political concerns also underlie his last major documentary, *A Diary for Timothy* (1945). Scripted by E. M. Forster and narrated by Michael Redgrave, the film interweaves the lives of several Britons during the last year of the war, finding a focus in the birth of young Timothy. The hope expressed for Timothy's future is explicitly linked to the need for greater social justice and seems to chime with the swell of public feeling at the end of the war which had led to the election of a radical Labour government. One of the most striking aspects of Jennings' outlook was his ability to successfully combine seeming opposites, so that his love of British traditions frequently sits next to his left-wing political sym-pathies. Although he continued to make documentaries after the war, the vision of Britain seen in *Dim Little Island* (1948) and *Family Portrait* (1950) already seems rather out of tune with the changing face of postwar Britain. The context of war had provided an arena in which his evocative meditations on the nature of Britishness, however ro-manticised, seemed precisely right. Jennings died on 24 September 1950 when he fell from a cliff while scouting locations for a film shoot on the Greek island of Poros.

**British Feature Films:** *Fires Were Started/I Was a Fireman* (1943); *Silent Village* (1943).

**Bibliography:** Kevin Jackson (ed.), *The Humphrey Jennings Film Reader* (Manchester: Carcanet, 1993); Geoffrey Nowell-Smith, 'Hum-phrey Jennings: Surrealist Observer', in Charles Barr (ed.), *All Our Yesterdays* (London: BFI, 1986); Mary-Lou Jennings (ed.), *Humphrey Jennings: Film-maker, Painter, Poet* (London: BFI, 1982).

# Roland JOFFÉ

Grandson of the sculptor Jacob Epstein, Roland Joffé was born in London on 17 November 1945. He began his career directing for the theatre, where he was one of the joint founders of the Young Vic, and in television where his credits include *Coronation Street* (1973–4) and a version of John Ford's *'Tis Pity She's a Whore* (1980). Work on radical TV dramas like Trevor Griffith's series *Bill Brand* (1976) and the single play *The Spongers* (1978) indicated his liberal political leanings. He made a considerable impact with his feature film debut *The Killing Fields* (1984) which tells of the friendship of an American reporter and his Cambodian translator against the backdrop of the American bombing of Cambodia and the subsequent takeover of the country by the murderous Khmer Rouge. Joffé handles the epic sweep of historical events with assurance, as well as conveying a strong sense of place. The performances by Sam Waterstone and Haing S. Ngor are affecting and the film doesn't stint from revealing the horror of what took place, yet there is something slightly too glossy, too superficial in its approach.

Joffé confirmed his forte for combining high production values (lush cinematography, big stars, exotic locales) with a social message in *The Mission* (1986) where the forces of colonialism in eighteenth-century Brazil are resisted by a Jesuit colony which has managed to live in peace with the indigenous population. Jeremy Irons tries to fight back peacefully, whereas Robert de Niro goes for his sword. The film certainly looks beautiful and there is sincerity in its purpose, but the complexity of history is only really suggested in Ray McAnally's subtle, ambiguous performance as one of the oppressors. His first two films successfully established Joffé's international reputation, as confirmed by Oscar and BAFTA nominations as Best Director for both films and a Palme d'Or at Cannes for *The Mission*.

These films took Joffé to Hollywood where he made *Shadow Makers* (1989) which depicts the building of the two atomic bombs dropped on Japan in the Second World War. The film did not repeat the success of his earlier efforts and he returned to Europe to fund *City of Joy* (1992) which follows an American doctor who goes to work in Calcutta and reawakens his moral perspective. The casting of Hollywood heart-throb Patrick Swayze in the title role seemed all too painfully to confirm the director's tendency to keep one eye on the box office while offering his message of social conscience. The results were overblown and unconvincing. Returning to Hollywood he made an execrable adaptation of Nathaniel Hawthorne's *The Scarlet Letter* (1995) with Demi Moore and the forgettable thriller *Goodbye Lover* (1998). *Vatel* (2000) was, like *City of Joy*, an Anglo-French co-production, this time set at the court of Louis XIV. Its reception by critics and audiences at Cannes was so hostile it has not yet been released. This stark decline can only be regretted. Whatever reservations might be voiced about the commercial compromises inherent in his first two films, there was enough cinematic flair and liberal good intentions on show to suggest that Joffé should be capable of more work of real substance.

**British Feature Films:** *The Killing Fields* (1984); *The Mission* (1986); *City of Joy* (1992); *Vatel* (2000).

## Neil JORDAN

Neil Jordan was born on 25 February 1950 in County Sligo, Ireland and raised in Dublin. He studied Irish History and English at University College, Dublin where he also founded the Irish Writers' Co-operative. He first established his reputation as a writer of short stories and novels, winning the Guardian Fiction Prize in 1976. Moving into films as a script consultant on John BOORMAN's *Excaliber* (1981), he made his debut as a writer/director with *Angel* (1982), which Boorman produced. The film tells the story of a musician (Stephen Rea, who has appeared in many of Jordan's films) who tries to avenge the murder by terrorists of a young girl. Jordan is less concerned with the politics of Northern Ireland than with the psychological and moral impact of violence on the individual. The film also adopts a stylised visual approach which has become a trademark of Jordan's work. He began his successful collaboration with producer Stephen Woolley on *The Company of Wolves* (1984), adapted from Angela Carter's short stories. Using traditional fairy tales and elements of the horror genre, the film explores issues of sexuality, violence and class in a fluently imaginative way. The richness and complexity of Jordan's vision is apparent in *Mona Lisa* (1986), where a crime story about an ex-con (Bob Hoskins), a prostitute (Cathy Tyson) and a gangster (Michael Caine) is a vehicle for a carefully worked out meditation on innocence and corruption. The audience shares the subjective viewpoint of Hoskins' character, and his romantic delusions, with the film again adopting subtle visual motifs drawn from fairy tales.

The considerable critical and popular success of *Mona Lisa* took Jordan to Hollywood where he made two light comedies, the supernatural farce *High Spirits* (1988) with Peter O'Toole and the gentle, sweet natured *We're No Angels* (1989) featuring Robert de Niro and Sean Penn. The comparative commercial failure of these films returned him to Ireland where he made *The Miracle* (1991), a modest coming-of-age drama with the American actress Beverly D'Angelo. This is the first film in which Jordan is explicitly concerned with the changing

nature of modern-day Ireland. *The Crying Game* (1992) is again set
against the backdrop of the 'Troubles' in Northern Ireland but, as
before, he uses this, along with the film's thriller elements, as little
more than a frame on which to hang a fascinating and thoroughly
unconventional love story. The film challenges the audience's assump-
tions about gender identity and sexuality in a way that is both funny
and tender, and it features another fine performance from the melancholy Stephen Rea. Seemingly to the surprise of all concerned, the film
was a phenomenal success at the American box office taking Jordan
back into the forefront of bankable international film-makers.

*Interview With a Vampire* (1994) marked his return to Hollywood, but
this time he achieved a commercial hit with this glossy, star-studded
adaptation of Anne Rice's neo-gothic novel. The film has Jordan's
trademark visual panache and dark humour, as well as his concern with
social outsiders. With American backing he was able to make the
ambitious *Michael Collins* (1996). The film takes us through the events
of the Easter Rising of 1916, the IRA's campaign to end British rule and,
following independence, the bloody civil war. The portrayal of Collins
(Liam Neeson) as the story's hero, an essentially pragmatic man who is
contrasted with the deviousness of Ireland's first President, Eamon de
Valera (Alan Rickman), caused controversy in Ireland and with de
Valera's descendents. The film was also attacked by Loyalists, not least
for its sly mockery of Ian Paisley. Jordan's attempts to steer a middle way
through such material proved a lost cause. He remained in Ireland for
*The Butcher Boy* (1997), an extraordinary adaptation of Patrick McCabe's novel. No description can really do justice to the hypnotic, surreal
imagery of the film as we are drawn into the internal world of its young
'hero', a boy who witnesses the demise of his entire family and dispatches
a nosey interloper with a meat cleaver. Through his eyes we see a world
out of kilter, a hyper-vivid nightmare place which teeters on the edge of
madness. The film interweaves many of Jordan's preoccupations with
outsiders, the nature of Irish society and issues of identity in a dazzling,
cinematically audacious manner.

He returned to the States to make the psychological thriller *In
Dreams* (1999) and then shot an adaptation of Graham Greene's *The
End of the Affair* (1999) with Ralph Fiennes and Julianne Moore.
Jordan skilfully navigates the moral intricacies of Greene's story of an
extramarital affair in wartime London, with its intensely Catholic
themes of self-sacrifice and renewed faith. *The Good Thief* (2002) is
a thoughtful reworking of Jean-Pierre Melville's classic French thriller
*Bob le Flambeur* (1956) which uses the genre to examine the possibility
of redemption. His latest film is *Breakfast on Pluto* (2005), a colourful,

flamboyant celebration of the glam-rock generation of the 1970s which again plays with notions of identity, gender and sexuality.

Neil Jordan is a genuinely international film-maker whose has worked in America, Ireland, Britain and continental Europe. His talents have been recognised with many awards, including an Oscar for the screenplay of *The Crying Game*, a BAFTA for directing *The End of the Affair* and the Golden Lion from Venice for *Michael Collins*. Eschewing realism, his films acknowledge the artificiality of the medium and exult in its opportunities for fantasy. They tackle serious, challenging themes within genre formats which have often made them accessible to a wide audience. His substantial body of work has already ensured his position as one of the most creative, exciting film-makers in contemporary cinema.

**British Feature Films:** *Angel* (1982); *The Company of Wolves* (1984); *Mona Lisa* (1986); *The Miracle* (1991); *The Crying Game* (1992); *Michael Collins* (1996); *The Butcher Boy* (1997); *The End of the Affair* (1999); *The Good Thief* (2002); *Breakfast on Pluto* (2005).

**Bibliography:** Ruth Barton, *Irish National Cinema* (London: Routledge, 2004); Martin McLoon, *Irish Film: The Emergence of a Contemporary Cinema* (London: BFI, 2000).

### Isaac JULIEN

Isaac Julien, who was born in London on 21 February 1960, is an important figure in the development of black British cinema and an internationally renowned artist who uses film as a central part of his aesthetic. His parents came to Britain from St Lucia and he grew up in London's East End. After studying at Goldsmiths College, London, where he made the angry documentary *Who Killed Colin Roach?* (1983), he went to St Martin's College of Art to study fine art and film. While here, in 1983, he was instrumental in founding Sankofa, a film and video collective which became a cornerstone in the growing network of independent black film-makers in Britain. Julien was one of the collaborators on Sankofa's most widely known project, *The Passion of Remembrance* (1986), which attempts to deal with the difficulties of constructing a documentary history of black political experience by foregrounding questions of chauvinism and homophobia. His first solo film, the visually striking *Looking for Langston* (1989), explores the work of the gay African-American poet Langston Hughes and deals directly with complexities of gender and sexual identity which go beyond simple racial politics. It received the award for best short film at the Berlin Film Festival. In this early work, Julien adopts a fragmentary technique, blending reconstruction, montage and documentary footage into a collage effect which compliments his questioning approach.

He crossed into the mainstream of fiction cinema with the BFI-funded *Young Soul Rebels* (1991), a fresh, vibrant film which manages successfully to mix its serious examination of interracial relationships, homosexuality and young black experience, with a celebration of club culture and diverse music styles. Set in 1977 against the backdrop of the Queen's Jubilee, it conveys the tensions and pleasures of Britain's increasingly hybrid cultural scene. The film was well received, winning the Critics Prize at Cannes. In the 1990s he began to work in television, making documentaries in both Britain and America frequently dealing with issues of black representation in the media. These include the series *Black and White in Colour: Television, Memory, Race* (1992) and for American television *The Question of Equality* (1995). He also made a number of music videos for artists as varied as Des'ree and Peter Gabriel.

More recently his work has moved from the cinema and television into galleries, with video installations and multi-screen pieces. These works are more layered and abstract, but still return to themes of identity whether through sexuality, ethnicity or gender. They also show his continuing concern for the formal pleasures offered by the moving image. In 2001 his *The Long Road to Mazatlan* (1999) was shortlisted for the Turner Prize. Julien is also Visiting Professor of Cultural Studies at Harvard and an honorary research fellow at Goldsmiths College, London.

**British Feature Films:** *Young Soul Rebels* (1991).

**Bibliography:** Kobena Mercer and Chris Drake, *Isaac Julien* (London: Ellipsis, 2001); Isaac Julien and Colin MacCabe, *Diary of a Young Soul Rebel* (London: BFI, 1991).

### (Sir) Alexander KORDA

Alexander Korda was one of the most charismatic figures in British film production from the early 1930s until his death in 1956. His reputation is principally based on his career as a producer and studio executive, but he directed more than sixty films with eight of them being made in Britain. The best of these have an obvious historical significance, but also show the cosmopolitan panache and love of Britishness which were often characteristics of his approach.

He was born as Sándor László Kellner on 16 September 1893 in the Hungarian village of Puszta Turpásztó. After the death of his father, the family moved to Budapest where he worked firstly as a journalist before entering the film industry as an assistant director. After making his directorial debut in 1914, he quickly established himself as the leading director in Hungarian cinema before anti-Semitism and the chaos of the postwar period led him into permanent exile. He worked successfully in Vienna and then Berlin during the 1920s, but suffered a setback with three frustrating years spent in Hollywood at the end of the decade. Back in France he made his finest film to date, a version of Marcel Pagnol's *Marius* (1931), before finally arriving in Britain in 1931. With typical aplomb he established himself as a director and producer with two technically polished comedies, *Service for Ladies* (1932) and *Wedding Rehearsal* (1932), then in 1932 launched his own production company, London Films. Korda set about challenging the parochial nature of much British film-making of the period by producing films which would appeal to an international audience. Sophisticated technique and a glossy finish were part of his strategy and to this end he employed other European émigrés, including his brothers, the director Zoltán KORDA and the gifted designer Vincent Korda, as well as cinematographer Georges Périnal. His own directorial debut for the company was another light comedy, *The Girl from Maxim's* (1933).

The first real fruit of his ambitions came with the landmark film *The Private Life of Henry VIII* (1933). Taking a fairly free hand with British history, Korda produced a Rabelaisian romp which looked good and showcased an outrageous performance from Charles Laughton, characteristically resplendent in his period costume hurling discarded chicken bones from dinner over his shoulder. The film proved an enormous success, particularly in America where it was the first British film to win an Academy Award (for Laughton as Best Actor). Made for a modest £60,000, it took £500,000 on its first international run proving that British films could compete with Hollywood at their own game. Korda tried to repeat the formula with *The Private Life of Don Juan* (1934), but the ageing Hollywood star Douglas Fairbanks wasn't able to replicate Laughton's popular appeal and the film was a commercial failure. He used Laughton to great effect again in his next film, *Rembrandt* (1936). This was probably Korda's finest achievement as a director. The film evokes the world of the painter through superbly controlled cinematography by Georges Périnal and Laughton brings a touching pathos to the role. Unfortunately it was not a box office success, its austere approach proving to be uncommercial.

In 1935 he built a studio at Denham along the lines of Hollywood's great production facilities and in the same year he signed a deal with Charles Chaplin, Douglas Fairbanks and Mary Pickford to make him a partner in United Artists. London Films continued to undertake ambitious projects such as the spectacular science fiction film *Things to Come* (1936) as well as costume films aimed at the American market, but the company became particularly associated with gung-ho imperial adventure films like *Sanders of the River* (1935, Zoltán KORDA) with a number being directed by Alexander's brother, Zoltán. He built a reputation as an indulgent, supportive producer, nurturing such talents as Michael POWELL and David LEAN.

By 1938 London Films was in serious financial trouble and Korda had lost control of Denham. He appears to have spent part of the war period acting as a special envoy for Churchill in America, leading to his knighthood in 1942. He had a hand in making the propaganda film *The Lion Has Wings* (1939) as well as the magical *The Thief of Baghdad* (1940) in Britain and directed the patriotic period romance *Lady Hamilton* (1941) in Hollywood with Laurence Olivier and Vivien Leigh. With a restructured London Films back in production, he made *Perfect Strangers* (1945) as his first postwar film as director. It's a charming comedy with appealing performances from Robert Donat and Deborah Kerr as a staid married couple who are brought out of their shells by wartime separation and then have to face the prospect of reestablishing their relationship when the conflict ends. His final film as director was a disappointingly uninspired adaptation of Oscar Wilde's *An Ideal Husband* (1948).

London Films continued to make prestigious and memorable films including Carol REED's *The Third Man* (1949) and OLIVIER's *Richard III* (1955). Korda also became involved as an executive with British Lion which ran into major financial problems in 1949 and was bailed out with substantial loans from the government. The company maintained studio facilities at Shepperton and continued to act as a distributor for smaller production companies. His work often reflected his complex personality, sometimes deeply conservative in its love for his adopted homeland (he liked to be seen wearing a bowler hat), at other times openly internationalist, looking out at the world with a distinctly European wit and cynicism. As a producer, his high-risk policies were reflected in the pattern of 'boom and bust' which typified his career and has been repeated by others since. If his work as a director has been overshadowed, it is only because he was such an important, influential producer and champion for British film-making. He died on 23 January 1956.

**British Feature Films:** *Service for Ladies* (1932); *Wedding Rehearsal* (1932); *The Girl from Maxim's* (1933); *The Private Life of Henry VIII* (1933); *The Private Life of Don Juan* (1934); *Rembrandt* (1936); *Perfect Strangers* (1945); *An Ideal Husband* (1947).

**Bibliography:** Charles Drazin, *Korda: Britain's Only Movie Mogul* (London: Sidgwick & Jackson, 2002); Karol Kulik, *Alexander Korda: The Man Who Could Work Miracles* (London: W. H. Allen, 1975).

## Zoltán KORDA

Younger brother of Alexander KORDA, Zoltán Korda was born as Zoltán Kellner on 3 May 1895 in the same village of Puszta Turpásztó in Hungary. Following active service in the First World War as a cavalry officer, he joined Alexander at the Corvin Studios in Budapest. Here he worked as an editor before making his debut as a director in 1918. He followed his elder brother on his European travels to Austria and Germany during the 1920s, then on to Hollywood and back again to Europe in 1930. During this period he worked in a variety of capacities including cameraman, art director and scriptwriter. In Britain from 1932, he assisted Leontine Sagan on *Men of Tomorrow* (1932) and then directed the quota quickie *Cash* (1933), but it was *Sanders of the River* (1935) which set him on a path of making imperial adventure films set in Africa or India; these were to become his trademark.

Unlike his more conservative, traditionally patriotic elder brother, Zoltán Korda harboured left-wing political sympathies and a genuine concern with the plight of native peoples in the developing world. The tension between the brothers often exploded into violent arguments and is also apparent in a number of the films they made together in the 1930s. With Zoltán employed as a director for his brother's London Films production company, their conflicting approaches formed the context within which their films were made. These contradictions work to the severe detriment of *Sanders of the River*, a chronically dated African drama with Leslie Banks as the benevolent colonialist and the long-suffering Paul Robeson misused as a 'noble savage'. The production difficulties frequently encountered in making these films could also undermine their potential, as seen in the Kipling-inspired *Elephant Boy* (1937) where Robert Flaherty's impressive location documentary footage sits awkwardly with the unconvincing studio scenes made at Denham. The condescending characterisations don't help, although the film did make a star of Sabu.

However, it is Zoltán's personality which emerges more strongly in both *The Drum* (1938) and *The Four Feathers* (1939). The former again

featured Sabu and is a briskly entertaining Raj adventure with the
British army working in collaboration with an Indian prince to see off
his wicked uncle (even if some of the Indian locations are actually
Wales). The latter is the most enjoyable of Zoltán's films, despite a
narrative full of imperial clichés, as our reluctant hero (John Clements)
proves that he really isn't a coward by travelling undercover to the
Sudan and rescuing his best friend (Ralph Richardson). The spectacular action scenes are handled with undeniable verve and there is a
surprising vein of satire at the expense of the British which goes some
way to counterbalancing the colonial propaganda. Both films benefited
from the magnificent colour cinematography of Georges Périnal and
the impressive set designs of younger brother Vincent Korda.

Zoltán went to America to make a rather heavy-handed version of
Kipling's *The Jungle Book* (1942) for Alexander, with Sabu as Mowgli,
and remained there to make his next four films without his brother. The
realistic war actioner *Sahara* (1943) was a popular vehicle for Humphrey
Bogart, but the resistance drama *One Against Seven* (1945) failed to
repeat its success. *The Macomber Affair* (1947) made a reasonably
effective job of adapting Hemingway's story of big-game hunting
and *A Woman's Vengeance* (1948) did a similarly efficient job with
Aldous Huxley's short story and play. His final two films were made for
Alexander's London Films back in Britain. *Cry the Beloved Country*
(1952) was finally the film he had always wanted to make in Africa, a
liberal anti-apartheid narrative which wears its heart on its sleeve a little
too obviously, although no one would question its sincerity. Poor health
meant that Terence Young took on most of the directorial duties for
*Storm over the Nile* (1955), a virtual remake of *The Four Feathers* using
Zoltán's original location footage distorted to fit the fashionable Cine-
mascope format. Following his brother's death in 1956 he effectively
retired from film-making. He died in California on 13 October 1961.
Changes in attitudes have rendered elements of his 1930s work fairly
unacceptable for many modern audiences, but in his best films there is a
considerable flair for spectacle and an eye for exotic locations, as well as a
surprisingly liberal streak often straining to emerge.

**British Feature Films:** *Cash* (1933); *Sanders of the River* (1935); *Forget
Me Not* (1936); *Elephant Boy* (1937, co-directed with Robert Flaherty);
*The Drum* (1938); *The Four Feathers* (1939); *Cry the Beloved Country*
(1952); *Storm over the Nile* (1955, co-directed with Terence Young).

**Bibliography:** Michael Korda, *Charmed Lives: A Family Romance*
(New York: Random House, 1979).

## Stanley KUBRICK

Few would question Stanley Kubrick's status as one of the most important directors in film history, but his career poses considerable difficulties when trying to place him within the context of British cinema. Kubrick came to Britain in 1962 and remained until his death in 1999. During that period he made eight films which technically qualify as being British. These films were shot in Britain with largely British crews, a degree of British funding and a number of British actors in the casts. However, with the exception of just two titles, these films have American settings and subjects, with Kubrick sometimes going to quite extraordinary lengths to make Britain stand in for America. Consequently, it seems reasonable to view Kubrick as an American director working in self-imposed exile in Britain whose contribution to the indigenous national cinema was actually relatively small.

By 1962 Kubrick had already established a considerable reputation in America. He was born in New York City on 26 July 1928 and had worked successfully as a photojournalist before moving into films in the early 1950s. After making three short documentaries, he scraped together funding from family and friends for two ultra-low-budget films, *Fear and Desire* (1953) and *Killer's Kiss* (1955), with Kubrick writing, editing and photographing the films as well as directing. These brought him to the attention of independent producer James Harris and together they made the taut caper film *The Killing* (1956). He moved into the studio system with *Paths of Glory* (1957), a powerful anti-war story starring Kirk Douglas. It was Douglas who then brought him in to replace Anthony Mann (who Douglas had fired) on the intelligent epic *Spartacus* (1960). The film marked the beginning of Kubrick's disenchantment with Hollywood as he battled over its content with Douglas who was both its star and producer.

The precise reasons for his decision to film *Lolita* (1962) in Britain remain unclear, but the comparative liberality of Britain's censorship regime seems to have been the principle incentive. Even so Kubrick still had to raise the age of Nabokov's nymphet to make the topic of a middle-aged man besotted with a pubescent teenager acceptable enough to be passed. He followed it with the bleakest of Cold War black comedies *Dr Strangelove* (1963). At a stretch, it is possible to point to some specifically British aspects in these two films. Both feature key performances from British actors, with James Mason and Peter Sellers appearing in *Lolita* and Sellers memorably taking three roles in *Dr Strangelove*. There is also something rather British about the humour in both films, whether in the literary word play of *Lolita* or the surreal, goonish farce of *Dr Strangelove*. The skills of British technicians such as Ken Adam, who designed the stunning sets for *Dr Strangelove*, certainly contributed to the success of these films. However, with the hallucinatory, spellbinding *2001: A Space Odyssey* (1968) it is not so easy to connect such an abstract, intellectual film to any national culture, let alone an explicitly British one.

With his next two films Kubrick did produce work which can usefully be related to a British context. *A Clockwork Orange* (1971) is a breathtakingly cynical adaptation of Anthony Burgess's dystopian novel, depicting a Britain of the near future which bares a considerable resemblance to the Britain of the early 1970s. The tightly controlled visual design captures a world at once strange and yet recognisable as the country currently emerging from the optimism of the 1960s into the violent fragmentation of the new decade. Kubrick discards the faint optimism of Burgess's final draft of the novel, preferring to confront audiences with a future in which the brutality of the individual is matched by that of the state. Here the necessity for human free will only brings about rape and murder. Following a spate of copycat violence, the film was withdrawn by Kubrick from the British market, only being re-released after his death in 2000. Kubrick's ability to switch between genres was never more startlingly apparent than with his next project, an adaptation of Thackeray's novel *Barry Lyndon* (1975). The film is visually sumptuous, painstakingly recreating the eighteenth century through a series of painterly compositions as it follows the eponymous hero on his ultimately futile journey through the class structures of European society. Some critics disapproved of the cold detachment with which Kubrick unfolds the story, barely allowing the audience any emotional engagement with the characters, but it is exactly this quality which marks it out from other 'heritage' films. In place of comforting nostalgia, Kubrick offers a chilling vision of a soulless society.

The remainder of Kubrick's output belongs firmly within the history of American cinema. *The Shining* (1980) is a disturbing adaptation of Stephen King's horror novel with a wildly stylised performance from Jack Nicholson, whereas *Full Metal Jacket* (1987) is a characteristically distanced account of the horrors and dehumanisation of the Vietnam War. His final film was the dreamlike, erotic drama *Eyes Wide Shut* (1999) which had a mixed critical reception. On these films Kubrick went to bizarre lengths to recreate his settings in Britain, with a disused gas works standing in for Vietnam and the streets of London redressed as New York for *Eyes Wide Shut*. Why he remained in Britain to make these films has been the source of speculation with suggestions varying from a fear of flying to his desire to keep the Hollywood studios which funded his work at arm's length.

The long periods of meticulous preparation carried out in secret between films only added to the mystique surrounding him, as did his obsessive control over every aspect of production from initial script to the design of publicity materials.

Stanley Kubrick died on 7 March 1999 leaving behind a body of work which will ensure his status as one of the most imperishable talents cinema has produced. He was awarded a posthumous BAFTA Fellowship in 2000 and a Lifetime Achievement Award from the Directors Guild of Great Britain in 1999. It can only be regrettable for British cinema that someone resident in the country for such a long time made such a limited direct contribution to its national film culture.

**British Feature Films:** *Lolita* (1962); *Dr Strangelove or: How I Learned to Stop Worrying and Love the Bomb* (1963); *2001: A Space Odyssey* (1968); *A Clockwork Orange* (1971); *Barry Lyndon* (1975); *The Shining* (1980); *Full Metal Jacket* (1987); *Eyes Wide Shut* (1999).

**Bibliography:** Alexander Walker, Sybil Taylor and Ulrich Ruchti, *Stanley Kubrick, Director: A Visual Analysis* (London: Weidenfeld & Nicolson, 1999); John Baxter, *Stanley Kubrick: A Biography* (London: Harper Collins, 1997); Michel Ciment, *Kubrick*, trans. Gilbert Adair (New York: Holt, Rinehart & Winston, 1983).

# L

## Frank LAUNDER and Sidney GILLIAT

Among the several film-making partnerships which have distinguished British cinema, that of Launder and Gilliat was the most enduring and productive. Frank Launder was born on 28 January 1906 in Hitchin, Hertfordshire. His first job was in the offices of the Official Receiver of Bankruptcy, but it was through his involvement with Brighton Repertory Company, for whom he had acted and written a play, that he entered the film industry in 1928. He started in the script department at British International Pictures (BIP) at Elstree and continued as a writer for a variety of British studios during the 1930s. At this time he met and began to collaborate on scripts with Sidney Gilliat. Gilliat was born 15 February 1908 in Stockport. The son of a journalist and newspaper editor, it was his father's former film critic on the London *Evening Standard*, Walter C. Mycroft, who helped Gilliat into the film industry when he took over the running of BIP's script department in 1928. They began to work together on comedy-thrillers which were often distinguished by their skill in observing the quirks of British behaviour. Typical of this is their witty screenplay for HITCH-COCK's *The Lady Vanishes* (1938) where they created the characters of the bumbling Charters and Caldicott who were to reappear in a number of later British films.

Their first chance to control their own feature film came at Gainsborough with the wartime propaganda piece *Millions Like Us* (1943) which they jointly wrote and directed. The film is unpatronising and sympathetic in its depiction of the impact of war on the lives of ordinary British people, particularly women. Although it extols the virtues of the 'people's war' where individuals of all classes and backgrounds pulled together for the greater good, it isn't afraid to ask questions about what might happen to that spirit in the postwar world. This was the beginning of a partnership which usually saw the two of them working together on the script and alternating the tasks of directing and/or producing. If comedy was their real strong point, then it was Launder who tended towards a broader style with the use of farce and slapstick while Gilliat showed a preference for gentle satire directed at the constraints of British life. They made populist en-tertainments which ranged across a number of genres, but which were distinguished by their intelligence, careful scripting, sympathetic characterisations and just the occasional hint of an anarchic streak.

Working separately, Gilliat made the realistically observed wartime romantic melodrama *Waterloo Road* (1944), while Launder directed the sober *Two Thousand Women* (1944) set in a women's internment centre in France. Back together they founded their own production company, Individual Pictures, under the Rank umbrella. They were at their peak in the late 1940s, beginning with *The Rake's Progress* (1945) where Gilliat's taste for social satire is to the fore in an acerbic comedy of upper-class misbehaviour. Rex Harrison excels in a role he seems born to play. *Green for Danger* (1946) returned them to the territory of *The Lady Vanishes*, offering a murder mystery which manages to remain gripping while adopting a lightly humorous tone. It benefits greatly from a deliciously whimsical performance by Alastair Sim. *I See a Dark Stranger* (1946) even manages the unlikely task of bringing a waspish humour to the story of an IRA sympathiser (Deborah Kerr) spying for the Germans who falls in love with an English officer (Trevor Howard). Launder showed an occasional taste for Celtic subjects, directing two Scottish comedies, *Geordie* (1955) and *The Bridal Path* (1959), as well as the straight drama *Captain Boycott* (1947) which was set in nineteenth-century Ireland. *London Belongs to Me* (1948) showed their populist touch in a rousing tale of residents in a boarding house who rally together to save a young man arrested for murder. Their biggest commercial success came with *The Blue Lagoon* (1949), a lushly photographed romance of two youngsters stranded on a desert island which successfully captured the imagination of the British public.

Launder's liking for broad comedy, which had its roots in his 1930s scripts for such classic music hall-style comedies as *Oh, Mr Porter!* (1937), is evident in many of the films he directed from the 1950s onward. It is seen at its best in the brilliantly organised farce *The Happiest Days of Your Life* (1950) where the pupils of a boys school and a girls school find themselves billeted in the same buildings. A perfect cast, including Alastair Sim, Joyce Grenfell and Margaret Rutherford, milk the situation for every laugh it can generate and Launder maintains tight control of the mayhem which ensues. Mayhem is barely a sufficient description for *The Belles of St Trinian's* (1954). Based on Ronald Searle's cartoons, this was the first in what turned out to be a series of five *St Trinian's* films which stretched on until 1980. The first manages to whip up a real frenzy of enjoyable chaos from its depiction of the goings-on at a wildly anarchic girls school presided over by Alastair Sim in drag. As the series went on, the formula grew increasingly stale, as evidenced by the Swinging London trappings of *The Great St Trinian's Train Robbery* (1966) and the descent into vulgarity in *The Wildcats of St Trinian's* (1980).

Gilliat's preference for more cerebral humour is best seen in three of their later films. *The Constant Husband* (1954) has Rex Harrison in another purpose-built role as an amnesiac who wakes to discover he is a bigamist married to five different women. *Left Right and Centre* (1959) is a mild parody of party politics somewhat in the mould of the BOUTLING brothers' topical comedies. The best of the three is *Only Two Can Play* (1961), adapted from the Kingsley Amis novel *That Certain Feeling*. Peter Sellers is unusually restrained as the Welsh librarian who finds himself embroiled in the back-stabbing world of provincial literati. Gilliat's eye for convincing detail gives the film a sense of social claustrophobia and sexual frustration.

Launder and Gilliat remained champions of the art of scriptwriting, helping to found the Screenwriters' Association in 1937, with Launder becoming its President in 1946. They also showed a genuine interest in the health of their native industry, becoming involved with the management of British Lion from 1958 until 1972. Launder and Gilliat effectively retired from film-making in 1972 after making the critically derided Agatha Christie thriller *Endless Night* (1972), only reappearing belatedly to make the last *St Trinian's* film in 1980, a project which Gilliat only had a limited involvement with.

Sidney Gilliat died in 1994, followed by Frank Launder in 1997. In their long career together they created a body of work which is unpretentious and relatively conventional in its use of cinematic technique. They worked across a range of genres, with a particular affinity for light thrillers and comedies, which are usually polished, witty and neatly executed. In their best work, a realistically observed *mise en scène* provides the backdrop for a humorous narrative which, whether slyly satirical or played for easier laughs, often points up the absurdities of British life and hints at an anarchic spirit lurking under the mundane surface.

**British Feature Films:**
**Frank Launder directing** – *Two Thousand Women* (1944); *I See a Dark Stranger* (1946); *Captain Boycott* (1947); *The Blue Lagoon* (1949); *The Happiest Days of Your Life* (1950); *Lady Godiva Rides Again* (1951); *Folly to be Wise* (1952); *The Belles of St Trinian's* (1954); *Geordie* (1955); *Blue Murder at St Trinian's* (1957); *The Bridal Path* (1959); *The Pure Hell of St Trinian's* (1960); *Joey Boy* (1965); *The Wildcats of St Trinian's* (1980).

**Sidney Gilliat directing** – *Waterloo Road* (1944); *The Rake's Progress* (1945); *Green for Danger* (1946); *London Belongs to Me* (1948); *State Secret* (1950); *The Story of Gilbert and Sullivan* (1953); *The Constant Husband* (1954); *Fortune Is a Woman* (1957); *Left Right and Centre* (1959); *Only Two Can Play* (1961); *Endless Night* (1972).

**Jointly directed** – *Millions Like Us* (1943); *The Great St Trinian's Train Robbery* (1966).

**Bibliography:** Bruce Babington, *Launder and Gilliat* (Manchester: Manchester University Press, 2002); Geoff Brown, *Launder and Gilliat* (London: BFI, 1977).

## Philip LEACOCK

Elder brother of the documentary film-maker Richard Leacock, Philip Leacock was born on 8 October 1917 in London. He grew up in the Canary Islands and was educated at Bedales, the liberal English boarding school. In the 1930s he began to be involved in documentary film-making, working with Harold Lowenstein, his brother-in-law, on *Out to Play* (1936) and assisting Thorold DICKINSON on his two pro-Republican films made in Spain, *Behind the Spanish Lines* (1938) and *Spanish ABC* (1938). He continued working in documentary during the Second World War for the Army Kinematograph Service and after it with the Crown Film Unit. After making two short fictional films, he made his debut as a feature director with *The Brave Don't Cry* (1952), which was shot for John Grierson's Group 3 production company and produced by John BAXTER. The film tells its moving story of a mass rescue attempt at a Scottish coal mine in a semi-documentary style.

He incorporated documentary elements into his mainstream debut for Rank, the routine Second World War drama *Appointment in London* (1953) featuring Dirk Bogarde, but it was with *The Kidnappers* (1953) that his more distinctive style began to emerge. The film centres on two orphaned children living with their stern grandfather in Nova Scotia in the early 1900s who kidnap a baby and hide it in the woods to bring up as their own. As well as exhibiting a strong sense of place (despite being shot at Pinewood), the film is remarkable for the sensitive handling of the child actors and for the sympathy with which they are portrayed. These qualities were to distinguish a series of films which feature children at the centre of their narratives. *Escapade* (1955) is a quirky tale about three children who steal an airplane in order to make an anti-war protest and *Innocent Sinners* (1958) is a touching story of a London teenager who makes a garden in the bombed-out remains of a church. *The Spanish Gardener* (1956), which was nominated for the Golden Bear at the Berlin Film Festival, is similarly affecting and understated in its depiction of the growing relationship between the neglected son of the British consul in Spain and his gardener, played with a gentle tenderness by Dirk Bogarde. These films display an empathy for the loneliness and vulnerability of children in an indifferent adult world which has helped them to retain a considerable appeal.

After making three films and completing some television work in the States, including the racially aware drama *Take a Giant Step* (1959), he returned to Britain and to familiar territory with *Hand in Hand* (1960) which is about the friendship between two young girls, one Jewish and the other Catholic. There is an uncharacteristically dark take on childhood in *Reach for Glory* (1961) where the jingoistic games of two wartime evacuees accidentally result in the death of a German refugee. Here the depiction of childhood innocence is considerably less benign than usual with Leacock and the results are unsettling. Something of a decline is apparent in the solemn Second World War drama *The War Lover* (1962) with Steve McQueen and in *Tamahine* (1962), a light comedy set in a public school which finds itself thrown into confusion by the arrival of the headmaster's Polynesian cousin (Nancy Kwan).

Following the commercial failure of these films he returned to America where he was to spend the rest of his career working efficiently in television on a variety of fairly routine projects from long-running series such as *The Waltons* to soap operas like *Dynasty*, as well as on innumerable made-for-TV movies. He died while on holiday in London on 14 July 1990. In his small body of film work Leacock carved a modest but distinctive niche for himself which is distinguished by his sensitive handling of actors, an obvious sympathy for children and a strong sense of moral purpose. These quiet qualities have stood the test of time well and his best work retains a surprising level of emotional engagement.

**British Feature Films:** *The Brave Don't Cry* (1952); *Appointment in London* (1953); *The Kidnappers* (1953); *Escapade* (1955); *The Spanish Gardener* (1956); *High Tide at Noon* (1957); *Innocent Sinners* (1958); *Hand in Hand* (1960); *Reach for Glory* (1961); *The War Lover* (1962); *Tamahine* (1962).

## (Sir) David LEAN

David Lean is unquestionably one of Britain's most important film directors. His career divides neatly into a series of quite distinct phases, but throughout there is a meticulous concern for the craftsmanship of film-making and visual storytelling, as well as a distinctly romantic sensibility at work.

Born in Croydon on 25 March 1908 of Quaker parents, after working in his father's office he entered the film industry in 1927 as a clapper-boy. He spent the 1930s employed as a film editor, building a

reputation which was unrivalled in British studios. He made his directorial debut assisting Noël Coward on his epic wartime flag-waver *In Which We Serve* (1942) which was the start of a four-film collaboration between the two. *In Which We Serve* is very much Coward's film (he produced, wrote the screenplay, co-directed, starred and composed the music) and Lean's function appears to have been confined to handling the action sequences. The film catches the mood of a country still coming to terms with Dunkirk but remaining defiant in the face of apparent defeat. Although immensely popular, its class stereotypes and stiff-upper-lipped bravery now feel decidedly dated. Lean then co-founded Cineguild (with Anthony Havelock-Allan and Ronald Neame), which allowed him to work semi-independently under the Rank umbrella. *This Happy Breed* (1944), written by Coward as a form of companion piece to *In Which We Serve*, focused this time on the British domestic scene by following the progress of a lower-middle-class family between the wars and extolling the everyday virtues of ordinary British people. Despite a strong cast, it suffered even more obviously from Coward's patrician attitude towards a class of people he clearly knew little about, but it did provide Lean with his first solo outing as director.

Over the course of his work with Coward it is possible to chart the emergence of Lean's personal signature. *Blithe Spirit* (1945) is certainly still more Coward than Lean in its characteristically waspish comedy of social manners. Undeniably stagey, Lean keeps things moving in a lively, light-hearted manner and obtains fine performances from Rex Harrison and the rest of a perfect cast, although it was poorly received at the time. *Brief Encounter* (1945) has become one of the most cherished British films of the 1940s and is perhaps the first time that Lean really emerges from under Coward's shadow. The deeply romantic story of a frustrated married woman (Celia Johnson) and the equally married young doctor (Trevor Howard) she falls in love with unfolds in the dullest of surroundings, amid tea rooms, city parks and a dingy railway station, but this only serves to heighten the intensity of feeling (Rachmaninov's music helps). The film has been subjected to a variety of interpretations (and parodies) but remains the quintessential British film of love versus duty with passions held in check.

Following his break from Coward, Lean made two extraordinary versions of Charles Dickens novels, *Great Expectations* (1946) and *Oliver Twist* (1948). The two films set a benchmark for adaptations of nineteenth-century literature which has rarely been matched. Lean's particular skill lies in the tight control he maintains over the sprawling narratives and in the visual panache with which he pictures the famous characters and episodes from the two novels. The casting is nearly always perfect, the set designs of John Bryan and the cinematography of Guy Green capture the dark claustrophobia of Dickens' London and Lean shapes the storytelling with an absolute fluency. *Great Expectations* has remained one of best regarded British films of all time. The reputation of *Oliver Twist* is almost as high, although the film suffered initially in America from concerns over the alleged anti-Semitism of its portrayal of Fagin. It was withheld until 1951 and then only released with heavy cuts.

The central, transitional phase of Lean's career is marked by some less well-remembered work. *The Passionate Friends* (1948) is an adaptation of H. G. Wells which reworks some of the same themes as *Brief Encounter*. It starred Lean's third wife, Ann Todd, who also appeared in the nineteenth-century courtroom melodrama *Madeleine* (1949). Both films are rather coldly executed and fared poorly with critics and the public, but *The Sound Barrier* (1952) is a more ambitious project detailing the first flight to pass the speed of sound. The balance between the flying sequences and the dialogue scenes is sometimes a little jarring and the cut-glass accents haven't aged well, but the film is exciting and at times moving in its low-key heroism. The film also marked Lean's move from Rank to their great rival Alexander KORDA. *Hobson's Choice* (1954) was adapted from Harold Brighouse's popular play and provides a showcase for Charles Laughton's wonderfully irascible performance as the ill tempered northern patriarch who is out manoeuvred by his equally strong-minded daughter (Brenda de Banzie). *Summer Madness* (1955) proved to be a pivotal film for Lean. In many respects, it is another return to the themes of repressed love found in *Brief Encounter*, but this film was shot in colour on location in Venice with a Hollywood star, Katherine Hepburn, in the lead. On its own merits, it is a relatively modest film, but its glossy production values were an indication of the direction Lean's career was to take.

The final phase of Lean's career saw him move into large-scale international co-productions, often featuring starry casts and made at great expense. His now infamous attention to detail frequently led to long period of location shooting which meant that over the next fifteen years he released only four films. These films did well at the box office and received many awards, but their critical standing has been the subject of a good deal of heated debate. *The Bridge on the River Kwai* (1957), adapted from Pierre Boulle's novel, is a spectacular war film whose genre elements sit rather uncomfortably with its more thoughtful aspects. These lie principally in the culture clash between Alec Guinness's pedantic, pompous Colonel Nicholson and Sessue Hayakawa's increasingly enraged Colonel Saito. The film achieved a new level of international recognition for Lean confirmed by his Academy Award as Best Director. He won the award again with *Lawrence of Arabia* (1962) which is broadly recognised as his late masterpiece. Its technical qualities, including Frederick A. Young's breathtaking cinematography and the innovative editing of Anne Coates, are remarkable and the performances of Peter O'Toole (as T. E. Lawrence), Omar Sharif and Anthony Quinn are suitably charismatic, but it's the hypnotic beauty of the film as a whole which haunts the memory.

The beginnings of a critical backlash were already apparent with *Dr Zhivago* (1965), adapted by Robert Bolt from Boris Pasternak's novel, although it was a considerable commercial success. Despite its epic sweep and some memorable set-pieces, Lean's usual sureness of touch seems missing. Some of the casting is anachronistic, particularly the Egyptian Sharif as a Russian doctor, the complex narrative frequently becomes confused and Lean shows little personal engagement with the depiction of some of the most important political development of the twentieth century. If the critical reception was poor, this was nothing in comparison with the roasting given to *Ryan's Daughter* (1970). In essence, this is a slight love story set against the backdrop of Irish resistance to British rule in the early 1900s, but Lean blows this up over nearly four hours into a gargantuan, melodramatic storm in a teacup. He built an entire village in Ireland for the film, but the odd casting, slow pace and air of indulgence proved unappealing.

Lean blamed the critical hostility to the film for a subsequent fourteen-year absence from film-making, although he tried to get a number of large-scale projects off the ground during this time. His final film, *A Passage to India* (1984), was adapted from E. M. Forster's novel and has many of Lean's characteristic qualities in its clear storytelling and visual splendour. It did a good deal to restore his reputation at the time, although seen now its simplification of Forster's novel into a story of sexual repression and cultural misunderstanding seems crude and the casting of Alec Guinness as the Indian mystic Godbole embarrassed a fine actor. Despite this, nothing is likely to diminish Lean's standing within British cinema. A consummate, painstaking craftsman and masterly storyteller, his surprisingly consistent thematic concerns place him, alongside Michael POWELL, as the great romantic of British cinema. He was knighted in 1984 and died in London on 16 April 1991 while preparing a film of Joseph Conrad's *Nostromo*.

**British Feature Films:** *In Which We Serve* (1942, co-directed with Noël Coward); *This Happy Breed* (1944); *Blithe Spirit* (1945); *Brief Encounter* (1945); *Great Expectations* (1946); *Oliver Twist* (1948); *The*

*Passionate Friends* (1948); *Madeleine* (1949); *The Sound Barrier* (1952); *Hobson's Choice* (1954); *Summer Madness* (1955); *The Bridge on the River Kwai* (1957); *Lawrence of Arabia* (1962); *Doctor Zhivago* (1965); *Ryan's Daughter* (1970); *A Passage to India* (1984).

**Bibliography**: Kevin Brownlow, *David Lean* (London: Faber & Faber, 1997).

## Mike LEIGH

Mike Leigh, who was born in Salford on 20 February 1943, has become one of Britain's most acclaimed contemporary directors. Along with Ken Loach, he has been responsible for keeping the flame of socially relevant, realist cinema alive in Britain. For his many admirers, the gallery of exceptional performances, the humanity of his stories and the ongoing political commitment of his cinema have made him a treasured figure. His detractors point to a tendency to drift into caricature and suggest his use of humorous stereotyping as an indication of a patronising attitude. However, few would deny his importance in British cinema of the last twenty-five years.

The son of a doctor and a nurse, he attended his local grammar school and in 1960 won a scholarship to RADA. After a spell at art college, he studied at the London Film School and from 1965 began to work in the theatre as an actor, writer and director. He made his feature film debut with *Bleak Moments* (1971) in which his distinctive methods are already apparent. Having established a basic dramatic premise, setting and possible characters, but working without a script, Leigh allows his actors to improvise over a period of extensive rehearsals, with a final screenplay emerging from this collaboration. He then shoots the script in a more formally conventional manner. The results have a vivid spontaneity and naturalness unusual even in realist films. *Bleak Moments* is also typical in its concern for lives stunted by emotional repression and the inability to communicate. The exchanges of banal dialogue between the characters which mask their loneliness make for a painfully raw experience for audiences.

The uncompromising harshness of his vision found few supporters initially and he didn't make another cinema film for seventeen years. Instead, he joined the BBC in 1973 and continued with his theatre work (as he does today), as well as making a number of short films. In his feature length television films there is a greater emphasis on comedy, frequently stemming from an acute observation of the social ineptitude of his characters. In the popular *Abigail's Party* (1977) the humour is at the expense of the class ambitions of the suburban would-be sophisticate Beverly, beautifully played by Leigh's then wife Alison Steadman. Beverly's ghastly lack of taste and shallowness are revealed in a sometimes excruciating comedy of social embarrassment. The temptation to draw on caricature and easy stereotypes is even more apparent in the camping holiday farce of *Nuts in May* (1976) which is often agonising to watch and yet in which a strain of real melancholy and sympathy keeps the characters just within the realm of naturalistic observation. The bleaker side of Leigh's sensibility is more to the fore in the superbly acted *Meantime* (1984).

With the help of Channel 4, Leigh finally returned to feature film-making with *High Hopes* (1988) which remains one of the highlights of his career. Leigh deftly interweaves a familiar drama of working-class family life into a wider commentary on the effects of Thatcherism on British communities. The political subtext grows naturally out of the everyday struggles of individuals who find it difficult to retain a sense of purpose in an increasingly materialistic, selfish culture. For his critics, Leigh's political sympathies lead him to portray the proletarian characters with a warmth which is denied to the grotesque yuppies, but nonetheless the film was a success, establishing Leigh's international reputation and giving him a place on the art house circuit which he has subsequently maintained.

He achieved his widest success with *Secrets and Lies* (1996) in which his characteristic themes of futile social aspiration, loss of community spirit and the damaging effects of materialism are explored in a moving story of family reconciliation. The film was awarded two BAFTAs and the Palme d'Or at Cannes and even obtained a degree of American success with Brenda Blethyn's exaggerated performance winning an Oscar nomination. One consequence of Leigh's methods is that his actors are sometimes pushed towards a heightened realism which produces performances full of amplified character quirks which can be grating. This contrasts with the subtlety which can be achieved, typified by Timothy Spall's acting here. The film is also a fine riposte to those who argue that Leigh has no visual style. His technique, although understated, is always artfully crafted, as is evident here in the flowing camerawork, careful compositions and occasional use of montage.

Both *Life is Sweet* (1990), his first film for his own independent production company Thin Man, and *Career Girls* (1997) are in the classic Mike Leigh mould, although the latter has a tenderness and mood of regret which belie its rather poor reception. *Naked* (1993) is Leigh's most controversial and extreme film. The charismatic, vio-lently misanthropic Johnny, played brilliantly by David Thewlis, seemed to some critics to personify a streak of misogyny which had always been there in Leigh's work. The real tension arises from the fact that Johnny's rants against modern life are likely to strike a chord with many in the audience, although they are emanating from such a dislikeable mouthpiece. Leigh surprised everyone with *Topsy-Turvy* (1999), an engaging, affectionate portrait of Gilbert and Sullivan which delights in the recreation of the backstage world of the theatre. With *All or Nothing* (2002) he returned to much more familiar territory with another fraught drama of working–class life featuring many of his favourite repertory company of actors.

With his most recent film, *Vera Drake* (2004), he has recaptured the art house success he previously experienced with *Secrets and Lies*. Imelda Staunton gives a moving, beautifully nuanced performance as the heroine who provides illegal abortions for poor working women who don't have the social contacts to access a doctor. The film's even-handed treatment of a potentially divisive subject enabled it to have some success in America (where he received two Oscar nominations) and even his detractors could hardly fail to be impressed by the evocative period recreation (on a very low budget) and the strength of the performances. The film's reception seemed to mark an acknowledgment of Leigh's status within British cinema. His work is instantly recognisable, its humour built on an acute perception of typically British traits and characterised by a mixture of sympathy and satire. By stretching the boundaries of naturalism towards a form of stylisation he has created a distinctive signature, but beyond the caricatures it is his ability to embed the political within believably human situations that gives his films such a powerful connection with their audience. He was awarded the OBE in 1993 and the Ordre des Arts et Lettres in 1998.

**British Feature Films:** *Bleak Moments* (1971); *High Hopes* (1988); *Life is Sweet* (1990); *Naked* (1993); *Secrets and Lies* (1996); *Career Girls* (1997); *Topsy-Turvy* (1999); *All or Nothing* (2002); *Vera Drake* (2004).

**Bibliography:** Raymond Carney and Leonard Quart, *The Films of Mike Leigh: Embracing the World* (Cambridge: Cambridge University Press, 2000); Michael Coveney, *The World According to Mike Leigh* (London: HarperCollins, 1996).

## Richard LESTER

Richard Lester, the film director most associated with the youth culture explosion of Swinging Sixties Britain, was born in Philadelphia on 19 January 1932. He studied clinical psychology at the University of Pennsylvania and then began work in American television as a stagehand, rising rapidly to become a director at the remarkable age of just twenty. He also gained crucial experience working on television commercials. Leaving the States in 1954, he travelled in Europe before settling in Britain in 1956. His early work in British television showed a liking for anarchic humour, as exemplified in the series *A Show Called Fred* (1956) featuring Peter Sellers and Spike Milligan. He worked closely with Milligan and Sellers again on the groundbreaking eleven-minute short *The Running, Jumping and Standing Still Film* (1959). Shot in two days at a cost of £70, the film gave full reign to the surreal inventiveness of both performers.

His feature film debut, *It's Trad, Dad!* (1962), was set against the backdrop of the British jazz revival and was an early indication of Lester's affinity with Britain's nascent youth scene. *The Mouse on the Moon* (1963) was a relatively tame mainstream comedy, but his third film, *A Hard Day's Night* (1964), took him firmly into the media spotlight. In this first film intended to show off Britain's new pop sensations the Beatles, Lester adopts a surprisingly naturalistic approach, imitating the gritty realism of the New Wave in a faux documentary following a few days in the life of the band. There is a sense of authenticity in the glimpse the film gives into the band's already chaotic lifestyle and, unlike so many pop music vehicles of the era, something of the group's mischievous, gently anti-establishment stance is retained. Lester's achievement is evident in the fact that the film still seems fresh, as well as influential, forty years on. He wasn't able to replicate this artistic success with the second Beatles vehicle, *Help!* (1965). Despite a plethora of zany gags and visual trickery, as well as the use of travelogue locations in the Alps and the Bahamas, the frenetic approach can't disguise the basic hollowness of the enterprise. Its musical set-pieces, however, do look like the precursor to the modern-day pop music video.

Of all Lester's work it is probably *The Knack* (1965) which ensured his association with Swinging London. The simple story of a young teacher (Michael Crawford) who wants to emulate his housemate's success with women provides the framework for a barrage of playful cinematic techniques, from silent movie title cards to a Greek chorus of disapproving adults. There is a real delight here in inventiveness for its own sake and the film certainly captures the energy and essential innocence of the time. While the film won the Palme d'Or at Cannes and critics like George Melly celebrated its youthful vigour, others were less enamoured with what they saw as an inherent superficiality in Lester's approach, which was sometimes blamed on his time working in advertising. There is a similar 'anything goes' mood to his review-style film of Stephen Sondheim's stage musical *A Funny Thing Happened on the Way to the Forum* (1966), but with the help of an appealing cast including Buster Keaton and Phil Silvers the film has as at least as many hits as misses.

Lester's films of the late 1960s take on a darker, more pessimistic tone in keeping with the gradual unravelling of the swinging scene. *How I Won the War* (1967), which gave John Lennon his first and only film appearance without the other Beatles, is a slightly scattergun attack on the horrors of war and the absurdities of the British class system. Lester was reunited with Spike Milligan for the bizarre *The Bed Sitting Room* (1969), adapted from the play by Milligan and John Antrobus. A surreal vision of a world ravaged by nuclear war where the survivors transform into items of household furniture, the film indicates the degree to which Milligan's humour often grew out of a sense of despair at human folly. Between these films Lester made *Petulia* (1968) in the States. Although little remembered now, the film is a potently disillusioned portrayal of false 1960s values made with real intelligence.

The commercial failure of *The Bed Sitting Room*, along with the increasingly parlous financial state of British cinema, pushed Lester away from experimentation and social commentary into more mainstream projects. Nonetheless, there is still a 1960s spirit of joyful irreverence in his adaptation of Dumas' *The Three Musketeers* (1973) and *The Four Musketeers* (1974). Originally shot as one film but due to overlength released as two, there are amiable performances, particularly from Oliver Reed, and the action scenes are staged with gusto. There are similar qualities in *Royal Flash* (1975), based on George Macdonald Fraser's *Flashman* novels and starring Malcolm McDowell, and he belatedly returned to the format once more with *The Return of the Musketeers* (1989), a lacklustre retread principally remembered for the accidental death during production of Roy Kinnear.

A good deal of his later work was completed in America including the enjoyable disaster movie *Juggernaut* (1974) set aboard a transatlantic liner. He demonstrated a sure commercial touch with two entertaining additions to the Superman franchise, *Superman II* (1980) and *Superman III* (1983). His other American projects, *The Ritz* (1976), *Cuba* (1979) and *Finders Keepers* (1984), failed to find anything like the same audience. The best of his later films are marked by a mood of nostalgia, as seen in the elegiac, engaging *Robin and Marion* (1976). Sean Connery and Audrey Hepburn are the legendary figures who we now find in their declining years. Admittedly sentimental, the film still has a powerfully melancholic longing for a time of heroism long vanished. A similar mood underlies the more routine

American-made prequel *Butch and Sundance: The Early Days* (1979) and is even intrinsic to his last film, *Get Back* (1991), a documentary record of a concert tour by Paul McCartney.

At his height in the 1960s, no other director seemed to have such a sure sense of the youthful mood of freedom which Britain was experiencing. These films, with their goonish humour and cinematic sleight of hand, may now seem rather dated, but few films of the era capture with quite such insouciant charm the optimism and sheer pleasure which were at the heart of the period. If his later work seems more conventional, it's only because these films were so successful in distilling the newness of their own time.

**British Feature Films:** *It's Trad, Dad!* (1962); *The Mouse on the Moon* (1963); *A Hard Day's Night* (1964); *Help!* (1965); *The Knack . . . and How to Get It* (1965); *A Funny Thing Happened on the Way to the Forum* (1966); *How I Won the War* (1967); *The Bed Sitting Room* (1969); *The Three Musketeers* (1973); *The Four Musketeers* (1974); *Juggernaut* (1974); *Royal Flash* (1975); *Robin and Marion* (1976); *The Return of the Musketeers* (1989); *Get Back* (1991).

**Bibliography:** Andrew Yule, *The Man Who Framed the Beatles: A Biography of Richard Lester* (New York: Donald J. Fine, 1994); Neil Sinyard, *The Films of Richard Lester* (London: Croom Helm, 1985).

## Ken LOACH

Ken Loach was born in Nuneaton, Warwickshire on 17 June 1936. After studying law at Oxford where he was President of the Dramatic Society, he worked firstly in reparatory theatre and then in 1963 moved into television with the BBC. After a spell on the popular police series *Z Cars*, he began to specialise in single-episode dramas which often tackled contemporary topics using a semi-documentary style. Working frequently for the *Wednesday Play* slot with producer Tony Garnett, Loach made challenging, socially conscious work like *Up the Junction* (1965) and *Cathy Come Home* (1966). The latter in particular hit the public nerve, bringing the issue of homelessness to many people's attention. The programme remains a landmark in the history of television drama. He moved into feature films with *Poor Cow* (1967), scripted by Nell Dunn, which deals with the difficulties of a single mother played by Carol White. The film's tone is slightly uncertain, with Loach's characteristic naturalism sitting slightly awkwardly with more conventional elements such as the casting of Terence Stamp.

It is with his second feature, *Kes* (1969), that his mature style can be

seen. Aiming to maximise authenticity, Loach typically shoots on
location using a cast which mixes professional actors with local
amateurs. Loach uses such strategies as only supplying each actor
with their own lines so that they react with genuine spontaneity or
providing just that day's dialogue so actors are unsure how the drama
will unfold. The results are raw and convincing, although for his critics
this approach is a sleight-of-hand intended to deceive the viewer into
believing they are actually watching a documentary rather than a
fictional drama. *Kes* sympathetically depicts the stunted life of a young
schoolboy in a working-class mining community whose only release is
through his training of a kestrel. The film is surprisingly funny,
particularly in the now classic football lesson, as well as touching
and lyrical. He followed it with *Family Life* (1971), scripted by David
Mercer, which he had previously made as the television drama *In Two
Minds* (1967). It deals in an understanding manner with the plight of a
mentally ill young woman, indicting an indifferent medical profession
and the pressures of contemporary life as contributing to her condition.
Loach is always drawn to the downtrodden and outcast, seeing them as
victims of a materialistic society.

In the depressed economic climate faced by 1970s British cinema,
Loach often found it difficult to work. With the exception of the rather
misjudged children's period adventure film *Black Jack* (1979), his
other work of the decade is for television. This includes the compelling
four-part *Days of Hope* (1975) dealing with the build up to the 1926
General Strike. The production situation wasn't greatly more encouraging for such a politically committed film-maker in the Thatcherite
1980s when his only two cinema films were *Fatherland* (1986), a slightly
confused drama contrasting life in West and East Germany, and *Looks
and Smiles* (1981), which returns to familiar territory in depicting the
lives of unemployed youngsters. The latter was written by Barry Hines,
the original author of *Kes* and the television drama *The Gamekeeper*
(1980). These films interweave their political subtext with a warm,
evocative view of their characters. He also made a number of more
directly political documentaries which address the crisis facing the
Labour movement in Britain during this period, including *Questions of
Leadership* (1981) and *The Red and the Blue* (1983). These controversial
projects faced an unprecedented degree of attempted censorship, but
Loach has remained impressively consistent in his dedication to using
cinema and television to explore his socialist beliefs.

Loach has re-emerged into the wider spotlight since the beginning of
the 1990s, benefiting from his increasing international status as one of
Britain's most important contemporary directors, as well as from more

consistent funding. *Hidden Agenda* (1990), which deals with the British 'shoot-to-kill' policy in Northern Ireland, unsurprisingly incurred the wrath of the political Right. The film is more significant for the way in which Loach combines his political concerns and realist strategies with a more conventional dramatic approach, here using a thriller format to encompass his themes. This approach has been used in a number of his subsequent films leading to further accusations that his realist aesthetic is designed to disguise an emotionally manipulative narrative technique. Given Loach's open political stance it is hardly a shock that his films attract a good deal of criticism. The beginnings of a renaissance started with *Riff-Raff* (1991) and *Raining Stones* (1993), the latter winning the Jury Prize at Cannes. The former is set on a building site and deals with the problems faced by casual labourers. Its social concerns are blended with a good deal of humour and there are charismatic performances from Robert Carlyle and Ricky Tomlinson. Humour is used again in *Raining Stones*, along with a degree of sentiment as its unemployed protagonist mires himself in debt to a brutal loan shark in a desperate attempt to buy a dress for his daughter's communion service. These deeply humane films make their political points by demonstrating how economic and social structures impinge on the everyday lives of their characters.

This approach reaches its zenith with the powerful *Land and Freedom* (1995). Set during the Spanish Civil War, it examines questions of political commitment through a young woman's discovery of her grandfather's letters home from Spain. Written by regular collaborator Jim Allen, the film must be unique in managing to make a group discussion of collectivisation into a totally gripping scene. It also succeeds in demonstrating how the historical issues depicted remain relevant today. *Ladybird, Ladybird* (1994) revisited similar territory to *Cathy Come Home*, while the art house success *My Name is Joe* (1998) looks at the problems of unemployment, petty crime, drug use and alcoholism. In Tony Blair's Britain, Loach's focus has increasingly been targeted towards those who remain outside the economic improvements enjoyed by the majority, his disillusionment with Blair's Labour government indicated by his abandoning the party and subsequent affiliation to alternative left-wing groups like the Socialist Labour Party for whom he directed a party political broadcast. His concern with the socially marginalised has continued in his two more recent films set in Scotland, *Sweet Sixteen* (2002) and *Ae Fond Kiss* (2004). The internationalism of his outlook was reflected in his first American film *Bread and Roses* (2000), depicting the plight of immigrant workers, *Carla's Song* (1996), which dramatises the struggles of the Sandinistas in Nicaragua, and his contribution to the portmanteau films *September 11* (2002) and *Tickets* (2005).

For forty years Ken Loach has been a clear, unflinching voice within British cinema. His films address the concerns of ordinary people struggling within an iniquitous economic system in a manner which is engaging and full of empathy. Naturalistic observation adds a raw power to his political cinema, drawing the viewer in. In Loach's film-making the personal truly is the political.

**British Feature Films**: *Poor Cow* (1967); *Kes* (1969); *Family Life* (1971); *Black Jack* (1979); *Looks and Smiles* (1981); *Fatherland* (1986); *Hidden Agenda* (1990); *Riff-Raff* (1991); *Raining Stones* (1993); *Lady-bird, Ladybird* (1994); *Land and Freedom* (1995); *Carla's Song* (1996); *My Name is Joe* (1998); *Sweet Sixteen* (2002); *Ae Fond Kiss* (2004).

**Bibliography**: Jacob Leigh, *The Cinema of Ken Loach* (London: Wallflower, 2002); Graham Fuller (ed.), *Loach on Loach* (London: Faber & Faber, 1998); George McKnight (ed.), *Agent of Challenge and Defiance: The Films of Ken Loach* (Trowbridge: Flicks Books, 1997).

## Joseph LOSEY

The American-born Joseph Losey belongs to a group of distinguished directors who came to Britain in the late 1950s and 1960s from abroad. Whereas some were attracted by a newly vibrant film culture, Losey had rather more pressing reasons as he was fleeing from Senator McCarthy's House UnAmerican Activities Committee (HUAC) which subsequently blacklisted him as a communist. Losey was born in La Crosse, Wisconsin on 14 January 1909. He briefly studied medicine at Dartford and then English at Harvard, before moving to New York where he became involved with New Deal theatre projects and made short films for the Rockefeller Foundation. After war service he returned to the theatre and in 1947 he directed a stage production of Bertolt Brecht's *Galileo* starring Charles Laughton. He started in the film industry making shorts with MGM, but quickly moved to RKO where he made his feature debut with the anti-war film *The Boy with Green Hair* (1948). He followed this with a series of taughtly directed 'B' movies, often in the crime genre, including *The Prowler* (1951) and a remake of Fritz Lang's *M* (1951). The liberal sentiments expressed in these films, along with his involvement with left-wing theatre groups, brought him to the attention of HUAC and led in due course to his departure from the US.

He arrived in Britain in 1952 and initially struggled to establish himself, firstly working on television and then being forced to make films under various pseudonyms. His early British films continue the pattern of his American work centring on genre subjects which he handles with style and individuality. *The Sleeping Tiger* (1954) was a modest British debut, but *The Intimate Stranger* (1956) was more confident, as well as having a plot which paralleled elements of Losey's own experiences of persecution. The period melodrama *The Gentleman and the Gypsy* (1958) was a mistake, but *Time Without Pity* (1957), *Blind Date* (1959) and *The Criminal* (1960) are crime dramas which show Losey's panache even working with low budgets. In these films many of his typical methods and themes are already apparent. *Sleeping Tiger* teamed him with Dirk Bogarde for the first time and *Blind Date* and *The Criminal* feature Stanley Baker; these two actors were to be central to his 1960s output. His visual style here leans towards the expressionistic, particularly in *The Criminal*, and there is a concern for social outsiders and injustice. *The Criminal* was also his first film with composer Johnny Dankworth who would score many of his 1960s films.

His mature period really begins with *The Damned* (1961), super-ficially a science fiction chiller made for Hammer about children deliberately contaminated by the government with radiation but characteristically used by Losey to attack the development of nuclear weapons and the idiocies of the Cold War. It was only released by Hammer after considerable re-editing. He ran into problems with producers again on the undervalued *Eve* (1962) featuring Stanley Baker and Jeanne Moreau. The film was initially released in a truncated form which Losey disowned; it was eventually re-released in a longer version which revealed more of its complexity. In 1964 he made the trenchant, moving anti-war film *King and Country* with Bogarde and Tom Courtenay, but his real leap into critical acclaim came with *The Servant* (1963). Adapted by Harold Pinter from Robin Maugham's novella, this is an intricately scripted dissection of the British class system, as Dirk Bogarde's brilliantly played manservant, Barrett, gradually achieves mastery over his weak employer (James Fox). The two play out a dizzying array of different relationships, from bored married couple to hints of homosexuality, while Losey creates a suitably menacing atmosphere with chiaroscuro lighting and an elaborate set. If the film becomes faintly absurd in its final orgy sequence, it remains a genuinely groundbreaking film of the period.

Losey made two further films with Pinter. The first, *Accident* (1967), is perhaps his masterpiece and was awarded the Jury Prize at Cannes. Directed and written with minimalistic precision, the film depicts the shallow lives of two Oxford dons (Bogarde and Baker) whose intellectualism and apparent sophistication mask petty jealousies and selfishness. These are revealed in a long, beautifully observed sequence of a Sunday dinner party in summer which disintegrates into cold, emotional cruelty. *The Go-Between* (1971), which won the Palme d'Or at Cannes, stars Alan Bates and Julie Christie and was adapted from L. P. Hartley's novel of Edwardian England. Its depiction of the forbidden affair between the daughter of the local landowners and a tenant farmer allows Losey to again examine the hypocrisies of the British class system. The film is constructed with a concern for formal symmetry, using an elaborate flashback structure to reveal the psychological damage done to the characters by class prejudices.

Losey's other films never quite captured the quality of his work with Pinter and were frequently criticised for their pretentiousness and overly baroque directorial style. *Modesty Blaise* (1966) is a wildly camp comic-strip spoof of James Bond with Bogarde fetching in a silver wig. *Boom* (1968) was a heavily symbolic, indulgent melodrama adapted from a Tennessee Williams play and featuring Richard Burton and Elizabeth Taylor. Taylor also featured in the bizarre, claustrophobic psychodrama *Secret Ceremony* (1968), while Burton appeared in the plodding *The Assassination of Trotsky* (1972). Clumsy symbolism and obscurity marred the allegorical *Figures in a Landscape* (1970), whereas both *A Doll's House* (1973) and *Galileo* (1975) are straightforward theatrical adaptations weakened by the miscasting of Jane Fonda in the former and Topol in the latter. After making *The Romantic English-woman* (1975), he left Britain to make films in continental Europe. The best of his European films is his ornate version of *Don Giovanni* (1979), but otherwise he continued to show a gradual decline. His last film, *Steaming* (1985), was made back in Britain. Adapted from Nell Dunn's play and set in a bath-house, it features a strong all-female cast including Diana Dors and Vanessa Redgrave. It was at least a partial return to form. Sadly, Losey's health deteriorated during the making of the film and he subsequently died on 22 June 1984.

In his best work, Losey brought an outsider's sense of distance to the nuances of British life, producing work which examined the workings of the class system and the mechanics of power in a highly formalised cinematic style. If his work sometimes misfired, it was due to over-ambition rather than lack of ability. His finest films opened up new avenues for British film culture, changing the national cinematic landscape for good.

**British Feature Films:** *The Sleeping Tiger* (1954); *The Intimate Stranger* (1956); *Time Without Pity* (1957); *The Gypsy and the Gentleman* (1958); *Blind Date* (1959); *The Criminal* (1960); *The Damned*

(1961); *Eve* (1962); *The Servant* (1963); *King and Country* (1964); *Modesty Blaise* (1966); *Accident* (1967); *Boom* (1968); *Secret Ceremony* (1968); *Figures in a Landscape* (1970); *The Go-Between* (1971); *The Assassination of Trotsky* (1972); *A Doll's House* (1973); *Galileo* (1975); *The Romantic Englishwoman* (1975); *Steaming* (1985).

**Bibliography**: David Caute, *Joseph Losey: A Revenge on Life* (Oxford: Oxford University Press, 1994); Foster Hirsch, *Joseph Losey* (Boston: Twayne, 1980).

## Len LYE

Len Lye is a unique figure, being one of the earliest experimental film-makers to emerge from British cinema. Born in Christchurch, New Zealand on 5 July 1901, he was interested in art from an early age and learned film-making in Australia before undertaking anthropological studies in Samoa (he had an abiding interest in aboriginal art). When he came to Britain in 1926 he joined the London-based modernist group the Seven and Five Society. He exhibited with the group, but retained a fascination for how movement could be incorporated into art. This eventually led to his first animated short, the largely abstract *Tusalava* (1929). Finding it difficult to obtain financial support, he joined the GPO Film Unit in 1934 where he began to experiment with painting directly on to celluloid, a technique later taken up by Norman MCLAREN. His first short for them, the award-winning *A Colour Box* (1935), is barely recognisable as a conventional advertisement. Instead we are confronted with colourful shapes which shimmer and dance in time to a soundtrack of Cuban music. The results are joyful and dynamic. He used puppets in *Kaleidoscope* (1935), made with Humphrey JENNINGS, combined silhouettes with colour back-grounds in *Rainbow Dance* (1936) and used found documentary footage for *Trade Tattoo* (1937). *Birth of a Robot* (1935), made for Shell Oil, is a magical animation celebrating the excitement of modern machinery in glowing colours and featuring a striking, cylindrical robot.

Lye was fascinated with the idea of trying to capture the non-rational in art, hence his participation in the 1936 International Surrealist Exhibition in London. However, with his last promotional film for the GPO, *N or N.W.* (1937), he moved into a slightly more conventional narrative live-action format, although even here he added camera tricks and elements of animation to create a more inventive effect. Subsequently he worked on newsreels, provided special effects sequences for the feature film *Stardust* (1938) and produced advertisements for companies such as Imperial Airways. During the war he worked on propaganda films for the Ministry of Information, including compiling the documentary *Cameramen at War* (1944). He left Britain for America in 1944 where he worked on educational shorts and the *March of Time* newsreel series, as well as continuing to explore the possibilities of cinematic abstraction. In the late 1950s he started to focus his energies on painting and sculpture again. He returned to New Zealand in 1968 where he continued to work as an artist.

In an industry where realism has often been the dominant aesthetic, Lye is a highly unusual film-maker. A pioneer of British animation and a precursor of the experimental structuralist film-making which was to take off in the late 1960s and early 1970s, he demonstrated the possibilities of cinema as a medium for abstract expression. Considering the potentially cerebral nature of his work, it is an added pleasure that so much of it is concerned with the simple joy of movement and colour. Len Lye died on 15 May 1980 in Rhode Island, USA.

**Bibliography**: Roger Horrocks, *Len Lye: A Biography* (Auckland: Auckland University Press, 2001); Deke Dusinberre, 'The Avant-Garde Attitude in the Thirties', in Don Macpherson (ed.), *Traditions of Independence: British Cinema in the Thirties* (London: BFI, 1980).

### Alexander MACKENDRICK

Among the talented team assembled at Ealing Studios by Michael Balcon two directors stand out for their individualism, Robert HAMER and Alexander Mackendrick. If Hamer's films are distinguished by their visual stylisation and melancholy tone, then it is Mackendrick who took the Ealing comedy style and pushed it into areas of satire and black humour which mark his films out from the more whimsical, optimistic approach usually favoured by Balcon.

Mackendrick was born in Boston, Massachusetts on 8 September 1912 of Scottish parents. With the death of his father in 1919, he returned to live in Glasgow with his grandfather. After studying at the Glasgow School of Art he went to work as an artist for the advertising firm J. Walter Thompson in London where he remained for the rest of the 1930s. In the late 1930s he scripted several cinema commercials and co-wrote his first feature film, *Midnight Menace* (1937). During the war he wrote a number of short propaganda films for the animators HALAS and BATCHELOR, directed some educational inserts for

Pathé newsreels and co-directed two propaganda documentaries for the British Army in Italy following the fall of Rome. After the war he founded Merlin Productions which made documentaries for the Ministry of Information, but when it floundered in 1946 he went to work for Ealing.

His first jobs at Ealing were as a writer and production designer, but he eventually made his feature debut as a director with the Scottish comedy *Whisky Galore!* (1949). Taken from Compton Mackenzie's novel, the plot is typical Ealing with its story of a small island whose inhabitants salvage a cargo of whisky from a shipwreck and then conspire to keep their booty out of the clutches of an English customs inspector. However, in what became characteristic of Mackendrick, he partially subverts the familiar Ealing format offering a degree of sympathy for the bewildered inspector and adding a darker edge to the depiction of the anarchic villagers than was the Ealing norm. This ability to introduce a level of moral ambiguity to the Ealing formula is even more apparent in his second classic comedy for them, *The Man in the White Suit* (1951). Alec Guinness is the boffin who invents a material which never wears out or needs cleaning, thus incurring the wrath of both factory owners and the workforce. The satire on capitalism takes pot shots at both sides in the class war but doesn't allow Guinness's hero off the hook either as it eventually becomes transparent that his naivety is every bit as dangerous as the more deliberately Machiavellian behaviour of those around him.

He took a break from comedy to make *Mandy* (1952), a sympathetic, sensitive portrait of the world of a little deaf girl struggling to learn to speak which was awarded the Special Jury Prize at Venice. With a touching central performance from Mandy Miller, the film is also an examination of an adult world of non-communication exemplified by the barren relationship of Mandy's parents. He returned to comedy, and to a Scottish setting, with *The Maggie* (1954). This is the slightest of his Ealing output and struggles to overcome the clichés in its story of a wily Scottish steamboat captain and the rich American employer whom he runs rings around. His final film for Ealing, and the last of their series of classic comedies, was *The Ladykillers* (1955). The film develops into a blackly surreal masterpiece as its gang of would-be train robbers falls foul of a sweet old lady (Katie Johnson) who proves to be more than a match for them. The film's love-hate relationship with aspects of Britishness, its ambiguous portrayal of Mrs Wilberforce (who is at once the film's moral centre and also a representative of the reactionary forces in British society) and its bleak escalation into murder make it a unique film in the Ealing canon, as well as one of the most complex, rewarding British comedies.

With the demise of Ealing, Mackendrick went to America where he made the brilliant *Sweet Smell of Success* (1957), a bitter depiction of the shallow world of New York society centred on a mendacious gossip columnist and his rat-like press agent, played superbly by Burt Lancaster and Tony Curtis respectively. The film was made for Hecht-Hill-Lancaster, for whom Mackendrick was to shoot *The Devil's Disciple* back in the UK, but he was fired early on in the film's production. None of his last three films matched the high standards he had previously set, but the first two have considerable interest. Both *Sammy Going South* (1963) and *A High Wind in Jamaica* (1965) have children at their centre. The former is an epic adventure film about an orphaned boy who hitchhikes the length of Africa to find his aunt. If the handling here is relatively straightforward, then the latter film is another ambiguous, and sometimes disturbing, contemplation of innocence and experience depicting the relationships between a group of children and their pirate captors. The film was dogged by clashes with its American backers, something that was becoming a regular occurrence for Mackendrick. His final film, the Hollywood-made *Don't Make Waves* (1967), was a disappointingly limp beach comedy starring Tony Curtis.

With the British industry in increasing disarray and little liking for Hollywood, Mackendrick abandoned film-making and in 1969 joined academia becoming the Dean of the Film School at the California Institute for the Arts. He taught here almost up to the time of his death on 23 December 1993. With their emphasis on narrative, it is easy to overlook the visual skill with which Mackendrick's films were made. His control of *mise en scène* in *The Man in the White Suit* or the striking use of exaggerated colour in *The Ladykillers* are just two examples of the meticulous control and attention to detail which he brought to his films. In the dark pessimism of their humour and their leaning towards social satire, Mackendrick's work went well beyond the self-imposed limitations of Balcon's house style at Ealing, creating films that have stood the test of time and which rank him in the forefront of British directors.

**British Feature Films:** *Whisky Galore!* (1949); *The Man in the White Suit* (1951); *Mandy* (1952); *The Maggie* (1954); *The Ladykillers* (1955); *Sammy Going South* (1963); *A High Wind in Jamaica* (1965).

**Bibliography:** Philip Kemp, *Lethal Innocence: The Cinema of Alexander Mackendrick* (London: Methuen, 1991).

# Norman MCLAREN

Norman McLaren was born in Stirling, Scotland on 11 April 1914. His interest in cinema first developed while a student at the Glasgow School of Art. Here he made two 'documentaries', *Seven Till Five* (1933), which depicts a typical day at the art school, and *Camera Makes Whoopee* (1935), about the staging of the art school ball. His taste for experimentation is already apparent in the use of montage, superimposition and animation effects in the latter. His left-wing political leanings – he was a member of the activist group Glasgow Kino and for a time of the Communist Party – are to the fore in his best-known British work *Hell Unltd* (1936). Co-directed with his Glasgow Art School colleague, the sculptress Helen Biggar, the film attacks the growing arms trade of the period and combines a wide variety of techniques, including animation and the use of found footage, into a highly innovative collage. He subsequently went to Spain to work as cameraman on Ivor Montague's pro-Republican *Defence of Madrid* (1936). After winning the Best Film Award at the 1935 Scottish Amateur Film Festival for *Colour Cocktail*, he was invited by John Grierson to join the GPO Film Unit. Here he joined the like-minded Len LYE, whose experiments with animation and abstraction had similarities to McLaren's work. He was later to take up LYE's technique of painting directly onto film stock. McLaren was never completely comfortable at the GPO and only produced one significant piece for them, the inventive colour animation *Love on the Wing* (1938) which advertises the joys of letter writing.

McLaren left for America in 1939 and then in 1941 went to work again for Grierson at the newly formed National Film Board of Canada where he headed the animation unit. Under his supervision it was to become among the most innovative and influential animation producers in the world. The extensive range and formal innovation of his own work with the National Film Board was to secure him a reputation as one of the most important animators in the history of cinema, as well as a key figure in avant-garde and experimental film. *Begone Dull Care* (1949) matches abstract patterns painted and scraped onto the film with jazz music by the Oscar Peterson Trio, while the Academy Award-winning *Neighbours* (1952) uses the technique of pixilation (stop frame animation of objects and people) to tell its moral parable about territorial violence. He was showered with awards internationally, including a BAFTA for the charming *Pas de Deux* (1968). In later years he also worked on educational programmes with UNESCO. Although McLaren's British work is relatively slight, particularly in comparison with his achievements in Canada, it was sufficient to make him a key figure in British experimental cinema between the wars. McLaren died on 27 January 1987 in Montreal, Canada.

**Bibliography:** Maynard Collins, *Norman McLaren* (Ottawa: Canadian Film Institute, 1976).

## Shane MEADOWS

Shane Meadows is one of the brightest new talents to have emerged in recent British cinema. He was born in Uttoxeter, Staffordshire on 26 December 1972 and raised in Nottingham. Self-taught as a film-maker, he made more than twenty amateur films on a borrowed camcorder while out of work. These include *Where's the Money Ronnie?* (1995) which first gained him some public attention, winning a short film competition sponsored by the National Film Theatre. The hour-long *Small Time* (1996), funded by the BFI, was set on a working-class council estate in the suburbs of Nottingham, the setting for all his films, and featured a number of his friends in the cast. Its authenticity and acute observation were rewarded with the Michael Powell Award at the Edinburgh International Film Festival.

He made his feature debut with *TwentyFourSeven* (1997). Set in a boxing club run by Alan Darcy (Bob Hoskins), the film focuses on the lives of a group of disaffected young men and their attempts to find some direction in life. The film is solidly in the tradition of British social realism, with location shooting and mobile camera work, the use of non-professional actors and semi-improvised dialogue. It has a rough, naturalistic feel, but Meadows brings to this familiar formula elements of humour and broad characterisation, as well as a more self-conscious cinematic vocabulary typified by long takes, wide shots and mono-chrome. The film is concerned with the impact of environment on the characters in a way which is reminiscent of Ken LOACH's *Kes* (1969). *A Room for Romeo Brass* (1999) is shot in a similar style but is more sombre in tone. Working with regular writing collaborator and long-time friend Paul Fraser, Meadows based the film in part on their shared childhood experiences. The film shifts between comedy and violence with startling effectiveness, showcasing a mesmerising performance from Paddy Considine as the unstable, increasingly menacing Morell. A political undercurrent is detectable in these films in their concern for social injustice and exclusion, although this is never overtly stated.

*Once Upon a Time in the Midlands* (2002) is in danger of being better remembered for its title than its content. The idea of playing out the conventions of a western in the modern-day Midlands is a neat enough concept, and the film has an attractive cast including Robert Carlyle and Rhys Ifans, but the premise tends to wear thin and the film quickly feels like just another undernourished contemporary British comedy. It is the only film Meadows has made to date on which he didn't have final cut. There are shades of the western genre again in *Dead Man's Shoes* (2004) with its dark, almost mythic story of revenge, but this was a real return to form. The film, which contains another fine performance from Paddy Considine, was well received. It also set a new precedent for Meadows in being his first film shot outside of Nottingham (it was made in and around Matlock in the Derbyshire Peaks). This darkly compelling film sees Considine as a kind of avenging angel who returns home to inflict a very rough justice on those who have been responsible for brutally bullying his brother. Subsequently, he has returned to the short film format with *Northern Soul* (2004).

In just four feature films Meadows has already established a considerable reputation (acknowledged by a small plethora of nominations and prizes at European film festivals) and forged a recognisable cinematic signature, bringing a distinctive visual style, warmth and idiosyncrasy to familiar material. The spirit of British realism appears to be in safe hands.

**British Feature Films:** *TwentyFourSeven* (1997); *A Room for Romeo Brass* (1999); *Once Upon a Time in the Midlands* (2002); *Dead Man's Shoes* (2004).

## Peter MEDAK

Peter Medak was born 23 December 1937 in Budapest, Hungary. He came to Britain in 1956 just before the Hungarian uprising was crushed by the Soviet Union. He entered the film industry in the late 1950s working as an editor and then as an assistant director. Working his way up from second unit director on *Funeral in Berlin* (1966) and associate producer on *Kaleidoscope* (1966), he finally made his directorial debut with *Negatives* (1968), a bizarre psychological drama featuring Glenda Jackson which centres on the sexual fantasies of the lead characters which include role-playing as the murderer Dr Crippen and his wife. His second film, *The Ruling Class* (1971), which was nominated for the Palme d'Or at Cannes, is very much a product of its time. A Pythonesque black farce adapted from Peter Barnes' successful play, it stars Peter O'Toole as a demented aristocrat who thinks he is Jesus and boasts a fine supporting cast of character actors including Arthur Lowe and Alastair Sim. The tone is wildly uneven and self-indulgent, but it does take some timely satirical swipes at the British class system. *A Day in the Death of Joe Egg* (1971) is also adapted from a play, this time Peter Nichols' sympathetic account of a couple trying to cope with the demands of raising a severely disabled daughter. The performances by Janet Suzman and Alan Bates are convincingly touching and the film offsets its despairing narrative with humour.

After this promising start as a director Medak had the misfortune to be involved in the disastrous *Ghost in the Noonday Sun* (1973), a lightweight pirate comedy that was blown off course by the egotistical behaviour of its star, Peter Sellers, and then virtually buried by its American backers. His career in British cinema stalled in the 1970s and he worked mainly on television with series like *The Professionals* and *Return of the Saint*. His only cinema film was another surreal comedy, *The Odd Job* (1978), made with ex-Python Graham Chapman, which only had a very limited release. He subsequently moved to Hollywood where he again worked in television on fairly routine projects and made three extremely varied but largely unremarkable films including the ghost story *The Changeling* (1980) and the misjudged pastiche *Zorro, the Gay Blade* (1981).

Returning to Britain he made two fine 'true life' crime films which did much to re-establish his reputation. *The Krays* (1990) is a sharply detailed portrayal of the notorious East End twin gangsters. It benefits from a strong sense of time and place, as well as surprisingly successful performances from the pop stars Martin and Gary Kemp and, more predictably, Billie Whitelaw as their monstrous mother. *Let Him Have It* (1991) is a sober, moving retelling of the tragic Derek Bentley case (Bentley was executed for the killing of a policeman although he wasn't the one who pulled the trigger). It again recreates its working-class milieu with considerable sureness of touch. Emboldened by this success he returned to the States where he made two interesting, if minor, films: the noirish black comedy *Romeo is Bleeding* (1993) and the family melodrama *Pontiac Moon* (1994). After the abysmal horror sequel *Species II* (1998), he returned to television working on popular series such as *Law and Order* and *House*. It can only be regretted that Medak's career has been so hit and miss; his liberal leanings, sensitivity in handling actors and strong sense of social context have only rarely found full expression in the cinema, but have on several occasions produced really interesting work.

**British Feature Films:** *Negatives* (1968); *The Ruling Class* (1971); *A Day in the Death of Joe Egg* (1971); *Ghost in the Noonday Sun* (1973); *The Odd Job* (1978); *The Krays* (1990); *Let Him Have It* (1991).

## Anthony MINGHELLA

Anthony Minghella first achieved acclaim as a television scriptwriter and playwright before coming into cinema in the 1990s. Of Italian parentage, he was born in Ryde, on the Isle of Wight, on 6 January 1954. After studying at the University of Hull, he moved into television as both a writer and script editor. He worked on popular series such as the children's soap *Grange Hill*, the adult soap opera *EastEnders* and the much-loved *Inspector Morse*, establishing a reputation for the sensitivity of his writing. He also wrote regularly for the stage and radio during this period. The London Theatre Critics named him their most promising new playwright in 1984 and recognised *Made in Bangkok* with their award as Best Play in 1986.

His debut as a writer-director of films came with *Truly, Madly, Deeply* (1991), which was made for the BBC but which obtained a limited theatrical release. The film deals with bereavement through the formula of a romantic comedy, with Alan Rickman's ghost returning to haunt his grieving lover (Juliet Stevenson). Genuinely touching and funny, the film achieved a degree of commercial success and was well received, winning him a BAFTA for its screenplay. This breakthrough took Minghella to Hollywood were he made another rom-com, *Mr Wonderful* (1993). Unfortunately it didn't replicate the success of his debut. However, he was to hit the critical and box-office jackpot with *The English Patient* (1996), adapted from Michael Ondaatje's acclaimed novel. The film is visually sumptuous and its deeply romantic story of love in wartime is reminiscent of David LEAN's later films, combining the epic with the intimate. If it lacks the subtle complexities of the novel, it nonetheless found a response with audiences and critics, winning innumerable international awards capped by nine Oscars including Best Director. In retrospect, his fourth film, the American-made *The Talented Mr Ripley* (1999), might actually be of more lasting merit. It manages to capture the unusual tone of Patricia Highsmith's novel with its combination of thriller and psychological drama. The story of the morally ambivalent Ripley (Matt Damon) and his relationship with the socialite Dickie Greenleaf (Jude Law) preserves the homoerotic undertones of the original as well as its air of detachment.

He returned to television for a version of Samuel Becket's *Play* (2000) and then made the big-budget western melodrama *Cold Mountain* (2003) starring Nicole Kidman, Renée Zellwegger and Jude Law. Although filmed in Europe and nominally British, the film's narrative and setting place it firmly within American cinematic traditions. Set during the American Civil War, it is made in Minghella's typically expansive style with emotions writ large, but again was showered with awards. Minghella's talents have also encompassed producing, with *Iris* (2001) and *The Quiet American* (2002), and in 2005 he made a party political broadcast for the Labour Party. He was made a CBE in 2001 and more recently took on the task of chairing the BFI.

For his critics, Minghella is a talented film-maker who has regrettably chosen to work on glossy, overblown international blockbusters which make limited use of abilities which were seen to better effect on smaller-scale, more intrinsically British subjects. For supporters, he brings intelligence, romanticism and visual panache to what might otherwise be routine commercial material. The jury may be out, but he is certainly a film-maker who is difficult to ignore.

**British Feature Films**: *Truly, Madly, Deeply* (1991); *The English Patient* (1996); *Cold Mountain* (2003).

$$\boxed{\text{N}}$$

## Ronald NEAME

In a directorial career stretching for over forty years, Ronald Neame proved to be a reliable and versatile commercial film-maker but also one who defies easy categorisation. Efficient and craftsman-like, his films are well made but have lacked the individualism seemingly required to achieve auteur status. Instead he has been the epitome of the mainstream studio director, a model of professionalism whose output has often mirrored the ups and downs of the industry.

He was born in London on 23 April 1911. His father was the noted portrait photographer and film director Elwin Neame and his mother the actress Ivy Close. After his father's early death in a car accident, he had to leave public school and went to work for an oil company. With his mother's help, he entered the film industry at the Elstree studios of British International Pictures in 1927 and worked his way up from clapperboy to focus puller and eventually cinematographer. He photographed many quota quickies in the 1930s, along with a number of George Formby vehicles at Ealing. He established a solid reputation, winning his first Oscar nomination for his work on POWELL and PRESSBURGER's *One of Our Aircraft Is Missing* (1942). With *Major Barbara* (1941), he began an association with the film's editor, David LEAN. He worked initially as his director of photography on three Noël Coward projects (he was nominated for a second Oscar for *Blithe Spirit* in 1945). In 1943 they founded the production company Cineguild with Anthony Havelock-Allen which operated under the Rank umbrella. After a fact-finding trip to Hollywood on behalf of Rank, Neame switched to producing and scriptwriting, making important contributions to LEAN's two Dickens adaptations and to the classic romance *Brief Encounter* (1945), picking up further Academy

Award nominations in these new roles. Unfortunately, his partnership with LEAN ended rather acrimoniously when LEAN took over the direction of *The Passionate Friends* (1948) from Neame.

He made his debut as a director for Cineguild with *Take My Life* (1947), a more than competent HITCHCOCK-style thriller which showed Neame's technical skill as a film-maker. Throughout his career his work was uneven, so that the routine action hokum of *The Golden Salamander* (1949) was followed by the excellent sub-Ealing comedy *The Card* (1952) featuring Alec Guinness. Based on Arnold Bennett's novel, it is a sympathetic account of the nefarious rise of a humble clerk as he finds various ways to take advantage of the hierarchies of the British class system. Neame showed a real lightness of touch handling comic subjects, spinning out the thin premise of *The Million Pound Note* (1953) with some style and again drawing a fine performance from Guinness as an idiosyncratic painter in his pleasing adaptation of Joyce Cary's novel *The Horse's Mouth* (1958). In the 1950s he also made the intriguing wartime espionage tale *The Man Who Never Was* (1955), as well as having a brief, unsuccessful stint in Hollywood where he was eventually replaced as director on *The Seventh Sin* (1957).

Neame's liking for non-conformist characters reaches its height in his most acclaimed film *Tunes of Glory* (1960), a compelling barrack-room melodrama which also shows his skill in handling actors; here he is rewarded with memorable performances by John Mills and Alec Guinness as the two officers engaged in a violent clash of personalities. Like *The Horse's Mouth*, it was made for his own production company Knightsbridge Films. His 1960s output continued to be extremely variable. It included two Swinging London films, the amiable caper movie *Gambit* (1966) with Michael Caine and Shirley MacLaine and the instantly dated risqué comedy *Prudence and the Pill* (1968), on which he worked uncredited. He directed Judy Garland in her last film, *I Could Go on Singing* (1963), and had another spell in the States where he completed two unremarkable projects, *Escape from Zahrain* (1961) and *A Man Could Get Killed* (1966). The best-received work from this period was *The Prime of Miss Jean Brody* (1969). This popular adaptation of the stage version of Muriel Spark's novel provided Maggie Smith with a show-off role which duly won her an Oscar, but the film has considerable difficulty dealing with the essential theatricality of the story and characters.

After the middling musical *Scrooge* (1970) with Albert Finney in the title role, Neame took up permanent residence in Hollywood, eventually becoming an American citizen. He was responsible for establishing the 'disaster movie' genre with the immensely successful

*The Poseidon Adventure* (1972), although he followed it with one of the worst examples of this cycle, *Meteor* (1979). He also made two enjoyable, lightweight pieces with Walter Matthau, *Hopscotch* (1980) and *First Monday in October* (1981). The best of his limited British work in this period is the tautly effective thriller *The Odessa File* (1974), from Frederick Forsyth's bestselling novel, with Jon Voight uncovering a Neo-Nazi group. Nothing can forgive the atrocious sex comedy *Foreign Body* (1986) which looks like a relic from another era. His final film was *The Magic Balloon* (1990), a children's adventure designed to show off the new ShowScan widescreen format which consequently only had a limited release.

Throughout his career Neame was always a smoothly professional film-maker, adopting an unostentatious approach which relied greatly on his actors and which frequently left him at the mercy of the script. When these were good he produced highly effective films which often showcased outstanding acting performances. Even on his poorer commercial assignments there is an ability to serve the narrative no matter how inadequate this might be. His achievements, which include his active role in the industry union ACT and with the British Society of Cinematographers, were recognised with a BAFTA Fellowship and the CBE, both awarded in 1996.

**British Feature Films:** *Take My Life* (1947); *The Golden Salamander* (1949); *The Card* (1952); *The Million Pound Note* (1953); *The Man Who Never Was* (1955); *Windom's Way* (1957); *The Horse's Mouth* (1958); *Tunes of Glory* (1960); *I Could Go on Singing* (1963); *The Chalk Garden* (1964); *Mister Moses* (1965); *Gambit* (1966); *Prudence and the Pill* (1968, co-directed with Fielder Cook); *The Prime of Miss Jean Brodie* (1969); *Scrooge* (1970); *The Odessa File* (1974); *Foreign Body* (1986).

**Bibliography:** Ronald Neame, *Straight from the Horse's Mouth* (Oxford and Lanham, MD: Scarecrow Press, 2002).

## Mike NEWELL

Mike Newell has established a reputation as one of the most reliably popular British directors currently at work. If his films tend towards the middle-of-the-road, then they reflect the contemporary commercial climate of British mainstream cinema. He was born in St Albans on 28 March 1942. After studying English at Cambridge, where he directed student theatre productions, he joined Granada Television's trainee directors scheme in 1963. Making his directorial debut with the documentary *Sharon* in 1964, he was to spend the next twenty years in television working on a wide range of programmes for commercial companies and the BBC. These included populist series like *Budgie*, a fine version of the Thomas Hardy short story *The Melancholy Hussar* and plays by David Hare and Jack Rosenthal. His polished television film of *The Man in the Iron Mask* (1977) obtained a limited theatrical release and suggested the possibilities of a film career. His first cinema film was *The Awakening* (1980), which was made with American backing. It is a rather muddled combination of borrowings from various Egyptian mummy films with elements of the then fashionable cycle of child-possession horrors. The gloomy, New Zealand-based chase thriller *Bad Blood* (1981) didn't fare a great deal better.

It was only with his third film, and his first wholly British subject, that he made an impact. Written by Shelagh Delaney and based on the life of Ruth Ellis, the last woman to be executed in Britain, *Dance with a Stranger* (1985) is a haunting evocation of a narrow, repressive 1950s Britain where the brash, working-class Ellis, played beautifully by Miranda Richardson, is as much a victim of circumstances as the wealthy lover who she kills. The film exposes a pervasive national culture of snobbery and moral decay. The more humorous *The Good Father* (1987) turns an equally acerbic eye on gender relationships in the avaricious Britain of the 1980s. Anthony Hopkins and Jim Broadbent are the unhappy men out for revenge on their apparently liberated ex-wives as the former enters into a child custody battle. *Soursweet* (1988), scripted by Ian McEwan, takes a similarly abrasive look at the experiences of an immigrant Chinese family in contemporary Britain. These three films show a developed sensitivity to questions of class, ethnicity and gender as they impact on British life, observed with a telling eye for detail.

Newell continued to work for British television and also made the low-budget, liberal-minded *Amazing Grace and Chuck* (1987) in America. *Into the West* (1992) is in many respects Newell's most interesting and unusual British feature film. Combining realism and fantasy, it depicts the frustrated lives of two Irish children living in a tower block whose imaginations are opened when their grandfather returns home with a white horse. Newell manages to pull off the not inconsiderable feat of integrating a metaphor for the freedom of the American West into the drab reality of the setting without losing credibility. *Enchanted April* (1991) deals with repressed lives in a very different manner. Set in the 1920s and focusing on the frustrations of four very different women who make their escape to an Italian castle, it balances its emotional conflicts with an eye for pictorial charm.

Nothing that Newell had made to that point could have predicted the extraordinary commercial success which was to greet *Four Weddings and a*

*Funeral* (1994). The film still divides opinion but is unquestionably one of the most significant British films of the 1990s. For supporters, this is a genuinely funny romantic comedy which was sophisticated enough to please international audiences while preserving its intrinsically British qualities. For critics, it was a personification of everything that was wrong with British films of that decade: vacuous, aimed blatantly at American audiences and riddled with outdated representations of class. No amount of argument can change the fact that it was the highest grossing British film ever at the time or that it won Newell a BAFTA as Best Director. Next he returned rather startlingly to the drab 1950s with *An Awfully Big Adventure* (1995), a low-key film set in a Liverpool theatre company with Hugh Grant cast diametrically against the image of infuriating niceness established by *Four Weddings*.

Newell's success inevitably took him to America where he made the minor drama *Pushing Tin* (1999) set in the macho world of air traffic controllers and the impressive *Donnie Brasco* (1997), a complex, strikingly well acted addition to the overworked Mafioso genre which may well be Newell's best film to date. *Mona Lisa Smile* (2003), although returning Newell to the subject of 1950s female repression with its story of an inspirational teacher at a tight-laced girl's college, is nonetheless a sentimental vehicle for Julia Roberts, filmed in Newell's glossiest style. Newell has been one of the most commercially successful directors working in recent British films, managing to secure a strong position within the mainstream while retaining an unusual intelligence and wit. If some of his work is overly conventional and safe, his best films have shown a sharp eye for the nuances of British life.

**British Feature Films:** *The Man in the Iron Mask* (1977); *The Awakening* (1980); *Bad Blood* (1981); *Dance with a Stranger* (1985); *The Good Father* (1987); *Soursweet* (1988); *Enchanted April* (1991); *Into the West* (1992); *Four Weddings and a Funeral* (1994); *An Awfully Big Adventure* (1995).

# O

## Laurence (Lord) OLIVIER

It is beyond the remit of this guide to do justice to the career of Laurence Olivier as much of his most important work lies in the theatre and in acting rather than as a film director. Olivier has widely been regarded as the finest classical actor of his generation (although not everyone shared this view) and he dominated British theatre for four decades. In the cinema, he moved from romantic leading roles to character parts in British and American films during a career that stretched across six decades. It is easy for his achievements as a film director to seem marginal in the circumstances, but the five films he directed include three of the most effective interpretations of Shakespeare on film.

The son of a clergyman, Laurence Olivier was born in Dorking, Surrey on 22 May 1907. He trained as an actor at the Central School and made his professional stage debut in 1922, going on to establish an unparalleled reputation as an interpreter of classical roles, particularly Shakespeare. He acted with the Old Vic, created the National Theatre on the South Bank, was a star in the West End and on Broadway and took part in prestigious tours to Russia and Australia. Although he began acting in films from the early 1930s, like many British stage actors he was initially dismissive of this populist medium. He admitted that it was only when he went to Hollywood and appeared as Heathcliff in William Wyler's *Wuthering Heights* (1939) that he began to really take film acting seriously. The film established his screen image as a suavely romantic figure, something which was confirmed by his role in HITCHCOCK's *Rebecca* (1940).

Olivier's debut as a film director came with his version of *Henry V* (1944), made for Two Cities under the Rank umbrella. With war still raging, Olivier milks the play for its full patriotic content, even prefacing it with a dedication to the British armed forces. The film is surprisingly adventurous stylistically: beginning on the stage of the Globe in Elizabethan London, as it progresses we shift into a less theatrical mode (although still with the use of painted scenery), until at the Battle of Agincourt the film has become fully cinematic with the camera out in the open fields. The bravura battle sequence is set to William Walton's stirring music, aided by fluent camerawork and tight editing. Olivier's own performance combines tenderness (while walking among his men on the night before battle) with a barnstorming delivery for the patriotic speeches. The American Academy instituted a special award to recognise his achievements as the film's director, producer, star and adaptor.

He followed it with a film of *Hamlet* (1948) which drastically cut the original text. Olivier adopts a much sterner tone here, shooting in black and white with the camera stalking him as he wanders the corridors of Elsinore. Hamlet's soliloquies are delivered in voice-over as internal monologues, with Olivier emphasising the psychological aspects of the play, focusing on Hamlet's inner turmoil. It became the first British film to win the Oscar as Best Picture and won Olivier the award for Best Actor. The third, and perhaps finest, of Olivier's Shakespeare films is *Richard III* (1955), a magnificently melodramatic reading of the play with a spellbinding performance from Olivier as the wicked king. Made for KORDA's London Films, it makes striking use of colour and *mise en scène*, and has a remarkable supporting case including Ralph Richardson and John Gielgud. Olivier plays Richard as a charismatic figure so that the audience is implicated in their enjoyment of his immoral activities.

In comparison, his last two films as a director are something of a disappointment. *The Prince and the Showgirl* (1957) was adapted from a Terence Rattigan play which Olivier had appeared in on stage with his second wife Vivien Leigh. The film is hampered by the lack of on-screen chemistry between Olivier and Marilyn Monroe, who actually gives the better performance. It seemed a rather tame project for Olivier to tackle. His final film was a modest version of Checkov's *Three Sisters* (1970) featuring himself and third wife Joan Plowright. Perfectly respectable, it lacks the verve and imagination which lit his Shakespeare adaptations. He continued to act in films and television well into the 1980s. Although some of his later roles were beneath him, he was memorable opposite Michael Caine in *Sleuth* (1972), chilling playing a Nazi dentist in John SCHLESINGER's *Marathon Man* (1976) and touching as a First World War veteran in Derek JAR-MAN's *War Requiem* (1989). He also did some fine work for television including appearing in John Mortimer's *A Voyage Round My Father* (1982) and playing *King Lear* (1983). He provided a suitably sonorous narration for the landmark television series *The World at* War (1974).

He was lauded with accolades throughout his life, being knighted in 1947 and then made a life peer in 1970. The film world celebrated him with an Honorary Oscar in 1979 and a BAFTA Fellowship in 1977. He died on 11 July 1989. Because of his remarkable achievements in the theatre, it is easy to underestimate Olivier's contribution to cinema. At the very least, his three Shakespeare films succeeded in bringing the plays to a wider audience and stand as benchmarks of how to transfer them to film. Even more so, they stand as remarkable films in their own right, showing a real fluency with cinematic technique that only makes it regrettable that he didn't have time to exploit his gifts as a film-maker more fully.

**British Feature Films:** *Henry V* (1944); *Hamlet* (1948); *Richard III* (1955); *The Prince and the Showgirl* (1957); *Three Sisters* (1970).

**Bibliography**: Laurence Olivier, *Confessions of an Actor: An Auto-biography* (London: Weidenfeld & Nicolson, 1982); Robert L. Daniels, *Laurence Olivier: Theatre and Cinema* (San Diego, CA: A. S. Barnes, 1980).

P

## Nick PARK

If the international reputation of British animation has never been higher than in the last ten years then much of the credit for this must go to the Bristol-based company Aardman and their most famous director Nick Park. Born in Preston, Lancashire on 6 December 1958, Nick Park's interest in animation began as a teenager; one of his early efforts was shown by the BBC in 1975. He took a degree in Communication Arts at Sheffield Hallam University and then studied animation with the National Film School. It was here that he first met David Sproxton and Peter Lord, founders of Aardman Animation, who invited him to join them on completion of his course. His first significant work for Aardman was the beguiling short film *Creature Comforts* (1989) which uses animated clay figures of animals synchronised to accompany a soundtrack of voices recorded from members of the public. The meticulous creation of the claymation animals, particularly their expressive faces, provides for rich, humorous characterisations. The film won an Oscar, the first of many awards to follow. Along the way Park also worked on various advertisements, television programmes and music promos, including the innovative video for Peter Gabriel's 'Sledgehammer' (1987).

*A Grand Day Out* (1989) was started while at the National Film School, but finally completed for Aardman. It was the first appearance of Park's finest creations, the endearing duo of Wallace and Gromit, a cheese-loving, absent-minded inventor (beautifully voiced by Peter Sallis) and his rather more streetwise canine sidekick. Park's characteristic attention to detail, including the wonderfully precise sets and props, as well as a taste for quirky humour, is well in evidence. Wallace and Gromit were to appear in two more shorts, *The Wrong Trousers* (1993) and *A Close Shave* (1995), both of which won Academy Awards as well as BAFTAs. *The Wrong Trousers* is a miniature masterpiece of stop frame animation with brilliantly timed gags and inventive recycling of a variety of genre movie clichés, here borrowed from science fiction and caper movie originals.

A central part of the appeal of Park's work lies in his ability to tap into well-loved British traditions, not least in the eccentric friendship of Wallace and Gromit. For British viewers at least, there is something of the quality of the Ealing comedies or of television series like *Dad's Army* in the warmth which Park extends to his oddball characters. It was a logical step to move into feature animation and this came with *Chicken Run* (2000), made in partnership with Steven Spielberg's Dreamworks. The partnership seems to have resulted in some compromises, such as using Hollywood star Mel Gibson for the main character's voice, which tend to take the film away from the intrinsically British qualities which were such a strength in the short films. There is still much to enjoy here, not least in the affectionate references to war movies like *The Great Escape* (1963) and in the dazzling set pieces. He returned to rather firmer ground with his second feature, *The Curse of the Were-Rabbit* (2005), which brings back Wallace and Gromit. The film is a delight, with its highly appropriate voices (Ralph Fiennes, Helena Bonham-Carter), borrowings from the Hammer horrors and slapstick climaxes. The carefully observed settings take us back to a very British world of allotments and prize-winning vegetables. Yet another Academy Award was soon on its way. One can only assume there will be more to come. Park was made a CBE in 1997.

**British Feature Films:** *Chicken Run* (2000, co-directed with Peter Lord); *The Curse of the Were-Rabbit* (2005, co-directed with Steve Box).

## (Sir) Alan PARKER

Alan Parker, who was born in Islington, London on 14 February 1944, has been an outspoken critic of British cinema yet ended up occupying some of its senior administrative positions. For someone with such passionate views about his native industry, it is ironic that the majority of his films have been made in America. He began his career in the early 1960s as a copywriter at the advertising company Collett Dickenson Pearce, where he met two of his future collaborators, David Puttnam and Alan Marshall. His first foray into filmmaking was the script for *S.W.A.L.K.* (1970), also released as *Melody*, which Puttnam produced. It showed a sympathy for young people which was to reappear in some of Parker's later films. That year he formed the Alan Parker Film Company with Marshall which was responsible for producing a string of stylish television commercials, most memorable of which are the series of dryly humorous Cinzano adverts featuring Leonard Rossiter and Joan Collins. In the early 1970s he also made two shorts films and worked in television for the BBC, where he won a BAFTA for directing Jack Rosenthal's touching wartime drama *The Evacuees* (1975).

After failing to get funding for several self-penned scripts, he finally made his feature film debut with *Bugsy Malone* (1976), a quirky musical set in prohibition-era America where the getaway cars are pedal powered, the machine guns fire ice cream and the cast is made up entirely of children (including a very young Jodie Foster). The film's success swiftly led him to Hollywood, from whence he has only rarely returned. Parker's inclination has been towards medium- to high-budget mainstream films and American cinema offered far more opportunity in this area than the poverty-stricken British cinema of the 1970s and 1980s. *Midnight Express* (1978) was a British-American co-production with Puttnam and Marshall producing (as with *Bugsy Malone*) and financial backing from Columbia. Its lurid depiction of a young American suffering the horrors of the Turkish prison system divided critics; despite outcries at its xenophobia and accusations that it wallowed in the violence it was condemning, it still won an Oscar for its scriptwriter Oliver Stone and a nomination for Parker.

*Fame* (1980) was Parker's first wholly American film. Its dynamic, feel-good story about students at New York's School for the Performing Arts proved to be an enormous commercial success. He followed it with the modest marital drama *Shoot the Moon* (1982) featuring Albert Finney and Diane Keaton and then returned to Britain for *Pink Floyd The Wall* (1982), a grossly overblown version of the group's self-pitying concept album with Bob Geldof in the lead role. Its one redeeming feature was Gerald Scarfe's strikingly cruel animation sequences. Far more interesting and entertaining was his highly personal television documentary *A Turnip-Head's Guide to the British Cinema* (1986), a funny, coruscating attack on the ineptitudes of British commercial film-making and the intellectual vanity of its art house output. Parker himself has been on the receiving end of a fair amount of criticism; some commentators have placed him alongside other directors whose training was in advertising (Hugh HUDSON, Ridley Scott) with the suggestion that this background has resulted in films which are stylistically impressive but devoid of real depth.

Returning to America he made *Birdy* (1984), an affecting drama of two childhood friends trying to come to terms with the trauma of serving in Vietnam, and the flashy, macabre thriller *Angel Heart* (1987), which seemed to confirm the criticisms of him. *Mississippi Burning* (1988) again divided the critics. Many praised its recreation of events from the 1960s civil rights movement and also the performance of Gene Hackman, but for others it was a typical white man's view of

African-American history, diluting its subject to make it palatable to mid-American audiences. A similar response met *Come See the Paradise* (1990) which told the neglected story of the internment of Japanese-Americans in the Second World War. These films at least showed the sincerity of Parker's liberalism. Of his two Irish-set films, *The Commitments* (1991) and *Angela's Ashes* (1999), the former is the more successful being a lively, engaging adaptation of Roddy Doyle's novel about a group of young Dubliners finding a way out of poverty through music. It won Parker a BAFTA as Best Director and has something of the inspirational qualities of *Fame*. *Angela's Ashes*, adapted from Frank McCourt's best-selling autobiographical novel, was too sentimental a view of childhood hardship to be really effective.

His other work includes two further American films, the bizarre but oddly fascinating *The Road to Wellville* (1994) with Anthony Hopkins as the eccentric advocate of healthy living, Dr Kellogg, and the unconvincing thriller *The Life of David Gale* (2003). *Evita* (1996), a lavish version of the Andrew Lloyd-Webber/Tim Rice musical with Madonna starring, was partly British-financed. Parker's frequently histrionic style for once seemed thoroughly suited to the melodramatic bad taste of the original show. Considering his views of the BFI, it was rather a surprise when he became its chairman in 1998. Subsequently, as head of the newly formed UK Film Council, he was tasked with the thorny job of utilising the Lottery money which Tony Blair's government had earmarked for the regeneration of British commercial cinema.

In Parker's best films he has shown an ability to anchor a progressive message within accessible, audience-pleasing entertainments. This has led to unsurprising accusations of philistinism which tend to underestimate the skill required to successfully pull off what he attempts to do. He is certainly a director with visual panache and one who isn't afraid to speak his mind. It's a pity that circumstances and personal inclination have so often taken his talents away from his native industry. He was awarded the CBE in 1995 and knighted in 2002.

**British Feature Films**: *Bugsy Malone* (1976); *Midnight Express* (1978); *Pink Floyd The Wall* (1982); *The Commitments* (1991); *Evita* (1996); *Angela's Ashes* (1999).

**Bibliography**: Jonathan Hacker and David Price, *Take Ten: Contemporary British Film Directors* (Oxford: Clarendon Press, 1991).

## George PEARSON

The pioneer film-maker George Pearson was born in Kennington, London on 19 March 1875. He trained as a teacher and spent close to twenty years in the profession, rising to be a headteacher. In 1913, married with three children, he abandoned his teaching career and entered the fledgling British film industry, his amateur efforts at scriptwriting having impressed Pathé sufficiently for them to appoint him as production head of their small British operation. He was at Gaumont from 1915 where he was successful in pushing forward the visual fluency of British narrative films, culminating in his series of dashing adventures featuring the character *Ultus: The Man from the Dead*, designed to rival the success of the French *Fantômas* serial. In 1918 he established his own production company, Welsh-Pearson, in conjunction with Thomas Welsh and built studios at Craven Park. He quickly became one of the leading figures in British film-making, achieving a popular success with a sequence of four films featuring the engaging Betty Balfour as chirpy working-class heroine Squibs. She was to become the top female star of the period.

Working from his own screenplays, Pearson developed a form of populist cinema which employed stylised techniques, making considerable use of the expressive possibilities of the medium. His creative status in Britain was recognised with a royal premiere in 1924 for his powerful study of the aftermath of the First World War on ordinary lives, *Reveille*. In his attempts to create a genuinely aesthetic approach to cinema, the sometimes melodramatic vision of films like *Nothing Else Matters* (1920) and *The Little People* (1926) didn't always meet with approval; the latter was eventually withdrawn for re-cutting. In 1926 he was forced to sell Craven Park and look for financial backing from the States. During his visits to America in the late 1920s he became interested in the development of sound technology, although he could find few takers back home. In 1930 he supervised the sound recording for James Whale's Hollywood version of *Journey's End*. Although he continued to direct, Welsh-Pearson eventually went bankrupt in 1930 and tragically a number of his films were subsequently lost. In 1934 he parted company with Welsh and made a living shooting quota quickies (which he had once campaigned against) for Twickenham. During the Second World War he worked under Cavalcanti at the GPO Film Unit and then was appointed Director of the Colonial Film Unit, where he later helped to establish film schools in emerging Commonwealth countries.

Pearson was a tireless campaigner for the medium that he had so dramatically entered in its early years, being a founding member of the London Film Society and President of the Association of British Film Directors. In 1951 he was awarded an OBE and became an Honorary Fellow of the British Film Academy. For extending the possibilities of cinematic narrative and visual expressiveness, Pearson has often been accorded the position of 'father of British film', a modest, home-grown equivalent to American cinema's D. W. Griffith. He died in Malvern on 6 February 1973, not far short of his ninety-eighth birthday.

**Selected British Feature Films**: *A Study in Scarlet* (1914); *Ultus: The Man from the Dead* (1915); *The Better 'Ole* (1918); *Nothing Else Matters* (1920); *Squibs* (1921); *Love, Life and Laughter* (1923); *Reveille* (1924); *The Little People* (1926); *Huntingtower* (1927).

**Bibliography**: Christine Gledhill, *Reframing British Cinema: 1918–1928* (London: BFI, 2003); George Pearson, *Flashback: An Autobiography of a British Filmmaker* (London: Allen & Unwin, 1957).

## Roman POLANSKI

Roman Polanski was among a group of distinguished European directors, including François Truffaut and Michelangelo Antonioni, who (briefly in some cases) were attracted to make films in Britain during the boom period of the 1960s. Born in Paris on 18 August 1933, he returned with his Jewish parents at the age of three to their native Poland. Following the Nazi invasion, he was smuggled out of the country to live with relatives in Paris. His parents were sent to concentration camps and although he was reunited with his father, his mother perished at Auschwitz. Little wonder that his films have so often been marked by pessimism and an acute awareness of human brutality. After attending the Łodz Film School, he made the surreal short film *Two Men and a Wardrobe* (1958) and the chillingly understated thriller *Knife in the Water* (1962) in Poland. The latter achieved international recognition, being nominated for an Oscar, but its chilly reception by the communist authorities at home led to his departure, initially to France and then on to Britain.

With only limited English, he managed to direct one of the most disturbing British films of the era, *Repulsion* (1965). Catherine Deneuve plays a repressed Belgian woman working in London who withdraws into her own, increasingly deranged world and eventually murders her boyfriend and landlord. With its sudden eruptions into violence, bizarre hallucination sequences and startling imagery, the film is an unnerving study of mental disintegration with the audience drawn into the mind of the central character. He followed it with the almost equally striking *Cul de Sac* (1966), a Pinterish, absurdist drama set on a Northumbrian island. The owners of a castle, an eccentrically feminised man (Donald Pleasance) and his wife (Françoise Dorléac), find themselves held captive by two gangsters and enter into a quirky, tense game of cat and mouse. The end of this fruitful period in Britain was marked by the rather disappointing *Dance of the Vampires* (1967), an attempt to spoof the Hammer horror films which proved less darkly amusing than the originals.

In America, Polanski made another stylish, unnerving horror piece, the commercially successful *Rosemary's Baby* (1968), but after the brutal murder of his pregnant wife Sharon Tate by the followers of Charles Manson he returned to Britain. It was hard not to see the effect of his personal experiences in his savage, bloody version of *Macbeth* (1971). He subsequently returned to America where he made the masterly neo-noir *Chinatown* (1974), winning himself a BAFTA, but following his arrest for statutory rape (as the result of an affair with an underage model) he fled America claiming that he would not receive a fair trial. Under American law he has not been able to return to the States, but this didn't stop him making three American-backed films in Europe, the Hitchcockian thriller *Frantic* (1988), an offbeat comedy-adventure *Pirates* (1986) and the overblown Gothic horror of *The Ninth Gate* (1999). He is also prohibited from setting foot in Britain due to an extradition treaty with America, but has still managed to make five European films which have British input. *Bitter Moon* (1992), a bizarre, erotic melodrama, and *Tess* (1979), a rather romanticised version of Hardy, are minor pieces, but two films offer a more characteristically edgy, sombre meditation on personal and political oppression: *Death and the Maiden* (1995), adapted from Ariel Dorfman's play, and *The Pianist* (2002), which took Polanski full circle back to the Poland of his childhood and which won him the Palme d'Or at Cannes and an Oscar as Best Director (which he could not collect in person). His most recent film, *Oliver Twist* (2005), is a handsome adaptation of Dickens which, surprisingly for Polanski, doesn't really do justice to the dark heart of the novel.

Polanski's direct involvement with British cinema has been relatively small, but in these films we still see his characteristic concern with disturbed psychology and violence, handled with a coolly detached sense of the absurdity of human existence. His vision is a distinctly European one, rather than specifically British, but he is clearly a major international film-maker who has produced some memorable work in Britain.

**British Feature Films:** *Repulsion* (1965); *Cul de Sac* (1966); *Dance of the Vampires* (1967); *Macbeth* (1971); *Tess* (1979); *Bitter Moon* (1992); *Death and the Maiden* (1995); *The Pianist* (2002); *Oliver Twist* (2005).

**Bibliography**: Roman Polanski, *Roman* (New York: Morrow, 1984); Barbara Leaming, *Roman Polanski: His Life and Films* (London: Hamish Hamilton, 1982).

## Sally POTTER

Sally Potter was born in London on 19 September 1949. She studied briefly at St Martin's School of Art and then trained with the London School of Contemporary Dance. Her interest in film-making led to her joining the London Filmmakers' Cooperative and she made a number of short films which explored her interest in dance. Her earliest short films have much in common with the structuralist movement in avant-garde cinema, with their use of multi-screen projection sometimes combined with music and performance. During the 1970s she worked

as a dancer and choreography, often with companies using performance as a means of exploring sexual politics. Her move into film-making coincided with the development of academic interest in feminist film theory. Influential work by writers like Laura Mulvey called for a rejection of the patriarchal practices inherent in mainstream cinema and the creation of new ways of making films which did not objectify women. Her landmark short film, *Thriller* (1979), funded by the Arts Council, uses the opera *La Bohème* as a means to explore these issues and adopts an experimental style using direct quotes from feminist writing as well as references to films like HITCHCOCK's *Psycho* (1960). Her first feature, *The Gold Diggers* (1983), extends these interests into a wider consideration of the commodification of women within capitalism, where the role of women as possessions is equated with the ownership of marketable materials such as gold. The film was made with an all-female crew and everyone involved, including Julie Christie, was paid at the same rate. These films are central to the emergence of a radical feminist cinema which occurred in Britain during this period.

Potter began to move more towards the mainstream in the late 1980s with the short film *The London Story* (1986) and then the feature length *Orlando* (1992), which took eight years to bring to the screen but which was rewarded with international art house success. Adapted from Virginia Woolf's novel and starring Tilda Swinton, it adopts a much more playful, accessible tone while still questioning how gender and sexuality are defined by society. Swinton's character reappears in a number of different time periods through British history, starting as a man and then changing into a woman. In a more affirmative manner than her earlier films, *Orlando* suggests the possibilities and varieties which gender might take. *The Tango Lesson* (1997) is Potter's most overtly personal film, with the director writing the music and appearing in front of the camera as a film-maker trying to make a Hollywood movie but increasingly distracted by her interest in the tango. The film indulges Potter's love of dance in beautifully shot sequences with the Argentinean dancer Pablo Verón and skilfully subverts the 'male gaze' as defined by Mulvey, but it was very poorly received by mainstream critics.

With *The Man Who Cried* (2000) she moved even more firmly into the mainstream using the Hollywood stars Christina Ricci and Johnny Depp in a glossy romantic melodrama. Ricci is a Russian Jew fleeing across a war-ravaged Europe who falls in love with Depp's exotic gypsy. It's not entirely successful in its attempt to mix intellectual concerns and entertainment values. With her most recent film, *Yes* (2004), she managed to pull off this same feat with considerable aplomb, producing a film which is both challenging, particularly in dealing with questions of identity and prejudice, and passionately affecting. With her work to date, Potter has established herself at the forefront of contemporary British art cinema.

**British Feature Films:** *The Gold Diggers* (1983); *Orlando* (1992); *The Tango Lesson* (1997); *The Man Who Cried* (2000); *Yes* (2004).

**Bibliography:** Anne Cieko, 'Sally Potter: The Making of a British Woman Filmmaker', in Yvonne Tasker (ed.), *Fifty Contemporary Filmmakers* (London: Routledge, 2002).

## Michael POWELL (and Emeric PRESSBURGER)

Although viewed with suspicion by film reviewers of the 1940s and 1950s, and occasionally the subject of controversy, Michael Powell's reputation now stands as high as any director to have emerged from British cinema. Only Alfred HITCHCOCK has attracted a similar level of regard, but, unlike HITCHCOCK, Powell's work is almost entirely associated with a British context. He is British cinema's foremost romantic, a visionary film-maker who, whether working with his long-time collaborator Emeric Pressburger or alone, produced films which elevate cinema to art and which reflect on the nature of British culture and identity.

Powell was born on 30 September 1905 in Bekesbourne, Kent. After attending Dulwich College and a stint working in a bank, his father enabled Powell to meet the American director Rex Ingram whom he went to work for as an assistant; Ingram had been filming in the south of France where Powell's father ran a hotel. On his return to Britain, Powell entered the industry and quickly worked his way up to director. During the 1930s he made more than twenty quota quickies, the low-budget fillers designed to meet government-set production levels. His shift into 'A' grade productions came with *The Edge of the World* (1937), a portrait of life on the remote Scottish island of Foula which owes a good deal to the documentarist Robert Flaherty in its location shooting but which also brings to its subject a personal, poetic sensibility.

Turning to more mainstream projects, Powell made two stylish espionage thrillers featuring the charismatic German actor Conrad Veidt: *The Spy in Black* (1939) and *Contraband* (1940). It was on these films that Powell first worked with the scriptwriter Emeric Pressburger. Pressburger was born on 5 December 1902 in Miskolc, Hungary. He had worked in Germany as a journalist and translator before becoming a scriptwriter in the 1930s. He came to Britain in 1935 and worked for another Hungarian émigré Alexander KORDA, who introduced him to Powell. Meanwhile, Powell was one of several directors employed by KORDA on both the patriotic morale-booster *The Lion Has Wings* (1939) and the spectacular *The Thief of Bagdad* (1940), but he returned to work with Pressburger for *49th Parallel* (1941), the first of many films they made together which reflect on the War. *49th Parallel* is an episodic, melodramatic affair, but the more sober *One of Our Aircraft Is Missing* (1942) is clearly influenced by the dominant style of documentary realism. Moving to the Rank Organisation in 1943, Powell and Pressburger formalised their working relationship by establishing their own production company, The Archers, with its memorable logo of arrows striking a target. Over a dozen years they were to make thirteen films together in which they share a joint credit as writing, producing and directing, although it was Powell who remained the director and Pressburger who largely fashioned the scripts.

Their first project as the Archers, *The Life and Death of Colonel Blimp* (1943), incurred the wrath of Churchill who tried to ban it. It is a gloriously romantic celebration of the life of a very British war hero, the eternally honorable Clive Wynne-Candy (Roger Livesey), taking in his friendship with a very sympathetic German, Theo Kretschmar-Schuldorff (Anton Walbrook). With its sumptuous colour and idealised depiction of women (with three roles played by Deborah Kerr), it has established many of Powell and Pressburger's typical traits. *A Canterbury Tale* (1944) is another highly idiosyncratic 'propaganda' piece, an extraordinary, mystical contemplation of the English landscape and traditions, with Eric Portman as Colpeper, the local magistrate who pours glue into the hair of young girls to deter them from going out with servicemen who should be concentrating on saving his beloved nation. The film becomes increasingly spiritual until its final, moving epiphany in Canterbury Cathedral. *I Know Where I'm Going* (1945) also has mystical overtones, as Wendy Hiller's thoroughly modern young woman is distracted from marrying sensibly when she encounters the landscape of Scotland and the charms of Roger Livesey. The film is full of visual invention and sly humour, as well as embracing Celtic romanticism in place of the Englishness of *A Canterbury Tale*.

Perhaps the summation of this period is *A Matter of Life and Death* (1946), a film overflowing with cinematic trickery and delighting in the triumph of imagination over reality. David Niven is the pilot accidentally allowed by heaven to survive the destruction of his aircraft, who then falls in love with an American girl (Kim Hunter) while a heavenly emissary (Marius Goring) tries to persuade him to return 'upstairs' where he belongs. With heaven in stark monochrome and earth in glorious Technicolor, the film takes a dryly humorous look at the changing relationship between Britain and America and offers a warm endorsement of the power of love to overcome even death. The consequences of suppressing emotion become the subject of *Black Narcissus* (1947) as a group of nuns succumb to the strange atmosphere of their isolated nunnery perched high in the Himalayas. The film benefits from the startling sets and superb colour cinematography of Jack Cardiff, particularly when Kathleen Byron's demented Sister Ruth wears a flaming red dress and scarlet lipstick to stalk Deborah Kerr's Sister Clodagh. Few British films have matched its charged atmosphere.

The height of their popular success came with *The Red Shoes* (1948), a richly colourful depiction of the world of ballet and Powell's ultimate declaration of the importance of art over life. Moira Shearer is the ingénue who comes under the mesmeric influence of Anton Walbrook's impresario, Lermentov. With its central ballet sequence, larger-than-life characters and sinister undercurrents, it was a vindication of the ambition of The Archers. Unfortunately Rank didn't share the public's enthusiasm and Powell and Pressburger subsequently moved back to KORDA. Their first film for him was *The Small Back Room* (1948), a tautly made story of a bomb disposal expert. Other than a bravura scene of alcoholic delirium, the film is unusually austere in its visual style. *Gone to Earth* (1950) was made in collaboration with American producer David O. Selznick and starred his wife Jennifer Jones. Selznick's interference seems to have been at least partly responsible for its disjointed effect, but it is still an enjoyably full-blooded melodrama. By comparison, *The Elusive Pimpernel* (1950) is a smoothly glossy production, but one which lacks Powell and Pressburger's usual resonance.

With *The Red Shoes*, Powell had begun to develop his idea of the 'composed film', in which image and sound are synchronised in a symphonic manner without recourse to conventional narrative or dialogue. With *The Tales of Hoffman* (1951), from Offenbach's operetta, we have the nearest he came to realising this concept. Its audacious combination of music, dance, luminous colour and stylised design confused contemporary critics, but its experimentation still seems fresh and exciting. Further attempts to explore these methods with *Oh . . .*

*Rosalinda!!* (1955), *Luna de Miel* (UK/Spain, 1957) and *Bluebeard's Castle* (UK/Ger. 1964) were hampered by the difficulties of international co-production and never matched the unity of *The Tales of Hoffman*. Powell and Pressburger's final two films together were rather a disappointment. *The Battle of the River Plate* (1956) and *Ill Met by Moonlight* (1957) are old-fashioned war films, although the former includes Peter Finch's depiction of yet another likeable German. They belatedly made one more film together, the sixty-minute *The Boy Who Turned Yellow* (1972), shot for the Children's Film Foundation.

Powell's later solo work seemed to indicate a decline, with two Anglo-Australian films – *They're a Weird Mob* (1966) from a script by Pressburger and *Age of Consent* (1969) – and the stiffly conservative *The Queen's Guard* (1961) adding little to his reputation. *Peeping Tom* (1960), however, is his late masterpiece. Savaged by contemporary critics for its bad taste, it is now recognised as a complex, disturbing meditation on the nature of cinema itself and its manipulation of the audience's voyeuristic tendencies. The dense layers of reference (Powell appears as the central character's father, while his son plays the hero as a child) and self-reflexivity reward repeated viewings.

If he was maligned in his prime, he had the last laugh as he became enshrined by film historians as perhaps the most important film-maker to have worked within British cinema. Late in life, he was able to enjoy the reassessment of his work which saw him hailed by film-makers like Martin Scorsese and Francis Ford Coppola. There is in Powell's work a celebration of the potential of film as an artistic medium on a level with any of the other arts, a medium capable of aesthetic beauty as well as dealing with profound ideas. There is also much that is intrinsically British about Powell, in his love of landscape, literature and tradition, as well as in his romanticism, so that he has become emblematic for a national cinema. Emeric Pressburger died in 1988, followed by Michael Powell on 19 February 1990.

**British Feature Films:*** *The Edge of the World* (1937); *The Lion Has Wings* (1939, co-directed with Brian Desmond Hurst and Adrian Brunel); *The Spy in Black* (1939); *Contraband* (1940); *The Thief of Bagdad* (1940, co-directed with Ludwig Berger and Tim Whelan); *49th Parallel* (1941); *One of Our Aircraft Is Missing* (1942); *The Life and Death of Colonel Blimp* (1943); *A Canterbury Tale* (1944); *I Know Where I'm Going* (1945); *A Matter of Life and Death* (1946); *Black Narcissus* (1947); *The Red Shoes* (1948); *The Small Back Room* (1948); *Gone to Earth* (1950); *The Elusive Pimpernel* (1950); *The Tales of Hoffman* (1951); *Oh . . . Rosalinda!!* (1955); *The Battle of the River*

*Plate* (1956); *Ill Met by Moonlight* (1957); *Luna de Miel* (1959); *Peeping Tom* (1960); *The Queen's Guard* (1961); *Bluebeard's Castle* (1964); *They're a Weird Mob* (1966); *Age of Consent* (1969); *The Boy Who Turned Yellow* (1972).

\* Powell also directed twenty-three quota quickies between 1931 and 1936.

**Bibliography**: Ian Christie and Andrew Moor (eds), *The Cinema of Michael Powell* (London: BFI, 2005); Ian Christie, *Arrows of Desire: The Films of Michael Powell and Emeric Pressburger* (London: Faber & Faber, 1994); Michael Powell, *Million Dollar Movie* (London: Heinemann, 1992); Michael Powell, *A Life in Movies* (London: Heinemann, 1986); Ian Christie (ed.), *Powell, Pressburger and Others* (London: BFI, 1978).

## Lynne RAMSAY

Lynne Ramsay is one of the brightest talents to have appeared in recent British cinema. She was born in Glasgow, Scotland on 5 December 1969 and studied photography at Napier College in Edinburgh. At the National Film and Television School she specialised in cinematography and directing, graduating in 1996. She began her career making short films including *Small Deaths* (1996), her graduation film, and *Gasman* (1997), both of which won prizes at the Cannes Film Festival. Her debut feature film, *Ratcatcher* (1999), clearly belongs in the tradition of British social realism, but like the work of her fellow Scot Bill DOUGLAS it transcends the limitations of naturalism to offer something more visually poetic. Set during the strike-ravaged 1970s, it presents a wholly unsentimental picture of the life of a young boy growing up on a grim housing estate in Glasgow. Its political message remains implicit as it is as much concerned with conveying the subjective experience of young James as recording the external realities of his life. Her achievement was recognised with the Carl Foreman Award as most promising newcomer at the BAFTAs.

Her second feature film, *Morvern Callar* (2002), adapted from Alan Warner's successful novel, again immerses us in the inner world of its central character, a supermarket worker who passes off her dead boyfriend's unpublished novel as her own and heads off to Spain with her friend on the proceeds. As with *Ratcatcher*, the narrative is only the bare bones of a film which is a sometimes abstract meditation on subjectivity, with image and music (Morvern takes with her a compilation tape made for her by her boyfriend) fusing into a beautifully composed, haunting whole. Her small output to date has already been recognised with a plethora of international awards and her further progress can only be awaited with considerable anticipation.

**British Feature Films:** *Ratcatcher* (1999); *Morvern Callar* (2002).

## (Sir) Carol REED

Few would dispute that Carol Reed is one of the most important directors to have worked in British cinema; his masterpiece, *The Third Man* (1949), was voted the greatest British film of all time in a BFI poll. Yet the qualities which distinguish his films remain difficult to categorise and perhaps this accounts for the lack of academic attention paid to his work. In his study of the director, Peter William Evans points towards such recurring themes as father–son relationships, class tensions, his sympathetic depiction of female characters and a concern with innocence versus experience. Reed was also a supreme stylist, whose famous tilted shots seemed to match his often sideways view of a world of shifting values and moral uncertainty.

Reed was born on 30 December 1906 in Putney, South London. His mother was the mistress of the married actor-manager Sir Herbert Beerbohm Tree and Reed was one of six children she bore him. Tree maintained his second family in solidly middle-class comfort, but the unusual relationship with his inevitably distant father seems to have had some impact on Reed. After public school, he spent a brief period in America (at his mother's insistence) working with his brother on a chicken farm, but then returned to Britain to take up a career as an actor. He eventually joined a theatre company formed by the thriller writer Edgar Wallace to stage some of his stories, working as an actor and stage manager. When Wallace became Chairman of British Lion in 1927, Reed joined him there as his assistant. With Wallace's death in 1932 he jointed ATP at Ealing and gradually worked his way up the ranks. He co-directed *It Happened in Paris* (1935) and then made his solo debut as director with *Midshipman Easy* (1936), a proficiently handled seafaring adventure.

Reed worked steadily as a director throughout the 1930s making a variety of mainly routine studio films. Most memorable among them is *Bank Holiday* (1938), which shows the growing influence of documentary realism in British cinema, the early screwball comedy *Climbing High* (1939) and *A Girl Must Live* (1939), which demonstrates Reed's sympathetic handling of female stars, in this case Margaret Lockwood.

As the 1940s began, Reed cemented his growing reputation. His adaptation of A. J. Cronin's *The Stars Look Down* (1939), the story of the rise of a miner's son to become an MP, softens the author's liberal political message and veers towards melodrama but is still a fine early example of socially aware British film-making. The much lighter *Night Train to Munich* (1940) is clearly indebted to HITCHCOCK's thrillers of the 1930s, particularly *The Lady Vanishes* (1938), but has considerable style on its own account. By comparison, both *Kipps* (1941) and the propagandist *The Young Mr Pitt* (1942) are relatively routine period dramas.

In 1942 Reed made a short educational piece for the War Office Film Unit called *The New Lot* (1942) which showed how a group of raw recruits could be moulded into a tough, loyal fighting unit. It was so popular that Reed was asked to expand it into a feature which became *The Way Ahead* (1944). Filmed in a semi-documentary style, the film is full of scenes and characters which have become clichés of the war movie genre but which were fresh at the time. It is moving nonetheless and its bleak ending is surprisingly downbeat for a propaganda piece. Following this Reed worked with the American director Garson Kanin on the documentary *The True Glory* (1945) which uses footage shot by allied cameramen to produce a lucid, powerful depiction of the final days of the war. It was rewarded with an Academy Award.

Reed's great period began with *Odd Man Out* (1947), an over-poweringly atmospheric account of the last days of a wounded IRA gunman played with melancholy charisma by James Mason. Reed adopts a highly stylised visual technique which perfectly suits the material and shifts the emphasis away from the politics of Ireland towards a story of love and salvation. Moving from Rank to KORDA's London Films, Reed was teamed with the novelist Graham Greene for his next two films. The relationship appears to have been sympathetic and Reed certainly got closer than any other director to capturing the mood of 'Greeneland'. *The Fallen Idol* (1948) was adapted from Greene's short story 'The Basement Room' and reverses its plot structure, but still offers a disturbing examination of the dangers of innocence with Bobby Henrey as the small boy left virtually alone in a London embassy who almost implicates the embassy's butler, whom he hero-worships, in a crime he didn't commit. Greene wrote an original screenplay for *The Third Man* and provided Reed with material perfectly suited to his talents. Its cynical story of postwar disillusionment marries together a number of wonderful elements, from the haunting zither score of Anton Karas to Robert Krasker's disorientating, skewed camerawork and the unforgettable performance of Orson

Welles as the seductive, but morally bankrupt, Harry Lime. Reed's use of canted shots and chiaroscuro perfectly convey the atmosphere of moral decay central to the narrative.

If Reed's subsequent work never quite captured the same heights as this trio of films, there is still plenty of interest. He worked with Greene again on *Our Man in Havana* (1960), a neatly acerbic adaptation of Greene's novel with well judged performances from Noël Coward and Alec Guinness, and revisited the themes of *The Third Man* with the Cold War thriller *The Man Between* (1953). *An Outcast of the Islands* (1952) is an ambitious attempt to film Joseph Conrad's novel which is only partially successful, while *A Kid for Two Farthings* (1955) is a slightly fantastical portrait of childhood imagination set in a romanticised East End. His two big budget international productions, *Trapeze* (1956), a circus story with Tony Curtis and Burt Lancaster, and *The Agony and the Ecstasy* (1965), with Charlton Heston's Michelangelo giving himself a bad neck painting the Sistine Chapel, are both dull, ponderous epics. He was fired from *Mutiny on the Bounty* (1962) after clashing with its star, Marlon Brando. There was, however, to be a final flourish. It's hard to resist *Oliver!* (1968). For all its bowdlerising of Dickens, Reed brings real zest to Lionel Bart's musical and the casting is, as usual, impeccable, including Reed's nephew Oliver Reed. The film was a huge box-office hit and won Carol Reed the Oscar as Best Director.

It is easy to dismiss Reed as the ultimate professional, reliant upon his writers, honing their scripts with the dedication of a painstaking craftsman. This is to seriously underestimate his achievements as his films are rarely without some merit. There may have been a decline in his later career, but at his peak, particularly with that magnificent trilogy of 1940s films, he won his place among the elite of British directors. These films, with their dark, soured romanticism, are a perfect counterpoint to the more optimistic vision of his contemporaries POWELL and LEAN. Reed was knighted in 1952, the first film director to receive such an honour. He died on 25 April 1976.

**British Feature Films:** *It Happened in Paris* (1935, co-directed with Robert Wyler); *Midshipman Easy* (1935); *Laburnum Grove* (1936); *Talk of the Devil* (1936); *Who's Your Lady Friend?* (1937); *Bank Holiday* (1938); *Penny Paradise* (1938); *Climbing High* (1938); *A Girl Must Live* (1939); *The Stars Look Down* (1939); *The Girl in the News* (1940); *Night Train to Munich* (1940); *Kipps* (1941); *The Young Mr Pitt* (1942); *The Way Ahead* (1944); *The True Glory* (1945, co-directed with Garson Kanin); *Odd Man Out* (1947); *The Fallen Idol* (1948); *The Third Man* (1949); *Outcast of the Islands* (1951); *The Man Between* (1953); *A Kid* *for Two Farthings* (1954); *The Key* (1958); *Our Man in Havana* (1959); *The Running Man* (1963); *Oliver!* (1968); *Follow Me!* (1971).

**Bibliography:** Peter William Evans, *Carol Reed* (Manchester and New York: Manchester University Press, 2005); Nicholas Wapshott, *The Man Between: A Biography of Carol Reed* (London: Chatto & Windus, 1990); Brenda Davies (ed.), *Carol Reed* (London: BFI, 1978).

## Michael REEVES

Michael Reeves is a rare cult figure in British cinema, a director of enormous potential whose career was cut tragically short. Born in London in 1944, he entered the industry in the early 1960s after attending public school. He made his way up through a variety of typical supporting jobs, including working for the American director Don Siegel and on two American-backed European films, *The Long Ships* (1963) and *Genghis Khan* (1965). European co-productions provided him with the chance to progress his career and in Italy he was first assistant director on *Castle of the Living Dead* (1964) and then made his directorial debut with *Revenge of the Blood Beast* (1965). These were strictly low-budget affairs, but *The Sorcerers* (1967), made back in Britain for the idiosyncratic exploitation company Tigon, is much more substantial. Boris Karloff and Catherine Lacey are the elderly couple who relive their youth vicariously by controlling the mind of the young Ian Ogilvy. Within the restricted budget, Reeves proves adept at both delivering an effective horror film and offering an examination of the voyeuristic nature of the medium, with nods towards Michael POWELL's *Peeping Tom* (1960).

Reeves' reputation rests squarely on his third feature film, *Witchfinder General* (1968). Vincent Price is chillingly ruthless as Matthew Hopkins, a lawyer who finds it profitable to exploit the hysteria over witchcraft which occurred during the English Civil War. The film relies for its impact on the juxtaposition of lyrical depictions of the English countryside with the realistically shot barbarity of its violent sequences. It generates a palpable sense of evil and tension rare in British horror films more typified by the romanticism of Hammer's output. He was signed to direct *The Oblong Box* for American International Pictures with Vincent Price and Christopher Lee starring, but during pre-production on 11 February 1969 he died from an overdose of alcohol and barbiturates. His death at the age of just twenty-five robbed British cinema, and particularly the horror genre, of a genuinely gifted talent.

**British Feature Films:** *Revenge of the Blood Beast* (1965); *The Sorcerers* (1967); *Witchfinder General* (1968).

**Bibliography:** Benjamin Halligan, *Michael Reeves* (Manchester and New York: Manchester University Press, 2003).

## Karel REISZ

One of the central figures in the British New Wave, Karel Reisz was born in Ostrava, Czechoslovakia on 21 July 1926. As a twelve-year-old he fled his homeland as war loomed and came to Britain to study at a Quaker school. The family he left behind were all to become victims of the Nazi Holocaust. He served in the Czech squadron of the RAF during the war and then studied chemistry at Cambridge before becoming a school teacher for two years. His interest in cinema first found its outlet in articles for the film magazine *Sequence*, co-founded by Oxford student Lindsay ANDERSON; Reisz was to co-edit the final edition with ANDERSON in 1952. He also wrote a landmark book on the aesthetics of editing, *The Technique of Film Editing* (1953), which was commissioned by the British Film Academy, as well as writing articles and reviews for journals such as *Sight and Sound*. He then worked as Programme Manager at the National Film Theatre where, with ANDERSON, he subsequently organised the Free Cinema programmes which provided a showcase for short films made by young British and continental directors, including work made by himself, ANDERSON and Tony RICHARDSON. With them he shared a desire to regenerate a moribund national film industry by making films which were both socially relevant and artistically challenging. This agenda shaped Reisz's initial entry into film-making with the documentaries *Moma Don't Allow* (1955), co-directed with Tony RICHARDSON and set in a jazz club, and *We Are the Lambeth Boys* (1959), a fresh, sympathetic account of the youngsters who congregate around a youth club in a working-class area of London. Its centrepiece is a visit by the club to a public school for a cricket match which captures a barely suppressed sense of class antagonism.

Working-class life was to provide him with the subject for his feature debut, *Saturday Night and Sunday Morning* (1960), a key film of the New Wave. Adapted by Alan Sillitoe from his novel and produced by his New Wave colleague Tony RICHARDSON for Woodfall, it presents an unpatronising picture of the life of a factory worker, Arthur Seaton (Albert Finney), who lives for his weekends of boozing and womanising. With its vivid location shooting by Freddie FRANCIS and Finney's bravura performance, audiences and critics responded warmly to the depiction of its young hero's anti-authoritarian anger.

It was a film which seemed to mirror the undercurrent of radical change beginning to sweep Britain and garnered a BAFTA as Best British Film. He went on to produce Lindsay ANDERSON's debut feature film, *This Sporting Life* (1963), which effectively marked the end of the New Wave.

*Night Must Fall* (1964) seemed an odd choice for his next film. An adaptation of Emlyn Williams's play which had previously been filmed in Hollywood in 1937, it abandons the straightforward chills of the earlier version for an attempt at psychological depth which rather misfired. Reisz moved even further away from the grim realities of the 'kitchen sink' films with *Morgan: A Suitable Case for Treatment* (1966), one of the archetypal films of Swinging London. Adapted from a television play by David Mercer and clearly influenced by the work of R. D. Laing, its 1960s trappings (white-on-white set designs, surreal dream sequences, goonish humour, jazzy score) don't entirely obscure its serious points about the way that society deals with its malcontents and dissenters. The film benefits from a beautifully observed performance by David Warner. Reisz made one further British film in the 1960s, *Isadora* (1968), a relatively straightforward biopic of the dancer Isadora Duncan co-scripted by Melvyn Bragg and starring Vanessa Redgrave. The film attempts, perhaps a little too heavy-handedly, to draw parallels between the radicalism of Duncan and the spirit of freedom spreading across Britain during the 1960s.

With British cinema entering a period of serious economic decline, Reisz made a living from television commercials and finally decamped to America where he made *The Gambler* (1974), an intense psychological study in self-destruction rather vaguely adapted from Dostoevsky and featuring a powerful central performance by James Caan. *Dog Soldiers* (1978) is an even gloomier, despairing meditation on the condition of America in the wake of the war in Vietnam. Reisz returned to Britain to make an adaptation of John Fowles' cerebral pastiche Victorian novel *The French Lieutenant's Woman* (1981). Reisz and his scriptwriter Harold Pinter manage the novel's complex structure by depicting its Victorian narrative as a film-within-a-film, with its romantic plot mirrored by a modern-day relationship between the two actors playing the characters in the period film. It looks beautiful, but is chillingly cold and ascetic. His last two films were again made in the States. *Sweet Dreams* (1985) is a highly effective study of the country singer Patsy Cline, played with conviction by Jessica Lange, but the political thriller *Everybody Wins* (1990), scripted by Arthur Miller, was poorly received. Following its failure Reisz worked mainly in the theatre, with some considerable success.

Reisz always claimed that he had no specific interest in realism as such, it was simply a convenient means with which to challenge the orthodoxies of 1950s British film production. Instead his real concern seems to have been with social outcasts, those who find themselves temperamentally outside of the mainstream and frequently suffer persecution as a result. Considering his childhood experiences, this might be seen as less than surprising. It is also confirms that there was a good deal more to Reisz than simply being a chronicler of working-class life. He died on 25 November 2002 in London.

**British Feature Films:** *Saturday Night and Sunday Morning* (1960); *Night Must Fall* (1964); *Morgan: A Suitable Case for Treatment* (1966); *Isadora* (1968); *The French Lieutenant's Woman* (1981).

**Bibliography:** Georg Gaston, *Karel Reisz* (Boston: Twayne, 1980); Karel Reisz, *The Technique of Film Editing* (London: Focal Press, 1953).

## Tony RICHARDSON

Along with Lindsay ANDERSON and Karel REISZ, Tony Richardson was a central figure in the British New Wave of the late 1950s and early 1960s which swept the cobwebs from a too cosy national film culture, introducing a youthful vigour and realism. He was born Cecil Antonio Richardson on 5 June 1928 in Shipley, Yorkshire where his father owned a chemist's shop. At Wadham College, Oxford he seems to have been more interested in amateur dramatics than his studies. On graduation, he was one of the first entrants on the BBC's new training scheme for directors. He became friends with REISZ and ANDERSON who wrote and edited the film magazine *Sequence*; Richardson would contribute idiosyncratic pieces to this and *Sight and Sound*. Through them he also contributed to the seasons of short documentary films which they organised at the National Film Theatre under the heading of 'Free Cinema'. With Reisz he co-directed *Moma Don't Allow* (1955), an attempt to capture the vibrancy of Britain's rejuvenated jazz scene.

In 1956 he was instrumental, along with George Devine, in establishing the English Stage Company at the Royal Court Theatre in London. Their agenda of providing a showcase for unknown young writers led to the staging of John Osborne's *Look Back in Anger* which was to become a landmark in postwar British theatre, ushering in a revolution in style and subject matter. Richardson continued to direct for the ESC until 1964 when Lindsay ANDERSON became their principal director. Among Richardson's other theatre work was the first staging of Osborne's *The Entertainer* with Laurence OLIVIER in the lead. He founded the production company Woodfall with Osborne and the Canadian producer Harry Saltzman with the intention of filming Osborne's plays. Richardson felt confined by the studio shooting which dominated his film versions of *Look Back in Anger* (1959) and *The Entertainer* (1960). The former is also hampered by theatricality, although the latter does preserve OLIVIER's performance for posterity. With *A Taste of Honey* (1961), adapted from Shelagh Delaney's play, Richardson finally got his wish to shoot entirely on location. With the unknown Rita Tushingham playing Jo, Richardson adopts a style which is more poetic than naturalistic, bringing a lyrical quality to his working-class subject. The film was also remarkable for breaking a number of censorship taboos, including featuring a sexual relationship between a white girl and a black man and having an obviously gay character in a sympathetic role.

*The Loneliness of the Long Distance Runner* (1962), adapted from the novella by Alan Sillitoe, was less well received. British reviewers baulked at its sometimes jarring combination of documentary realism and cinematic flamboyance (with devices borrowed from the French Nouvelle Vague). In retrospect, Richardson elicits another fine performance, this time from Tom Courtenay, and retains much of the anger of Sillitoe's writing. As a loyal member of the New Wave team he produced Karel REISZ's feature debut, *Saturday Night and Sunday Morning* (1960). His next film was a startling change of direction which clearly indicated the end of Richardson's interest in social realism and the New Wave. *Tom Jones* (1963) was a bawdy, energetic version of Henry Fielding's eighteenth-century novel which proved an enormous critical and commercial success, winning Richardson the Oscar as Best Director. He adopts an irreverent style, throwing every kind of cinematic trick available at the audience and ushering in the mood of Swinging London.

The popularity of *Tom Jones* gave Richardson international status, but his next few films are uneven. He had already worked in Hollywood with an unsuccessful version of William Faulkner's *Sanctuary* (1961) and he now returned to make an adaptation of Evelyn Waugh's black comedy about the funeral parlours of California, *The Loved One* (1965). The film has developed a cult reputation on the basis of some bizarre cameos, particularly one from Liberace, but the film is very hit and miss. Two indulgent films with Jeanne Moreau followed, both shot in France, but neither *Mademoiselle* (1966), adapted from Jean Genet, or *The Sailor from Gibraltar* (1967), based on Marguerite Duras' novel, made much impact. On his return to Britain he made the short film *Red and Blue* (1967) and then completed the ambitious *The Charge of the*

*Light Brigade* (1968). Richardson reverses the usual heroic version of events handed down to us by Tennyson and Hollywood and instead builds a bleak satirical attack on the idiocies of the British military elite and the anachronisms of the Victorian class system. With Charles Wood's deliberately archaic dialogue, brilliantly realised cartoon inter-ludes by Richard Williams and a series of fine comic turns by Harry Andrews, John Gielgud and Trevor Howard, Richardson creates the ultimate anti-heritage film.

The film had a mixed response and Richardson found himself working on more modest projects, with literary adaptations predomi-nating as they did throughout his career. *A Delicate Balance* (1973) and *Laughter in the Dark* (1969) are relatively straightforward adaptations of Edward Albee and Vladimir Nabokov respectively, but the film of his own stage production of *Hamlet* (1969) is a greater success, its low budget forcing Richardson into a minimalist style which suits the material surprisingly well. With a heavily cut text, extensive use of close-ups and inventive handling of the spaces in the Roundhouse Theatre, London, Richardson produces an intense, claustrophobic adaptation which draws a powerful performance from Nicol William-son. Unfortunately, his Australian epic *Ned Kelly* (1970), with Mick Jagger out of his depth as the outlaw hero, was a critical and box office failure. Richardson's final British films confirmed a downward spiral, with the routine Dick Francis racetrack thriller *Dead Cert* (1974) and a rather desperate attempt to revisit Henry Fielding with the tired romp *Joseph Andrews* (1977).

Richardson resurfaced in America in the 1980s where he made a living directing mini-series for television. He completed three further feature films, all of which are relatively minor, but which offer pleasures. *The Border* (1982) is an effective depiction of Mexican illegal migration into America with a restrained Jack Nicholson and *The Hotel New Hampshire* (1984) is an honourable attempt to film John Irving's quirky novel. *Blue Sky*, made in 1991 but not released until 1994 (after Richardson's death from AIDS on 14 November 1991), belatedly won an Oscar for its star Jessica Lange. Richardson aroused criticism in some quarters with his intermingling of realism and modernism, raising the ire of British critics who believe these approaches should not be mixed. This seems unfair; although Richardson's work is patchy, he was a director of real vision, an individualist whose films are often about outsiders at odds with their own society. He is a film-maker desperately in need of re-evaluation. He was married to the actress Vanessa Redgrave and his daughters, Joely and Natasha, are also actors.

**British Feature Films:** *Look Back in Anger* (1959); *The Entertainer* (1960); *A Taste of Honey* (1961); *The Loneliness of the Long Distance Runner* (1962); *Tom Jones* (1963); *Mademoiselle* (1966); *The Sailor From Gibraltar* (1967); *The Charge of the Light Brigade* (1968); *Laughter in the Dark* (1969); *Hamlet* (1969); *Ned Kelly* (1970); *A Delicate Balance* (1973); *Dead Cert* (1974); *Joseph Andrews* (1977).

**Bibliography:** James M. Welsh and John C. Tibbetts (eds), *The Cinema of Tony Richardson: Essays and Interviews* (New York: State University of New York Press, 1999); Tony Richardson, *Long Distance Runner: A Memoir* (London: Faber & Faber, 1993).

## Guy RITCHIE

Few contemporary British directors have made as much public impact or grabbed as many headlines as Guy Ritchie. Born in Hatfield, Hertfordshire on 10 September 1968, he entered the film industry as a runner in 1993 and graduated to directing commercials and music videos. He made the short film *The Hard Case* (1995) and then hit the box-office jackpot with his feature debut *Lock, Stock and Two Smoking Barrels* (1998). Ritchie takes the template of the traditional, working-class British gangster film and forces it through a fashionable stylistic rebranding, exaggerating the ludicrous street patois of its likeable villains, speeding up the editing and utilising every visual sleight of hand he had learned in his apprenticeship on pop promos and commercials. This is gangster pastiche, and a riot of unreconstructed male stereotyping typified by the casting of the bullet-headed ex-footballer Vinnie Jones, but it certainly touched a nerve with young audiences in a manner which few recent British films have achieved. Its popularity spawned a revival in the genre leading to a plethora of violent crime movies, one or two rather good, the majority quite awful.

He revisited the same territory with *Snatch* (2000), this time import-ing American star Brad Pitt to bolster the formula. It has the same postmodern knowingness in its jokey plundering of genre clichés and the same testosterone-driven energy, but although still a commercial success the strain of repetition was already beginning to show. Press revelations of his decidedly establishment background also tended to undermine Ritchie's claims for working-class authenticity. By this time the media was as interested in his marriage to Madonna as in his films, which probably didn't help the reception for *Swept Away* (2002). In this remake of Lina Wertmüller's 1974 allegorical film, Ritchie removes the politics and turns the story into a thoroughly unconvincing and self-indulgent vehicle for his wife. It was rapidly withdrawn following its

American release and only emerged in Britain on straight-to-video some time later. With his most recent film, *Revolver* (2005), he returned to more familiar ground with another fast-moving crime film. Slightly more low key and restrained than his earlier work, it didn't fare as well commercially but did a good deal to restore a critical reputation which had taken a hammering after *Swept Away*.

For his critics – and he certainly has them – Ritchie is an ersatz film-maker, recycling the conventions of old gangster movies with a thin veneer of flashy technique. For fans, he brought life back into a genre that was flagging, taking it into the age of MTV. With only a handful of credits the jury may be out, but he is still a director whose films attract exceptional levels of media interest.

**British Feature Films:** *Lock, Stock and Two Smoking Barrels* (1998); *Snatch* (2000); *Swept Away* (2002); *Revolver* (2005).

**Bibliography:** Steve Chibnall, 'Travels in Ladland: The British Gangster Film Cycle, 1998–2001', in Robert Murphy (ed.), *The British Cinema Book* (London: BFI, 2001).

### Bruce ROBINSON

Bruce Robinson was born in North London on 2 May 1946 but spent most of his childhood in Kent. He trained as an actor with the Central School of Speech and Drama in London and made his film debut while in his graduation year as Benvolio in Franco Zeffirelli's film of *Romeo and Juliet* (1968). He continued as a struggling actor for the best part of ten years, before eventually switching to writing in the late 1970s. His first produced screenplay was for Roland JOFFÉ's *The Killing Fields* (1984), a drama set during the violence of the Khmer Rouge era in Cambodia, which won him a BAFTA and an Oscar nomination. He then wrote and directed *Withnail and I* (1987), a frequently hilarious tale of two out of work actors on a chaotic weekend's holiday in the country. It made stars of Paul McGann and Richard E. Grant, becoming the cult film of choice for a generation of students. Among the witty wordplay and perversely joyful squalor of its two reprobate heroes is a finally moving story of friendship and loss which also acts as a lament for the death of 1960s idealism.

None of Robinson's subsequent work has achieved the kind of audience response which *Withnail and I* attracted, but his next film, *How to Get Ahead in Advertising* (1989), largely succeeds as an acid satire of 1980s materialism with Richard E. Grant again taking the lead role. The hectoring tone of the film, along with the abrupt shifts into manic fantasy, occasionally proved alienating. He produced another script for Joffé with *Shadow Makers* (1989), before making *Jennifer 8* (1992) in the United States. A surprisingly conventional thriller, it was a critical and commercial failure. Subsequently he returned to screenwriting, including the script for Neil JORDAN's American-made *In Dreams* (1999), but seems to have become increasingly disillusioned with the film business. More recently he has had considerable success as a novelist. His apparent withdrawal from directing has to be regretted, but the anarchic, melancholy splendour of *Withnail and I* lingers in the memory.

**British Feature Films:** *Withnail and I* (1987); *How to Get Ahead in Advertising* (1989).

**Bibliography:** Alastair Owen (ed.), *Smoking in Bed: Conversations with Bruce Robinson* (London: Bloomsbury, 2000).

## Nicolas ROEG

Amid the general gloom of 1970s British cinema, Nicolas Roeg seemed to represent one of the few real chinks of light. A gifted cinematographer, he moved to directing and quickly established a reputation as a distinctively personal film-maker. With their jagged cutting and disconcerting time shifts, his films didn't look like the work of any one else and their dark themes of destructive sexuality and confused identity made them sharply provocative.

Roeg was born on 15 August 1928 in London. Following National Service, he entered the industry in the late 1940s in the traditional manner as a general runabout. During the 1950s he worked his way up from clapperboy to camera operator to director of photography and his credits included second unit work on David LEAN's *Lawrence of Arabia* (1962) as well as the occasional scriptwriting jobs. During the 1960s he became regarded as one of the finest cinematographers available, noted for his expressive use of colour. He photographed *The Masque of the Red Death* (1964) for exploitation master Roger Corman, *Fahrenheit 451* (1966) for Truffaut and John SCHLESINGER's *Far From the Madding Crowd* (1967), for which he was BAFTA nominated. It was his technical prowess that led to his involvement with *Performance* (1970) when he was brought in to provide assistance to first-time director Donald Cammell, who had also written the film. Roeg finished as the film's cinematographer and co-director. It is a film of distinct halves, the first a violent gangster story which draws parallels between crime and big business. The second follows Chas (James Fox) as he becomes immersed in the world of jaded rock star Turner (Mick Jagger). Under the influence of sex and drugs, his sense of identity collapses and his latent homosexuality and femininity emerge. Its complex themes are mirrored by an elaborate cinematic style with the use of stylised *mise en scène* and fractured editing. Shelved by Warner Brothers, it finally appeared and became an instant cult success.

Identity is also at the centre of Roeg's first solo directorial effort, *Walkabout* (1970), where two English children find themselves stranded in the Australian outback and are befriended by an aboriginal boy. The film contrasts the natural spirituality of the aboriginal way of life with the shallowness of contemporary society in a slightly simplistic manner, but the film's conclusion remains shocking and Roeg's cinematography is stunning. The high quality of Roeg's work continued with the much acclaimed *Don't Look Now* (1973), starring Julie Christie and Donald Sutherland as a couple who go to Venice to recover from the death of their young daughter. The film resolves itself into a slightly preposterous supernatural chiller, but for most of its length Roeg is more concerned with themes of sex and death. Again beautifully photographed, this time by Anthony Richmond, the film is hauntingly enigmatic. Roeg's characteristic manipulation of time through montage editing is seen at its height in the scene where the couple's love-making is intercut with shots of them dressing to go out.

In *The Man Who Fell to Earth* (1976) the other-worldly David Bowie is appropriately cast as an alien who arrives on earth seeking water for his drought stricken planet but finds himself corrupted by the greedy materialism of human beings. The film's classic sci-fi themes are rather buried under the mannerisms of Roeg's directing style and, not for the last time, he found himself accused of pretentiousness. Sex and death are again at the heart of *Bad Timing* (1980), a coldly executed examination of a destructive sexual relationship featuring yet another music star, Art Garfunkel, starring opposite Roeg's future wife, Theresa Russell. The underlying pessimism of much of Roeg's work is particularly apparent here. The intricacies of *Eureka* (1983) proved too much for distributors who were reluctant to release it. Although guaranteed to provoke accusations of pretentiousness from Roeg's critics, it is a mesmerising analysis of false materialistic values with Gene Hackman as a driven gold prospector. *Insignificance* (1985) portrays an imagined meeting between Marilyn Monroe, Joe DiMaggio, Senator Joseph McCarthy and Albert Einstein. Stagey and relentlessly talkative, Roeg's usual visual pyrotechnics are largely missing and the fascination of the metaphysical discussions don't always overcome the contrivance of the basic set-up. Nonetheless, it won him an award at the Cannes Film Festival.

After contributing a section to the portmanteau opera film *Aria* (1987), Roeg shifted more into the mainstream with *Castaway* (1987). Based on a true story, it follows Oliver Reed and Amanda Donohoe as their attempt to live out an idyll on a beautiful desert island falls foul of natural hazards and the tensions inherent in their relationship. As she discovers her affinity with the landscape, Reed descends into a mire of sexual frustration which, in a surprisingly affecting performance, elicits some sympathy. *Track 29* (1988), from an original screenplay by Dennis Potter, took Roeg firmly back into the arena of art cinema. It is one of Roeg's most impressive later films, a disturbingly ambiguous meditation on the shifting nature of identity and the difficulties of fully knowing another person. Following it, Roeg made his most mainstream film to date with *The Witches* (1990). Adapted from Roald Dahl's children's story, the film successfully captures the author's distinctive combination of light and dark, with broad humour cut through by genuinely sinister elements. The film has a lightness of touch which is not usually associated with Roeg.

Since the 1990s, Roeg's work has gone into quite a steep decline. *Cold Heaven* (1991), made in America and adapted from Brian Moore's novel, is a supernatural thriller which works well for its first half and then fizzles out to an unbelievable ending, while *Two Deaths* (1995) sets another story of sexual obsession rather jarringly against the backdrop of the bloody Ceauşescu regime in Romania. Other than the bizarre, erotic short film *Hotel Paradise* (1995), most of his subsequent work has been for American television or straight-to-video release, including an uninspired version of Conrad's *Heart of Darkness* (1994), the strictly routine *Samson and Delilah* (1996) and the inanities of *Full Body Massage* (1995). It is probably best to overlook this fall from grace and remember his outstanding work from the 1970s and 1980s, which was among the most startlingly innovative and daring to have been produced within British cinema.

**British Feature Films:** *Performance* (1970, co-directed with Donald Cammell); *Walkabout* (1970); *Don't Look Now* (1973); *The Man Who Fell to Earth* (1976); *Bad Timing* (1980); *Eureka* (1983); *Insignificance* (1985); *Castaway* (1986); *Track 29* (1988); *The Witches* (1990); *Two Deaths* (1995).

**Bibliography:** John Izod, *The Films of Nicolas Roeg* (Basingstoke: Macmillan, 1992); Neil Sinyard, *The Films of Nicolas Roeg* (London: Letts, 1991).

## Ken RUSSELL

The perpetual 'enfant terrible' of British cinema, even now in his eighties, Ken Russell has infuriated critics and provoked controversy for most of his film-making career. He is also one of the most original talents in British cinema, a genuinely maverick director whose passion and flamboyance have brought vivid colour to a national film culture frequently accused of playing it safe.

Ken Russell was born on 3 July 1927 in Southampton. His early years were spent drifting through a variety of occupations including spells in the Merchant Navy and in the RAF during the Second World War, working as an actor and ballet dancer and then as a professional photographer. On the strength of a number of amateur short films he had made, particularly the charming *Amelia and the Angel* (1957), he was hired by the BBC. He established himself on the arts documentary series *Monitor*, hosted by Huw Wheldon, for whom he worked extensively throughout the 1960s. He attracted considerable attention for his studies of classical composers including the masterly *Elgar* (1962) and *Song of Summer* (1968), which depicted Delius at work. These short films balanced factual information, provided by Wheldon's voice-over, with lyrical imagery shot by Russell. He felt increasingly confined by the strictures imposed by *Monitor* and its successor *Omnibus* (e.g. keeping dramatised sequences and dialogue to a minimum) and began to kick against their regulations with more experimental work such as *The Debussy Film* (1965), with its film-within-a-film structure, and *Dance of the Seven Veils* (1970) about Richard Strauss.

His first feature film was the rather tame seaside comedy *French Dressing* (1963), followed by *Billion Dollar Brain* (1967), the third in the 'Harry Palmer' spy series starring Michael Caine. An indication of things to come was provided by a finale borrowed outrageously from Eisenstein's classic *Alexander Nevsky* (1938). His real breakthrough as a cinema director came with *Women in Love* (1969), adapted from D. H. Lawrence's novel. Some critics took umbrage at his rather casual way with the more intellectual aspects of Lawrence's work but the strong sense of period and impressive performances by Alan Bates, Oliver Reed and Glenda Jackson won a great deal of critical praise, including BAFTA and Oscar nominations for Russell. The film's naked male wrestling scene was just the first of many taboo-breaking sequences which would earn Russell notoriety. This controversy was nothing compared to the outrage which greeted *The Devils* (1971). A lapsed Catholic convert, Russell filled this attack on religious intolerance with shocking images of masturbating nuns and priests being tortured. The censors wielded their scissors, but with the advantage of hindsight the film has emerged as Russell's masterpiece, a savage black comedy of sexual repression and violence with a powerful central performance by Oliver Reed and memorable set designs by Derek JARMAN.

In the 1970s Russell produced a series of film biopics of composers and artists beginning with another controversial film, *The Music Lovers* (1970). The focus on Tchaikovsky's repressed homosexuality and his unhappy marriage created another press furore. The film shows an almost complete reversal of Russell's previous view of the romantic artist, from one of veneration to a repudiation of their human frailties, the majesty of the music being contrasted with the squalor of their personal lives. The excess, self-indulgence and intellectual shallowness of *The Music Lovers* is also evident in *Lisztomania* (1975), with Roger Daltrey in the lead, and *Valentino* (1977) which has Rudolf Nureyev as the silent star. More effective, and considerably more restrained, were *Mahler* (1974) and *Savage Messiah* (1972), about the sculptor Gaudier-Brzeska, which returned Russell to the style of his 1960s television work. This was by far Russell's most productive period and it also included an overblown version of Sandy Wilson's pastiche musical *The Boy Friend* (1971) and an adaptation of The Who's rock opera *Tommy* (1975). The latter shows Russell near his best, with his wildly idiosyncratic visual style matching the eccentricities of Pete Townsend's writing. Among the many striking images are Elton John's Pinball Wizard in his enormous Dr Marten boots and the iconic depiction of Daltrey as the messianic hero.

He made three films in America beginning with *Altered States* (1980), a hallucinogenic and intermittently impressive variation on *Dr Jekyll and Mr Hyde* over which he had major clashes with its producers. However, both *Crimes of Passion* (1984) and *Whore* (1991) are luridly sensationalist exercises. Back in Britain, he filmed two surprisingly conventional adaptations of Lawrence novels, *The Rainbow* (1989) and *Lady Chatterley* (1993), the latter serialised for television. His characteristic excess is more apparent in *Gothic* (1986) which centres on the decadent lives of the poets Byron and Shelley as well as on the writing of *Frankenstein* by Mary Shelley. The baroque visuals can't disguise the dubious nature of Russell's premise that the book was inspired by the author's loss of a baby. Far more enjoyable is the camp delirium of *The Lair of the White Worm* (1988) and *Salomé's Last Dance* (1988). The former is a highly entertaining, tongue-in-cheek gothic horror which wouldn't have gone amiss as a production of Hammer Studios.

Finding it increasingly difficult to attract funding, Russell has worked largely for television in recent years, particularly for *The South Bank Show*. Some of this work has been decidedly egocentric, allowing Russell to voice his opinions on a variety of subjects, e.g. *Ken Russell's ABC of British Music* (1988) and *Ken Russell's Treasure Island* (1995). Frustrated with the lack of support he has received from British producers, he has taken to shooting films on digital video tape, using his house and garden as sets and his family and friends as the cast. These 'home movies', frequently available only on the Internet, have taken him back to his roots making short films on 8 mm in the 1950s.

*The Fall of the House of Usher* (2001) received a limited release but was mauled by the British critics.

Through much of his career Russell has railed at the philistines in the film industry who refuse to fund his projects and at the narrow-minded critics who castigate his perceived vulgarity. At his worst, his films are undisciplined, crude and poorly thought-through, although they are rarely dull. He has remained unswervingly dedicated to a cinema of excess, of feeling and imagination communicated through images and music rather than dialogue or conventional narrative. The results have been uneven, but never less than memorable.

**British Feature Films:** *French Dressing* (1963); *Billion Dollar Brain* (1967); *Women in Love* (1969); *The Music Lovers* (1970); *The Devils* (1971); *The Boy Friend* (1971); *Savage Messiah* (1972); *Mahler* (1974); *Tommy* (1975); *Lisztomania* (1975); *Valentino* (1977); *Gothic* (1986); *The Lair of the White Worm* (1988); *Salomé's Last Dance* (1988); *The Rainbow* (1989); *The Fall of the House of Usher* (2001).

**Bibliography:** Gene D. Philips, *Ken Russell* (Cranbury, NJ and London: ASU Presses 1999); Ken Russell, *A Very British Picture* (London: Heinemann, 1989); John Baxter, *Ken Russell – An Appalling Talent* (London: Michael Joseph, 1973).

## Victor SAVILLE

Victor Saville was born on 25 September 1897 in Birmingham as Victor Salberg. He was invalided out of the army during the First World War after sustaining serious wounds. On his return home he entered the nascent British film industry, becoming the manager of a small cinema in Coventry. He worked for Pathé in London and then in 1920 he formed a film rental company with the young Michael Balcon. This led in turn to an interest in production and in 1923 he and Balcon co-produced *Woman to Woman*. At Gaumont-British he formed a successful partnership with the director Maurice Elvey for whom he produced five films including *Hindle Wakes* (1927). Later the same year he made his directorial debut with *The Arcadians* and in 1928 established his own production company, Burlington, for whom he directed *Tesha* (1928). In 1929 he went to America to add sound sequences to *Kitty* and while there directed a remake of *Woman to Woman* (1929) with sound.

Returning to Britain, he made the popular spy movie *The W Plan* (1930) and then joined Gainsborough, where Balcon was head of production. Saville made sixteen films in five years working for Balcon, proving to be a reliable, proficient director who could turn his hand to most genres. He made a sound version of *Hindle Wakes* (1931), two vehicles for the comic Leslie Hanson – *A Warm Corner* (1930) and *The Sport of Kings* (1931) – and one for Jack Hulbert, *Love on Wheels* (1932), as well as historical dramas and romances. Most memorable are the five films he made with Jessie Matthews which turned her into a major star. These include a lively version of J. B. Priestley's story of a travelling vaudeville troupe, *The Good Companions* (1933), the charming musical *Evergreen* (1934) and *First a Girl* (1935), a playful cross-dressing comedy with Matthews disguising herself as a boy. He achieved a similar success for the actress Madeleine Carroll with the espionage thriller *I Was a Spy* (1933).

In 1936, with the backing of Alexander KORDA's London Films, he and screenwriter Ian Dalrymple established Victor Saville Productions. This resulted in another entertaining spy drama *Dark Journey* (1937), a whimsical comedy with anti-fascist undercurrents, *Storm in a Teacup* (1937), and *South Riding* (1938), which is perhaps his finest achievement as a director. Adapted from Winifred Holtby's successful novel and set in the Yorkshire Dales, its multi-stranded plot is a little too near soap opera at times, but Saville handles the narrative with considerable assurance to produce an engaging, socially aware film. Its political message may seem watered down now but was radical enough in the context of the period.

Saville had established himself as a highly competent, frequently stylish director of middlebrow entertainments, often with a softly-peddled liberal message, but he wanted to return to producing. In the late 1930s he was responsible for the production of two of the most popular films of the era, *The Citadel* (1938) and *Goodbye Mr Chips* (1939), both made in Britain for MGM and directed by Americans. Their formula of sentiment and social conscience proved a box-office winner. During the war years he was in Hollywood where he produced eight films for MGM, including the anti-Nazi *The Mortal Storm* (1940) which was made before America entered the war and caused a considerable controversy. Remaining in America, he directed a section for the portmanteau film *Forever and a Day* (1943); produced to raise money for war charities, it featured contributions from the European contingent in Hollywood. He then returned fully to directing with the musical *Tonight and Every Night* (1945), which recreates London's Windmill Theatre in America in an utterly unconvincing manner. He went on to make a further three films as a director at MGM in Hollywood, none of them very memorable.

Saville remained based in America, but made occasional forays home to direct. This unfortunately resulted in such routine fare as *Calling Bulldog Drummond* (1951) and the Cold War thriller *Conspirator* (1949). Things reached a low point with his famously woeful American biblical epic *The Silver Chalice* (1954) starring a young Paul Newman. It was to be his last film as a director, although he continued to produce. He returned to Britain to live in the early 1960s and produced two more films there. He died in London on 8 May 1979. Saville was an unusual figure in that he worked successfully as a director and a producer in both Britain and Hollywood. Although much of his work was routinely commercial, his films of the 1930s remain a fascinating glimpse into the period. Rich in sentimentality and the glamour of stardom, they nonetheless contain a solid sense of social purpose, pointing to the class tensions and economic resentments of the depression era.

**British Feature Films:** *The Arcadians* (1927); *Tesha* (1928); *Kitty* (1929); *Woman to Woman* (1929); *The W Plan* (1930); *A Warm Corner* (1930); *Hindle Wakes* (1931); *Michael and Mary* (1931); *The Sport of Kings* (1931); *Sunshine Susie* (1931); *The Faithful Heart* (1932); *Love on Wheels* (1932); *Friday the Thirteenth* (1933); *The Good Companions* (1933); *I Was a Spy* (1933); *Evensong* (1934); *Evergreen* (1934); *The Iron Duke* (1934); *First a Girl* (1935); *The Dictator* (1935); *Me and Marlborough* (1935); *It's Love Again* (1936); *Dark Journey* (1937); *Storm in a Teacup* (1937); *South Riding* (1938); *Conspirator* (1949); *Calling Bulldog Drummond* (1951); *Twenty-Four Hours of a Woman's Life* (1952).

**Bibliography:** Cyril Rollins and Robert J. Wareing, *Victor Saville* (London: BFI, 1972).

### John SCHLESINGER

John Schlesinger was born on 16 February 1926 in London. His study of English Literature as an undergraduate at Balliol College, Oxford was cut short by war service with the Combined Services Entertainment Unit. Back at Oxford, he joined the Dramatic Society, was President of the Experimental Theatre Company and started to make his own amateur short films. After graduation, he worked as a professional actor in theatre and film but continued his interest in directing by making the short documentary *Sunday in the Park* (1956) which led to a job as an assistant director with the BBC. He went on to direct more than twenty documentaries for the BBC working on the current affairs series *Tonight* and the arts programme *Monitor*. For Edgar Anstey's British Transport Films he made *Terminus* (1961), a sharply observed fly-on-the-wall portrait of life at Waterloo Station in London which won awards from BAFTA and at Venice.

Schlesinger's first feature film, *A Kind of Loving* (1962), adapted from Stan Barstow's novel by Keith Waterhouse and Willis Hall, was sufficiently in the social realist mode to be considered part of the British New Wave. It is one of the quieter entries in this cycle, but is distinguished by the portrayal of a more white-collar milieu than is usual with the 'kitchen sink' films and by its frank, sympathetic account of a young couple (Alan Bates and June Ritchie) struggling with their own naivety about adult relationships. The film won the Golden Bear at Berlin and marked the beginning of Schlesinger's fruitful relationship with producer Joseph Janni which continued throughout the 1960s. He worked with Waterhouse and Hall again on *Billy Liar* (1963), an adaptation of Waterhouse's novel and their stage success. Tom Courtenay is engaging as Billy, a young man trapped in a dead-end job who compensates for the routine of his life with a very vivid imagination. The film marks a key moment in the development of British cinema, bridging the naturalism of the New Wave with the fantasy of the Swinging Sixties. It also introduced audiences to the ultimate Sixties girl, Julie Christie.

Christie appears again in *Darling* (1965) in which a shift into full Swinging London mode is apparent. Scripted by Frederic Raphael and containing such would-be daring elements as an orgy sequence, the film is a chilly dissection of fashionable lifestyles and attitudes of the period. By Schlesinger's standards, the depiction of the central character is surprisingly unforgiving, bordering on misogyny, and there is something uncomfortable about a film which frequently wallows in a moral depravity it appears to be condemning. Nonetheless, it was a significant British film of its era and won many plaudits on release, including Oscars for Christie and Raphael. Critics and audiences were less forgiving of the expensively produced Hardy adaptation *Far from the Madding Crowd* (1967) which again featured Christie and Alan Bates, and another Swinging London icon Terence Stamp. Despite the faithfulness of Frederic Raphael's script and sumptuous photography by Nicolas ROEG, reviewers objected to what they saw as the imposition of too contemporary a tone onto period material. Seen now, the chemistry between Stamp and Christie seems more appealing.

By this time Schlesinger was regarded as among the brightest talents British cinema had to offer, so it is all too typically ironic that much of his subsequent career was to be spent in Hollywood. His first American film, *Midnight Cowboy* (1969), is widely regarded as his finest work. A cruelly acerbic portrait of modern American values, it benefits from the poignant performances of Jon Voight as a young hustler and Dustin Hoffman as his sleazy, tragic friend. Briefly, Schlesinger was the darling of American critics and won the Academy Award as Best Director. Back in Britain, he made the low-key *Sunday Bloody Sunday* (1971) which was groundbreaking in its depiction of a triangular love affair where both Peter Finch and Glenda Jackson share the same male lover. Typically for Schlesinger, its two central characters are depicted with a warmth which is not extended to the portrait of the shallow, middle-class society in which they exist. It won him his second BAFTA as Best Director. Schlesinger's international standing was confirmed by his selection to direct one of the eight segments of *Visions of Eight* (1973), a record of the 1972 Munich Olympics.

Back in the States he made the uneven, but often visually striking, *Day of the Locust* (1975). Adapted from Nathanael West's novel, it presents a scathing attack on the values of classic-era Hollywood and builds to a surreal, disturbing climax. *Marathon Man* (1976) is a stylish, brutal thriller which obliquely links the Nazis to the persecution of liberals by Senator McCarthy. Its directorial flourishes attracted some criticism but it has gone on to attain a kind of cult status. Those with a phobia for dentists should avoid it. Back again in Britain he made *Yanks* (1979), a beguiling, multi-stranded depiction of the impact of American troops stationed in Britain during the Second World War. It is openly nostalgic, but all the more likeable for that. And then the bubble abruptly burst. *Honky Tonk Freeway* (1981) is an overblown, modestly entertaining small-town comedy which cost a fortune to make and fared so badly at the box office that it almost bankrupted the American studio which backed it. Schlesinger's film career never fully recovered. His best later work was for British television where he made *An Englishman Abroad* (1983). It is a dryly observed portrait of the British spy Guy Burgess who went to live in communist Russia, played with careworn cheerfulness by Alan Bates from a beautifully crafted Alan Bennett script.

He returned to feature production in America with the minor political drama *The Falcon and the Snowman* (1985). A gradual slide into routine commercial projects is apparent with the tolerable horror film *The Believers* (1987) and the yuppies-in-peril suspense thriller *Pacific Heights* (1990), which also betrayed an increasingly right-wing tone in Schlesinger's work. He made a couple of European co-productions, the theatrical *Madame Sousatzka* (1988) with an over-the-top Shirley MacLaine and *The Innocent* (1993), a routine Cold War thriller. Two further American films followed, the crudely exploitative revenge drama *Eye for an Eye* (1996) and the superficially trendy romantic drama *The Next Best Thing* (2000), with Madonna and Rupert Everett as the gay man who fathers her baby. Schlesinger continued to produce polished, if slightly predictable prestige fare for British television such as *A Question of Attribution* (1992), which revisits similar territory to *An Englishman Abroad*, and *Cold Comfort Farm* (1995). He also worked successfully in the theatre and turned his hand to opera.

The latter part of Schlesinger's career shows a considerable decline in form, but at his height he was a director who regularly elicited memorable performances from his actors, showing a real sensitivity towards society's victims and outcasts. His finest work combines cynicism towards the wider society with a real humanity for the individual. He was also a film-maker who could use the medium with a genuine sense of style and flamboyance. He was made a CBE in 1970 and received a BAFTA Fellowship in 1996. He died on 25 July 2003 in Palm Springs, California.

**British Feature Films:** *A Kind of Loving* (1962); *Billy Liar* (1963); *Darling* (1965); *Far from the Madding Crowd* (1967); *Sunday Bloody Sunday* (1971); *Yanks* (1979); *Madame Sousatzka* (1988); *The Innocent* (1993).

**Bibliography:** Gene D. Phillips, *John Schlesinger* (Boston: Twayne, 1981).

# George Albert SMITH

George Albert Smith was born in London on 4 January 1864. He moved to Brighton where he subsequently became, with James Williamson and Esme Collings, a central contributor to the most important group of British film pioneers known as the 'Brighton School'. He had initially achieved public notoriety in the 1880s as a stage hypnotist, but his interest in optical illusions led him to developing elaborate lantern slide shows which involved switching between images to aid story-telling in a manner which foreshadows the methods of film editing. After working as a portrait photographer, in 1896 he purchased an early moving image camera and the following year established a studio in the gardens of his home in Hove which he dubbed his 'film factory'. Here he processed films as well as producing his own work. By the end of the century he had gone into partnership with another pioneer, the American Charles Urban, who ran the Warwick Trading Company. His films of this period are largely simple slapstick comedies, actualities or fairy-tale adaptations and often featured his wife, Laura Bayley, who had already been a successful performer in comic revues.

In 1900 Smith produced a number of films which indicate his significance to the development of film in Britain as a narrative form and an entertainment. With films such as *The Kiss in the Tunnel* and *As Seen through the Telescope* he developed techniques of editing which built on his earlier magic lantern shows. In a simple sequence containing just a handful of shots he used such methods as dissolves, cutting between wide shot and close-up, superimposition and point-of-view. These enabled him to construct simple narratives in purely cinematic terms which the audience could follow. Smith particularly established a reputation for his trick films involving the manipulation of the new medium to produce startling visual effects. This included the use of reverse motion in *The House that Jack Built* (1900) and dream sequences in *Let Me Dream Again* (1900). Most famous of these is the charming *Grandma's Reading Glass* (1900), which makes imaginative use of close-ups to draw the audience into the internal world of the film; we share the young protagonist's viewpoint as he looks at various objects through a magnifying glass. The sophistication of these films put him light years ahead of most other British pioneers and gives him a place in the development of British cinema equivalent to that of Méliès in France.

For the remainder of his career he focused on developing colour techniques. His two-colour Kinemacolor process was patented in 1906 and publicly launched in front of the Royal Society of Arts in 1908. It became the basis for Urban's creation of the Natural Color Kinematograph Company in 1910, although the two were to part company in

1914 as they became embroiled in ownership disputes. With studios in Hove and Nice, the company produced more than 100 short films between 1910 and 1913 which demonstrated the possibilities of colour, including *Tartans of Scotland* and *Woman Draped in Handkerchiefs*. They even produced a feature-length film using the process, *The Durbar at Delhi* (1911). Unfortunately, Smith's rival pioneer William Friese-Greene sued over the patent for Kinemacolor leading to the collapse of the company and effectively brought Smith's remarkable career to an end, although he was to re-emerge as a low-budget producer in the 1930s. He lived to see film historians rediscover his work and was an honoured guest at the opening of the National Film Theatre in 1952. He died in Brighton on 17 May 1959.

**Bibliography:** John Barnes, *The Beginnings of the Cinema in England 1894–1901, Vols 2–5* (Exeter: Exeter University Press, 1996–8); Frank Gray, 'George Albert Smith's Visions and Transformations: The Films of 1898', in Simon Popple and Vanessa Toulmin (eds), *Visual Delights: Essays on the Popular and Projected Image in the 19$^{th}$ Century* (Trowbridge: Flicks Books, 2000).

# T

## Pen TENNYSON

Penrose Tennyson is a minor but appealing figure in British cinema history whose considerable promise was cut short by an early death. Born in London on 26 August 1912, he was a great-grandson of the poet Alfred, Lord Tennyson and his father was a senior government official. After Eton, he studied briefly at Oxford, but swiftly left to pursue a career in the cinema. He started work with Michael Balcon (who was a friend of the family) in the script department at Gaumont-British in 1932 and then became an assistant director. He worked with Victor SAVILLE on *The Good Companions* (1933) and with HITCH-COCK on a number of films including *The 39 Steps* (1935). He then followed Balcon as he went to MGM British and then on to Ealing. It was here that he made his debut as a feature director with *There Ain't No Justice* (1939) which he also wrote, as with all of his films as a director. He was the youngest director then working in British films. The film's depiction of corruption in the world of boxing indicated Tennyson's preference for films with a strong social conscience, which was to become his trademark.

He made a greater impact with *The Proud Valley* (1940), a drama set in the South Wales coalfields which clearly takes the side of the unemployed miners against the self-serving pit owners. The film's radicalism was toned down with the outbreak of war and it was turned into something of a flag waver, but it still generates considerable power in its depiction of working-class solidarity. The great American singer Paul Robeson is rather unconvincingly cast in the role of a migrant worker, but is nonetheless a charismatic presence. His third film was the wartime propaganda piece *Convoy* (1940). Its characteristic story of self-sacrifice, as a merchant ship is destroyed saving a Royal Navy convoy, and obvious sincerity cemented Tennyson's growing reputation. It was to be his last film. He joined the Navy as an officer and was given the job of running the Admiralty's Educational Film Unit when, on 7 July 1941, his flight to the naval base at Rosyth went down and he was killed along with everyone else on board. His death robbed British cinema of a director of enormous talent and future potential.

**British Feature Films:** *There Ain't no Justice* (1939); *The Proud Valley* (1940); *Convoy* (1940).

**Bibliography:** Michael Balcon, 'Sub-Lieutenant F. Penrose Tennyson', in Derek Tangye (ed.), *Went the Day Well* (London: Michael Joseph, 1995); C. T. (Charles Tennyson), *Pen Tennyson* (London: A. S. Atkinson, 1943).

## Gerald THOMAS

The place of Gerald Thomas in the history of British cinema is secured by the series of thirty-one Carry On films which he directed over the best part of twenty-five years. Reviled by critics, but loved by filmgoers, they occupy a special place in British popular culture, bringing to the screen the vulgar humour and broad stereotypes of the music hall. With their working-class layabouts, busty blondes and nagging wives, they recall the world of Donald McGill's saucy seaside postcards, achieving an almost unrivalled level of audience affection.

Gerald Thomas was born on 10 December 1920 in Hull. At university he studied medicine, but his student days were cut short by wartime service in the army. After being demobbed, rather than return to his studies he went into the film industry. He initially trained as an editor at Denham, where he worked on OLIVIER's *Hamlet* (1948). In the early 1950s he worked as an editor and second unit director for his elder brother Ralph, who was already established as a director. This included cutting Ralph's major commercial success

*Doctor in the House* (1954). He made his directorial debut with *Circus Friends* (1956) for the Children's Film Foundation and his first mainstream feature with *Time Lock* (1957), a neatly handled suspenser. The film marked the beginning of his collaboration with producer Peter Rogers with whom he would make the Carry On series. They made a handful of fairly undistinguished films together in the late 1950s including *The Duke Wore Jeans* (1958), a vehicle for British rock 'n' roll singer Tommy Steele, before releasing *Carry on Sergeant* (1958), a routine National Service farce. It turned out to be surprise box office success and started the pair on the long running series which would dominate both their careers.

The formula for the Carry Ons was established with their second outing, *Carry on Nurse* (1959). Made cheaply at the rate of about two a year, their broad comedy relied heavily on sexual innuendo which remained just the right side of blue to keep the censors happy. Their popularity rested on the enjoyably stereotyped characters played by the team of comic actors which Thomas and Rogers assembled, including Sid James (working-class wide boy), Joan Sims (battleaxe), Hattie Jacques (sexually predatory older woman), Kenneth Williams (camp authority figure) and Charles Hawtrey (manically camp eccentric). The early films were dominated by send-ups of British institutions – *Teacher* (1959), *Constable* (1960) – and scripted by Norman Hudis. When Talbot Rothwell took over writing duties they turned to parodies of film genres and historical subjects, including *Cleo* (1964), *Spying* (1964), *Cowboy* (1965) and the high watermark of the series, *Carry On Up the Khyber* (1968). Film academics like Marion Jordan critiqued the series for its use of sexist and homophobic stereotyping, but Andy Medhurst defended them as the ultimate proletarian entertainment which attained a kind of democracy by mocking everyone equally. Far from being reactionary, he pointed to their gleeful subversiveness.

By the 1970s the series seemed to loose its way, crossing the line into genuinely adult humour and subsequently losing the sense of inno- cence which had endeared the films to audiences. A low point came with the crude *Emmanuel* (1978) but the series was belatedly revived one more time for the disastrous *Columbus* (1992), with most of the original cast long dead and a new group of 'alternative' comedians failing to recapture the glories of the old team. At the time of going to press, *Carry on London* is threatened.

Outside of the Carry Ons, Thomas's other work rarely ventured far from the same style of suggestive, knockabout comedy. These include *Please Turn Over* (1959) with Leslie Philips, *Watch your Stern* (1960) and *Raising the Wind* (1961). The titles tell you everything you need to know. In later years he made television spin-offs from the Carry Ons and various compilations of clips, as well as directing stage productions featuring the team. Despite the obvious decline of the Carry Ons, in their prime they provided a riposte to British cinema's obsession with worthy period dramas and gritty social realism. Their warm humour and mocking of British inhibitions hit a nerve with audiences, ensuring Thomas's place of honour in the roll call of British popular culture. He died on 9 November 1993.

**British Feature Films**: *Circus Friends* (1956); *Time Lock* (1957); *The Vicious Circle* (1957); *Chain of Events* (1957); *The Solitary Child* (1958); *The Duke Wore Jeans* (1958); *Carry On Sergeant* (1958); *Please Turn Over* (1959); *Carry On Nurse* (1959); *Carry On Teacher* (1959); *Watch Your Stern* (1960); *No Kidding* (1960); *Carry On Constable* (1960); *Raising the Wind* (1961); *Carry On Regardless* (1961); *Twice Round the Daffodils* (1962); *The Iron Maiden* (1962); *Carry On Cruising* (1962); *Nurse On Wheels* (1963); *Carry On Cabby* (1963); *Carry On Spying* (1964); *Carry On Jack* (1964); *Carry On Cleo* (1964); *The Big Job* (1965); *Carry On Cowboy* (1965); *Carry On Screaming* (1966); *Carry On Don't Lose Your Head* (1966); *Carry On Follow That Camel* (1967); *Carry On Doctor* (1967); *Carry On Up the Khyber* (1968); *Carry On Camping* (1969); *Carry On Again Doctor* (1969); *Carry On Up the Jungle* (1970); *Carry On Loving* (1970); *Carry On Henry* (1971); *Carry On at your Convenience* (1971); *Bless This House* (1972); *Carry On Matron* (1972); *Carry On Abroad* (1972); *Carry On Girls* (1973); *Carry On Dick* (1974); *Carry On Behind* (1975); *Carry On England* (1976); *That's Carry On* (1977): *Carry On Emmanuel* (1978); *The Second Victory* (1986); *Carry On Columbus* (1992).

**Bibliography**: Robert Ross, *The Carry On Companion* (London: B. T. Batsford, 1996).

## Ralph THOMAS

Ralph Thomas was born in Hull on 10 August 1915. After studying at Middlesex College, he entered the film industry in 1932 as a clapperboy at Sound City studios. He worked his way up as a camera assistant and then as an editor at British Lion before distinguished army service in the Second World War. After the war, he joined the Rank Organisation working initially in their trailers department. It was here that he met Betty Box who was to become his producer in a partnership which lasted for twenty-five years. He began directing in the late 1940s with some unremarkable comedies made for Rank at their Gainsborough studios base, including the bizarre screwball farce *Helter Skelter* (1949), but he proved adept at a variety of genres. Particularly striking among his early films is the Hitchcockian chase thriller *The Clouded Yellow* (1950), which was the first of his films to be produced by Betty Box.

During the 1950s, while working for Rank at Pinewood, he became a pillar of mainstream commercial production, bringing professionalism and polish to a wide range of subjects. His commercial breakthrough came with the amiable and enduringly popular hospital comedy *Doctor in the House* (1954) for which he remains best known. With a fine cast including Dirk Bogarde, Kenneth More and James Robertson Justice, Thomas showed a gift for mixing gentle humour, romance and characterisation into a highly successful formula. Six sequels followed, with Michael Craig and Leslie Philips taking over the central role of Simon Sparrow, although the comedy progressively coarsened over the years. His other work in this period included location action films such as the cod-western *Campbell's Kingdom* (1957), the romantic melo-drama *The Wind Cannot Read* (1958) and tasteful literary adaptation with *A Tale of Two Cities* (1958). All of these featured Rank's favourite leading man Dirk Bogarde, although he seemed more comfortable in the romances than as an action hero. Other interesting films include *Appointment with Venus* (1951), a quirky wartime comedy set in the Channel Islands, and the typically stoic naval drama *Above Us the Waves* (1955). Less well advised was a lifeless remake of HITCH-COCK's *The 39 Steps* (1958).

Thomas's most impressive work came at the start of the 1960s. *Conspiracy of Hearts* (1960), about Italian nuns rescuing Jewish children from the Nazi camps, is certainly sentimental but manages a real emotional impact. Most striking is the acerbic political fable *No Love for Johnnie* (1961), with an excellent Peter Finch as the mere-tricious Labour MP who puts his career above his principles. It was nominated at the Berlin Film Festival. However, the new decade ushered in the beginning of a decline as Thomas seemed increasingly out of step with changing attitudes. There was some mileage in *Deadlier Than the Male* (1966), an update of Bulldog Drummond for Swinging London, and the spy spoof *Hot Enough for June* (1964). The thriller *Nobody Runs Forever* (1968) works well enough, but by the 1970s he had hit rock bottom entering the world of the British sex comedy with the penis-transplant antics of *Percy* (1971) and its even worse sequel, *Percy's Progress* (1974). It was a tawdry final chapter for a director who had always shown an unerring eye for the box office, but who usually combined this with restraint and some regard for the audience.

Thomas may have lacked the visual style and distinctive approach required by the auteur theory, but for the whole of the 1950s he and Betty Box seemed to have an uncanny ability to produce solidly entertaining mass entertainment films which on occasions pushed beyond this into something more ambitious. His brother was Gerald THOMAS, director of the Carry On films, and his son Jeremy became an accomplished producer and Chairman of the BFI. Ralph Thomas died on 17 March 2001.

**British Feature Films:** *Helter Skelter* (1949); *Once Upon a Dream* (1949); *Traveller's Joy* (1949); *The Clouded Yellow* (1950); *Appointment with Venus* (1951); *Venetian Bird* (1952); *The Dog and the Diamonds* (1953); *A Day to Remember* (1953); *Doctor in the House* (1954); *Mad About Men* (1954); *Doctor at Sea* (1955); *Above Us the Waves* (1955); *Checkpoint* (1956); *The Iron Petticoat* (1956); *Campbell's Kingdom* (1957); *Doctor at Large* (1957); *A Tale of Two Cities* (1958); *The 39 Steps* (1958); *The Wind Cannot Read* (1958); *Upstairs and Downstairs* (1959); *Conspiracy of Hearts* (1960); *Doctor in Love* (1960); *No Love Johnnie* (1961); *No, My Darling Daughter* (1961); *A Pair of Briefs* (1961); *The Wild and the Willing* (1962); *Doctor in Distress* (1963); *Hot Enough for June* (1964); *The High Bright Sun* (1965); *Deadlier Than the Male* (1966); *Doctor in Clover* (1966); *Nobody Runs Forever* (1968); *Some Girls Do* (1969); *Doctor in Trouble* (1970); *Percy* (1971); *Quest for Love* (1971); *It's 2' 6"* Above the Ground (1973); *Percy's Progress* (1974); *The Biggest Bank Robbery* (1980).

**Bibliography:** Brian McFarlane, *An Autobiography of British Cinema* (London: Methuen, 1977).

## J. Lee THOMPSON

Born in Bristol on 1 August 1914, (John) Lee Thompson went on to establish a reputation as a director of genre movies with a strongly masculine character. Born into a theatrical family, his career started as an actor with Nottingham Repertory Company, but he achieved greater success as a writer and his play *Double Error* became a West End production. He moved into cinema in the mid-1930s, initially adapting his own plays and then writing original screenplays. He was dialogue coach on HITCHCOCK's *Jamaica Inn* (1939) and was influenced by the efficiency of the master's preplanning of shots. He served with the RAF during the Second World War and then returned to work at Elstree. His directorial debut came with *Murder Without Crime* (1950) for ABPC, another adaptation of one of his plays.

For the first half of the 1950s he was a reliable studio director turning out a variety of films, from the tepid newly weds comedy of *For Better, For Worse* (1954) with Dirk Bogarde, to the Jack Buchanan vehicle *As Long as They're Happy* (1955) and the zany animal-on-the-loose farce of *An Alligator Named Daisy* (1955). He began to establish a distinctive style with the powerful *Yield to the Night* (1956) which gave Diana Dors her finest screen opportunity playing a character uncannily similar to Ruth Ellis, the last woman to be hanged in Britain. The film is lean and realistic but not without elements of effective melodrama and had a considerable impact on the public attitude to capital punishment. After a forgettable version of J. B. Priestley's *The Good Companions* (1956), Thompson's returned to social realism with *Woman in a Dressing Gown* (1957), a stark portrait of a disintegrating marriage adapted from Ted Willis's breakthrough television play. He worked with Willis again on *No Trees in the Street* (1958), a tough portrait of life in London during the depression of the 1930s. The depiction of Cardiff's docklands in *Tiger Bay* (1959) had a characteristic sense of authenticity, vividly capturing its teeming, multi-ethnic streets. In many respects it's the quintessential Lee Thompson film of this period, combining elements of the crime genre with a documentary filming style and a liberalism apparent in the sympathetic depiction of the young murderer played by Horst Buchholz. The film was a box office hit and made a star of child actress Hayley Mills. The quality of his output in this period was recognised with a series of nominations at Cannes, Berlin and the BAFTAs.

In the late 1950s Thompson changed direction, becoming known internationally for a number of smartly handled, big-budget adventure yarns beginning with the compelling *Ice Cold in Alex* (1958), a taut combination of character-driven drama and atmospheric desert action. More exotic adventures followed with the dashing *Northwest Frontier* (1959) and the enormous commercial success of *The Guns of Navarone* (1961), which won him an Oscar nomination. Produced and scripted by the blacklisted American Carl Foreman, the film combines spectacular set-pieces with surprisingly thoughtful dialogue, the tension neatly maintained to an impressively explosive finale. The film's popularity established Thompson with Hollywood and he continued in similar vein with *Taras Bulba* (1962), an epic of battling Cossacks and Poles, with Yul Bryner and Tony Curtis as a feuding father and son.

The remainder of Thompson's career belongs largely to American cinema. His flare for genre and disciplined direction made him ideal at bringing films in on time and within budget. His commercial acumen was proved by the success of many of his Hollywood films. Particularly notable is his superbly menacing *Cape Fear* (1962) with Gregory Peck as the lawyer stalked by a suitably alarming ex-con played by Robert Mitchum. With its sweaty southern locales and Bernard Herrmann score, it brought the most creative period of Thompson's career to a close. His reputation declined in the mid-1960s with a couple of frenetic comedies featuring Shirley MacLaine. He returned to Britain to make *Return from the Ashes* (1965), a suspense thriller with darker themes of postwar angst. This was followed by *Eye of the Devil* (1967), a bizarre gothic melodrama which went through a variety of production difficulties as well as clashes with the censors. He continued to work intermittently in Britain in the late 1960s making the well intentioned *Before Winter Comes* (1968), with David Niven as a British officer dealing with displaced persons in the wake of the Second World War, and *Country Dance* (1969) with Peter O'Toole going mad as an aristocrat with incestuous designs on his sister.

In America he worked with Carl Foreman again on the starry, spectacular western *McKenna's Gold* (1969), made a saccharin musical version of *Huckleberry Finn* (1974) and directed the final two films in the Planet of the Apes cycle. *Battle for the Planet of the Apes* (1973) is strictly a low-budget filler, but the allegorical aspects of *Conquest of the Planet of the Apes* (1972), with its timely story of a 'racial' uprising, sufficiently frightened its American producer for the film to be toned down. The final stage of Thompson's career was dominated by his partnership with the stony-faced Charles Bronson. They made nine films together, with Bronson typically cast as a macho avenger violently bringing the bad guys to book. From *St Ives* (1976) to the lamentable *The Evil That Men Do* (1984) and the dire *Death Wish 4: The Crackdown* (1987), the liberalism of Thompson's earlier work is replaced by an increasingly reactionary strain. He also made an overblown version of *King Solomon's Mines* (1985) and a thinly veiled portrait of Aristotle Onassis in *The Greek Tycoon* (1978) starring Anthony Quinn. He directed his last film in 1989 and died in British Columbia, Canada on 30 August 2002. His critical reputation has been rather unfairly hampered by the poor quality of some of his later American films and his tendency to fit in with prevailing commercial trends, but a more recent re-evaluation has acknowledged the remarkable quality of his best work which combines populist elements with humanitarian concerns and a tough realism with a considerable visual flair.

**British Feature Films:** *Murder Without Crime* (1950); *The Yellow Balloon* (1953); *The Weak and the Wicked* (1953); *For Better, For Worse*

(1954); *As Long as They're Happy* (1955); *An Alligator Named Daisy* (1955); *Yield to the Night* (1956); *The Good Companions* (1956); *Woman in a Dressing Gown* (1957); *No Trees in the Street* (1958); *Ice Cold in Alex* (1958); *North West Frontier* (1959); *Tiger Bay* (1959); *The Guns of Navarone* (1961); *Return from the Ashes* (1965); *Eye of the Devil* (1967); *Before Winter Comes* (1968); *The Most Dangerous Man in the World* (1969); *Country Dance* (1969); *The Passage* (1978).

**Bibliography:** Steve Chibnall, *J. Lee Thompson* (Manchester: Manchester University Press, 2000).

## Wendy TOYE

Wendy Toye was born on 1 May 1917 in London. She achieved early fame after appearing on stage at the Albert Hall as a three-year-old dancer. She was something of an infant prodigy, performing in music hall and starring at the Palladium at the age of nine in a ballet she had choreographed herself. This was followed by engagements with a number of international ballet and stage companies as a choreographer and performer, including Diaghilev's Ballet Russe, while she continued also to work in the music hall. Her career as a stage choreographer was to continue successfully into the 1950s. She made her first appearance in films with Anthony ASQUITH's *Dance Pretty Lady* in 1931, but she was more interested in working behind the camera and soon found employment as a choreographer with credits for distinguished directors such as Carol REED and Herbert WILCOX.

She finally made her debut as a film director in 1952 with the celebrated short *The Stranger Left No Card* made for producer George K. Arthur. Directed with real visual flair and imagination, it picked up an award at the Cannes Film Festival and won her a contract with producer Alexander KORDA. She worked on three films for him, providing one episode in the portmanteau chiller *Three Cases of Murder* (1955), directing the Francis Durbridge adaptation *The Teckman Mystery* (1954) and the popular comedy *Raising a Riot* (1955). All were handled with professionalism and a degree of style. On KORDA's death in 1956 her contract moved to Rank where she continued to show an aptitude for making box-office hits with the romantic comedy *All for Mary* (1956) and a nautical farce *True as a Turtle* (1956). Her last completed feature film was *We Joined the Navy* (1962) which mined a similar vein. After one further short film, she crossed over into television eventually filming a second version of *The Stranger Left No Card* (1981) as part of the successful *Tales of the Unexpected* series. She continued to direct for the theatre well into the 1990s.

Although her output may appear relatively modest (she was certainly constrained by the requirements of the studio system of the 1950s), Wendy Toye is an important, groundbreaking figure in the male-dominated world of British cinema. With her consummate profession-alism and instinct for populist entertainment, she proved categorically that a woman could work efficiently in the role of director and helped to pave the way for later generations of women film-makers.

**British Feature Films:** *The Teckman Mystery* (1954); *Three Cases of Murder* (1955, one segment); *Raising a Riot* (1955); *All for Mary* (1956); *True as a Turtle* (1956); *We Joined the Navy* (1962).

**Bibliography:** Caroline Merz, 'The Tensions of Genre: Wendy Toye and Muriel Box', and Wheeler Winston Dixon, 'An Interview with Wendy Toye', in Wheeler Winston Dixon (ed.), *Re-Viewing British Cinema 1900–1992* (Albany, NY: State University of New York Press, 1994).

## Marcel VARNEL

Of all British directors, Marcel Varnel is probably the one most closely associated with the musical hall comedy style which was in its heyday in the 1930s. He directed three vehicles for Arthur Askey, eight for Will Hay and nine for George Formby as well as four featuring the Crazy Gang. For a director known for such characteristically British fare it's ironic that Varnel was actually born in Paris on 16 October 1894 as Marcel Hyacinth Le Bozec. He attended Charterhouse and the French Conservatory of Dramatic Arts, before starting his career as a stage actor in Paris. He switched to directing musical comedies and in 1925 made a successful move to Broadway. His first films were made in Hollywood in the early 1930s and were mainly stage adaptations, but in 1934 he moved again, this time to Britain.

His British career started with a series of long forgotten musicals and comedies, but his future path was cemented by *Good Morning, Boys!* (1937) which made a big screen star of music hall comedian Will Hay. Varnel's theatrical training stood him in good stead and he was able to fashion sympathetic vehicles for British comics of the period which effectively displayed their individual talents. Askey's chirpy persona is at its best in *Band Waggon* (1940), based on his long-running radio show, while *Alf's Button Afloat* (1938) is a fine record of the surreal anarchy of the Crazy Gang. The Formby vehicles were too often threadbare productions which mechanically overworked George's already well established character as a cheerfully gormless northerner, but audiences couldn't get enough. The best of the bunch are *Turned Out Nice Again* (1941) and the entertaining wartime propaganda piece *Let George Do It!* (1940). The most memorable of all Varnel's work was done with Will Hay. His cynical, bumbling persona, usually in the form of some disreputable authority figure (teacher, policeman, stationmaster), has survived changes in audience tastes better than the other comics Varnel worked with. *Ask a Policeman* (1939) is a briskly handled farce, but their finest hour together came with the joyful *Oh, Mr Porter!* (1937) which probably encapsulates the music hall comedy better than any other film. An unofficial reworking of Arnold Ridley's *The Ghost Train*, it builds up a fine head of steam with some skilfully executed slapstick routines and caustically dry one-liners.

Varnel neatly adapted his approach to the patriotic demands of wartime cinema with films like Will Hay's *The Ghost of St Michael's* (1941), but by the end of the war the genre was already losing its popular appeal, not helped by the rather tired-looking later vehicles for Formby. With his career in decline Varnel returned to the theatre, but his progress was brought to a violent end when he was killed in a car accident on 13 July 1947. In his best work, Varnel preserved on film the talents of a generation of top British comedians and provided audiences with some of the most popular films of the 1930s and early 1940s. Although this type of humour may be out of favour with current audiences, it has an inventiveness and anti-authoritarian vigour which certainly hit a nerve with contemporary audiences. Its legacy can be seen in the Norman Wisdom films of the 1950s and the much-loved Carry On series in the 1960s.

**British Feature Films:** *Freedom of the Seas* (1934); *Girls Will Be Boys* (1934); *Dance Band* (1935); *No Monkey Business* (1935); *I Give My Heart* (1935); *Royal Cavalcade* (1935, co-director); *All In* (1936); *Public Nuisance No. 1* (1936); *Good Morning, Boys!* (1937); *Oh, Mr Porter!* (1937); *O-Kay for Sound* (1937); *Alf's Button Afloat* (1938); *Convict 99* (1938); *Hey! Hey! USA!* (1938); *Old Bones of the River* (1938); *The Frozen Limits* (1939); *'Where's That Fire?'* (1939); *Ask a Policeman* (1939); *Band Waggon* (1940); *Gasbags* (1940); *Let George Do It!* (1940); *Neutral Port* (1940); *The Ghost of St Michael's* (1941); *South American George* (1941); *Turned Out Nice Again* (1941); *Hi, Gang!* (1941); *I Thank You* (1941); *The Net* (1941); *King Arthur Was a Gentleman*

(1942); *Much Too Shy* (1942); *Get Cracking* (1943); *He Snoops to Conquer* (1944); *Bell-Bottom George* (1944); *I Didn't Do It* (1945); *George in Civvy Street* (1946); *This Man Is Mine* (1946)

**Bibliography:** Robert Murphy, *Realism and Tinsel: Cinema and Society in Britain, 1939–49* (London: Routledge, 1989); David Sutton, *A Chorus of Raspberries: British Film Comedy 1929–1939* (Exeter: University of Exeter Press, 2000).

$$\boxed{W}$$

### Pete WALKER

In the 1970s, with Hammer studios in decline, the fate of the British horror film fell to a group of film-makers schooled in the lower reaches of exploitation cinema. Rising to the top was Pete Walker, who brought a sufficiently individual approach to the genre to establish a blood-soaked cult reputation. His sombre, macabre oeuvre is testament to a strikingly pessimistic sensibility, perfectly mirroring the dreary disillusionment of the 1970s.

Walker was born in Brighton in January 1939. His father was the popular comedian Syd Walker and his mother a chorus girl, but following his father's death in 1945 he spent a dislocated childhood in orphanages, foster homes and Catholic schools. From the late 1950s he worked intermittently as a film actor and a stand-up comedian, as well as behind the camera on television commercials, before establishing his own low-budget production company, Heritage Films (he went on to produce and finance all but one of the films he directed). In the 1960s he churned out 8 mm 'glamour' films, before making his first properly distributed feature with *I Like Birds* (1967). He continued to work independently in soft-core sexploitation with *School for Sex* (1968) and *Cool It Carol* (1970), gradually moving into suspense thrillers with *Man of Violence* (1970) and *Die Screaming, Marianne* (1971). He even tried his hand with 3D on *Four Dimensions of Greta* (1972).

It was with the baroque Grand Guignol and dark humour of *The Flesh and Blood Show* (1972) that Walker's characteristic approach to horror first really emerged. He followed it with the three films on which his reputation is based: *House of Whipcord* (1974), *Frightmare* (1974) and *House of Mortal Sin* (1975). Their graphic violence pushed them into territory where Hammer had never ventured, but their critical standing rests more on their allegorical qualities and the visual flair which Walker brought to potentially tawdry material. With their stories of cannibalistic families, institutional violence and psychotic priests, these films offer a commentary on 1970s Britain, balancing an attack on hypocritical authority with an almost equally grim portrait of a liberal, self-indulgent counterculture. The former is represented by ex-judges, Catholic priests and family matriarchs (these usually played chillingly by Sheila Keith) whose public morality hides acts of perverse cruelty, while the latter takes the form of well-meaning psychiatrists and naive do-gooders, as well as the immoral young, who usually underestimate the power of the corrupt establishment they are up against. The shocking images and deliberately grisly *mise en scène* also seem to capture eloquently the mood of the period. There are no reassuringly happy endings either, as the audience is left to ponder the triumph of the malevolent over the benign.

With *Schizo* (1976) and *The Comeback* (1978) Walker moved toward more conventional genre material, foreshadowing the development of the slasher movie of the 1980s. The latter film also exhibits his sense of irony in its use of the American crooner Jack Jones and by introducing an element of self-parody. Pastiche has largely taken over with *House of the Long Shadows* (1983) which rather wastes its larger than usual budget and an extraordinary cast of horror icons including Christopher Lee, Peter Cushing and Vincent Price. Walker's disillusionment with British film production in the 1980s led to his early retirement from film-making, as he turned to property dealing and restoring classic cinemas. His legacy is an exceptional contribution to a genre that Britain has frequently made its own, memorably reinventing the gothic horror to address the climate of the 1970s.

**British Feature Films:** *I Like Birds* (1967); *Strip Poker* (1968); *School for Sex* (1968); *Man of Violence* (1970); *Cool It Carol* (1970); *Die Screaming, Marianne* (1971); *Four Dimensions of Greta* (1972); *The Flesh and Blood Show* (1972); *Tiffany Jones* (1973); *House of Whipcord* (1974); *Frightmare* (1974); *House of Mortal Sin* (1975); *Schizo* (1976); *The Comeback* (1978); *Home Before Midnight* (1979); *House of the Long Shadows* (1983).

**Bibliography:** Steve Chibnall, *Making Mischief: The Cult Films of Pete Walker* (Guildford: FAB Press, 1998).

## Herbert WILCOX

Herbert Wilcox was born on 18 April 1890, probably in Cork, Ireland and was brought up in England. He worked as a journalist and served in the First World War before entering the industry in 1918 as a distributor. In the 1920s he formed the production company Graham-Wilcox with the director Graham Cutts and proved to be a pioneering producer and director, arranging German co-productions and using American stars like Dorothy Gish and Will Rogers to help market British films in the States. He was instrumental in creating British National and was later Head of Production at British and Dominions, as well as helping to establish Elstree Studios. His commercial acumen was apparent in his pursuit of technical innovation, which included early experiments with sound and colour. He made his directorial debut with a silent version of the stage musical *Chu Chin Chow* (1923) and scored a critical hit with *Dawn* (1928), the first of two films he was to make about the nurse Edith Cavell.

Wilcox was a prolific film-maker, directing over fifty films and producing twice that number. More than thirty of these films were vehicles for his wife, the actress Anna Neagle, whom he married in 1943. Their first film together was the musical romance *Goodnight Vienna* (1932) and they made a number of films in the same vein during the 1930s including *Limelight* (1936) and *London Melody* (1937). However, their most popular films were reverential biopics of historical figures, particularly *Victoria the Great* (1937) and its sequel *Sixty Glorious Years* (1938) which was shot in Technicolor. Rather less tasteful but more lively was *Nell Gwyn* (1934) which Wilcox had previously filmed in the silent period. He also continued to be a successful producer throughout the 1930s, filming a number of the Aldwych Farces starting with *Rookery Nook* (1930) and producing a series of comedy vehicles for Jack Buchanan.

During the early war years, Wilcox and Neagle worked for RKO in Hollywood, but they returned to Britain to make *They Flew Alone* (1942) about the aviator Amy Johnson. Although *Yellow Canary* (1943) offered more in the way of patriotic drama, their most memorable work of the 1940s was the so-called 'London romances' which began with *I Live in Grosvenor Square* (1945). Neagle was cast initially opposite the American Dean Jagger, but in *Piccadilly Incident* (1946), *Spring in Park Lane* (1948) and *Maytime in Mayfair* (1949) she was partnered by Michael Wilding. The series became increasingly fantastical, offering the austerity audiences of postwar Britain escape into a fantasy of upper-class life, replete with lavish ball scenes and aristocrats disguised as butlers. *The Courtneys of Curzon Street* (1947) offered a period variation on the style, with its depiction of three generations of romances that break class divides. Although dated now, these films were among the most successful of the period.

Wilcox's work in the 1950s seemed to ape the impact of his earlier films, with *The Lady with a Lamp* (1951) portraying Florence Nightingale in typically romanticised manner and *Lilacs in the Spring* (1955) allowing Neagle to play Nell Gwyn and Queen Victoria again in one film. The strongest of his later films is *Odette* (1950), a surprisingly tough, moving portrait of a French resistance agent played with considerable power by Neagle. Wilcox's final throw of the dice came with a series of ill-advised films in the late 1950s that tried to cash in on the emerging youth culture. These began with the lurid *My Teenage Daughter* (1956) and continued with vehicles for the pop singer Frankie Vaughan including *These Dangerous Years* (1957) and *The Heart of a Man* (1959). He found it difficult to get ventures off the ground in the 1960s and was eventually declared bankrupt. He died in London on 15 May 1977.

Wilcox the director is rather overshadowed by Wilcox the producer, who always retained his independence and kept afloat financially for four decades, a record rivalled by very few other British producers. As a director, he was a more than serviceable craftsman with an astute eye for commercial trends. With his wife he formed one of the most unusual partnerships in British cinema, offering audiences escapist entertainment which often harked back to an imagined golden age of class deference and national pride.

**British Feature Films:** *Chu Chin Chow* (1923); *Decameron Nights* (1924); *Southern Love* (1924); *Nell Gwyn* (1926); *The Only Way* (1926); *London* (1926); *Madame Pompadour* (1927); *Mumsie* (1927); *Dawn* (1928); *Tiptoes* (1928); *The Bondman* (1929); *The Woman in White* (1929); *The Loves of Robert Burns* (1930); *The Chance of a Night-Time* (1931); *Carnival* (1931); *Goodnight Vienna* (1932); *The Blue Danube* (1932); *Money Means Nothing* (1932); *Bitter Sweet* (1933); *The King's Cup* (1933); *The Little Damozel* (1933); *Yes Mr Brown* (1933); *Nell Gwyn* (1934); *The Queen's Affair* (1934); *Peg of Old Drury* (1935); *Limelight* (1936); *This'll Make you Whistle* (1936); *The Three Maxims* (1936); *London Melody* (1937); *Victoria the Great* (1937); *Sixty Glorious Years* (1938); *They Flew Alone* (1942); *Yellow Canary* (1943); *I Live in Grosvenor Square* (1945); *Piccadilly Incident* (1946); *The Courtneys of Curzon Street* (1947); *Elizabeth of Ladymead* (1948); *Spring in Park Lane* (1948); *Maytime in Mayfair* (1949); *Into the Blue* (1950); *Odette* (1950); *The Lady with a Lamp* (1951); *Derby Day* (1952); *Trent's Last Case* (1952); *Laughing Annie* (1953); *Trouble in the Glen* (1954); *King's Rhapsody* (1955); *Lilacs in the Spring* (1955); *My Teenage Daughter* (1956); *The Man Who Wouldn't Talk* (1957); *Wonderful Things* (1957);

*These Dangerous Years* (1957); *The Lady Is a Square* (1958); *The Heart of a Man* (1958).

**Bibliography:** Herbert Wilcox, *Twenty-Five Thousand Sunsets: The Autobiography of Herbert Wilcox* (London: Bodley Head, 1967).

## Michael WINNER

Michael Winner is one of the best known British film-makers with the general public, as recognisable these days for his appearances in television commercials as for his films. He has been a largely un-pretentious director of mainstream entertainment films throughout his career, riding the waves of changing public taste with considerable commercial acumen. Critics have tended to either ignore his work or revile it as crude exploitation, but in a national cinema often accused of timidity, his has been a notably blunt, brash contribution.

Winner was born on 30 October 1935 in London. His parents were Jewish immigrants, his mother Polish and his father Russian. He was educated at a Quaker boarding school and then read law at Cambridge. From an early age he showed the self-confidence and determination that have marked his career, becoming a newspaper gossip columnist at fourteen. He worked in television with the BBC from the mid-1950s and then served his apprenticeship in the film industry on shorts and 'B' movies, working as assistant director, scriptwriter and eventually director. In his later career he often had a hand in the scripts he filmed and liked to produce for his own company. His willingness to take on low-rent commercial chores without flinching was apparent from the beginning with the soft-porn 'nudie' *Some Like It Cool* (1961).

He moved into the mainstream with *Play It Cool* (1962), a musical aimed at the emerging youth market and featuring British pop stars Billy Fury and Helen Shapiro. Winner has always shown an ability to latch on to current audience trends, so this was followed by *The Cool Mikado* (1962), an updated version of Gilbert and Sullivan's operetta. He tried for New Wave-style social realism in *West 11* (1963), a portrait of London's homeless drifters, and for more traditional knockabout comedy with *You Must be Joking!* (1965), featuring such reliable performers at Terry-Thomas and Lionel Jeffries. He really hit his stride as Swinging London began to take off, directing several films that have verve as well as an eye for the changing social scene. He shows assurance and lightness of touch with the ironic seaside farce *The System* (1964), panache on the caper film *The Jokers* (1966) and an easy-going warmth with *Hannibal Brooks* (1969), where Oliver Reed is the Second World War POW escaping across the Alps on an elephant.

Reed also starred in both the earlier films and in *I'll Never Forget What's 'Is Name* (1967), a more serious, critical depiction of 1960s values. *The Jokers* and *Hannibal Brooks* benefited from tight scripting by television sitcom veterans Dick Clement and Ian Le Frenais. These films are sometimes flashy and superficial, but they also manage a degree of charm, as well as capturing the current British scene with some veracity. They remain the most agreeable of Winner's output.

With Winner's approach to film-making, it was perhaps inevitable that he would move onto a wider stage. *The Games* (1969) is a big-budget international film depicting preparations for the Olympics and finishing with an excitingly staged marathon race. Having proved his professionalism, Winner headed for Hollywood where, during the 1970s and 1980s, he was a reliable producer of formulaic genre movies covering horror, westerns, film noir and particularly action films. His regular star was the stony-faced Charles Bronson who plays a succession of tough loners meeting out justice at the point of a gun to a world full of malevolent bad guys. Most controversial of these films was *Death Wish* (1974), a violent vigilante movie which gave full expression to the reactionary political and moral views which Winner was to make public on a number of occasions. The liberal press was horrified, but that didn't stop Winner from churning out two sequels as the customers kept coming. The hypocrisy of making films which condemn violent crime while simultaneously exalting in gratuitous brutality as entertainment seems to have completely bypassed Winner.

He made regular visits to Britain during the 1970s, including the lurid shocker *The Nightcomers* (1971) with Marlon Brando and a version of Raymond Chandler's *The Big Sleep* (1978) which curiously shifted its setting from California to London. He returned on a more permanent basis in the 1980s as his Hollywood career waned. He made a crude, but vigorous remake of Gainsborough's *The Wicked Lady* (1983), complete with a female whip-fighting sequence, while *Appointment with Death* (1988) was a proficient Agatha Christie adaptation. *A Chorus of Disapproval* (1989) offered a surprisingly well-judged, sympathetic version of Alan Ayckbourn's play, but he courted controversy again with *Dirty Weekend* (1993), a reworking of *Death Wish* with a female rape victim handing out the instant justice this time. His most recent outing was the inept revenge black comedy, *Parting Shots* (1998).

In more recent years Winner's interest in cinema seems to have taken second place to leading campaigns to recognise police heroism and writing restaurant reviews for Sunday newspapers. Winner's films have frequently antagonised with their simplistic values, predictable genre elements and gleeful brutality. His directorial style has won him few friends, veering from the extravagance of his 1960s movies to the pared down, anonymous approach of his more recent work. None of this criticism is likely to cut much ice with Winner, who has consistently defied the brickbats and got on with making the films that he believes audiences want to see.

**British Feature Films:** *Shoot to Kill* (1960); *Old Mac* (1960); *Out of the Shadow* (1961); *Some Like It Cool* (1961); *Play It Cool* (1962); *The Cool Mikado* (1962); *West 11* (1963); *The System* (1964); *You Must be Joking!* (1965); *The Jokers* (1966); *I'll Never Forget What's 'Is Name* (1967); *Hannibal Brooks* (1969); *The Games* (1969); *The Nightcomers* (1971); *The Big Sleep* (1978); *Firepower* (1979); *The Wicked Lady* (1983); *Appointment with Death* (1988); *A Chorus of Disapproval* (1989); *Dirty Weekend* (1993); *Parting Shots* (1998).

**Bibliography:** Bill Harding, *The Films of Michael Winner* (London: Frederick Muller, 1978).

## Michael WINTERBOTTOM

Michael Winterbottom, who was born on 29 March 1961 in Blackburn, is one of the most impressive talents to have emerged from contemporary British cinema. After studying English at Oxford and then taking a film course at Bristol University, he began his professional career working in television. He graduated from editing to direction,

working on a number of television series and films including *Forget About Me* (1990), the first of several collaborations with writer Frank Cottrell Boyce, and the IRA drama *Love Lies Bleeding* (1993). In 1995 he formed the production company Revolution Films with Andrew Eaton and made his theatrical debut with *Butterfly Kiss* (1995). An original talent is already apparent in this haunting depiction of the relationship between two women, one of whom is revealed to be a serial killer and the other her eventual accomplice and lover. The film never quite lives up to its own pretensions, but elicits strong performances from its two leads (Amanda Plummer and Saskia Reeves) and captures a cinematically unfamiliar England of dreary motorway service stations and chance meetings.

An iconoclastic temperament is evident in *Jude* (1996), a version of the first half of Thomas Hardy's classic novel. The author's Victorian tragedy is rendered in suitably austere, melancholy images which are a long way from the picturesque Merchant-Ivory approach to literary adaptation. Christopher Eccleston plays the eponymous hero with memorable intensity. Hardy also provides the basic narrative for *The Claim* (2000), loosely adapted from *The Mayor of Casterbridge*. The setting has been shifted from rural Dorset to America's Sierra Nevada during the nineteenth-century gold rush, but there is a similar concern for individuals destroyed by a combination of their own character traits and the unavoidable forces of progress. Winterbottom returned to contemporary subject matter in *Welcome to Sarajevo* (1997). Drawn from the experiences of journalist Michael Nicholson, it depicts the war in the Balkans through a mixture of fact and fiction, cinematic recreation and archive footage, creating an overpowering sense of immediacy and emotional involvement. The film is direct in its criticism of the West's failure to act quickly enough to stop the suffering taking place.

Winterbottom is nothing if not eclectic. His next film, *I Want You* (1998), was an unsettling account of romantic obsession set against a backdrop of asylum-seekers in the coastal town of Hastings, with elements of violence and voyeurism. Again, he seemed as interested in the location, which is used atmospherically, and the sympathetic depiction of social outsiders as in any standard generic formula. Location is also key to *Wonderland* (1999), a partially experimental portrait of the lives of three young Londoners which vividly captures the capital as a place of possibility and frustration, teeming with life and yet lonely. Using grainy digital video, jagged editing and fluid camera-work, the film is another meditation on individuals estranged from their surroundings and each other, searching for meaning in their lives. London is exchanged for Manchester in *24 Hour Party People* (2002), a nostalgic journey through the city's illustrious pop music scene over the course of twenty years, based on the career of pioneering record company executive Tony Wilson played by comedian Steve Coogan.

The experiences of the socially excluded are again central to *In This World* (2002), which follows the journey of an Afghan refugee from Pakistan to London. The topicality of the story is reinforced by having the central role played by a real-life, fifteen-year-old refugee. For *Code 46* (2003) Winterbottom moved into the genre of science fiction, setting its love story in a futuristic totalitarian state with echoes of George Orwell. The film makes characteristically striking use of the cityscape of modern-day Shanghai. He courted controversy with the sexually explicit *9 Songs* (2004) which charts the progress and disintegration of a relationship purely through its physical dimension, with the narrative structured by nine concerts which the couple attend together. Despite tabloid outrage, the film is surprisingly restrained and even austere in its depiction of the characters.

He worked with Steve Coogan again on *A Cock and Bull Story* (2005), an updated version of Laurence Sterne's *Tristram Shandy* which handles the novel's considerable complexities by portraying two actors involved in the making of an adaptation of the novel. The conceit works neatly, preserving the original's meditations on the nature of storytelling while allowing Winterbottom to play with the established comic personas of Coogan and his co-star Rob Brydon. Winterbottom has continued to work in television making *With or Without You* (1999), a bleak account of marital breakdown which was given a limited cinema release, and most recently *The Road to Guantánamo* (2006) which mixes documentary and reconstruction to tell of the three British Muslims held by the American authorities following 9/11 who were subsequently released without charge. Again the director shows a concern with those caught up in the machinations of international politics. As an executive producer he has helped to foster the work of other young British film-makers including Marc Evans.

Winterbottom is a remarkably prolific film-maker, with eleven features completed in the same number of years. The range of subjects has been highly diverse, incorporating genre elements, literary adaptation and stories torn from the headlines. His films often combine realism with an experimental aesthetic which mirrors his passion for European art cinema giants like Fassbinder and Fellini. They have been showered with international awards, including a Golden Bear at Berlin for *In This World* and three nominations for the Palme d'Or at Cannes. The result is a body of work which has already established him as the outstanding new director working in Britain since the 1990s.

**British Feature Films:** *Butterfly Kiss* (1995); *Jude* (1996); *Welcome to Sarajevo* (1997); *I Want You* (1998); *Wonderland* (1999); *The Claim* (2000); *24 Hour Party People* (2002); *In This World* (2002); *Code 46* (2003); *9 Songs* (2004); *A Cock and Bull Story* (2005).

**Bibliography:** Neil Sinyard and Melanie Williams, ' "Living in a World That Did Not Want Them": Michael Winterbottom and the Unpopular British Cinema', *Journal of Popular British Cinema*, 5 114–23.

$$\boxed{Y}$$

## Terence YOUNG

Terence Young enjoyed a lengthy career as a solidly proficient director of mainstream entertainment films but preserves a special niche in the history of British cinema for his central involvement in the creation of the long-running series of James Bond films. He was born in Shanghai, China on 20 June 1915, studied at Cambridge and entered the industry as a scriptwriter in 1936. After service as a paratrooper during the Second World War (he was wounded at Arnhem), he made his directorial debut with *Corridor of Mirrors* in 1948, a psychological melodrama featuring Eric Portman. He quickly established himself as a safe pair of hands in a variety of genres ranging from war adventures like *They Were Not Divided* (1950) and *The Red Beret* (1953) to musical comedy with *One Night With You* (1948), period solemnities in *That Lady* (1955) and imperial heroics with *Storm Over the Nile* (1955).

Little of Young's work from the 1950s is of any lasting interest, although the 'social problem' film *Serious Charge* (1959) handled the topical issue of homosexuality with restraint and thoughtfulness. The relatively routine job of helming a modestly budgeted adaptation of Ian Fleming's *Dr No* (1962) turned out to be one of the defining moments of British cinema. The casting of Sean Connery as Bond was crucial, but Young showed more than mere proficiency in balancing the action, sex and exotic locales which distinguished the formula. The result was a cultural phenomenon and Young was to return to Bondage on two further occasions. *Thunderball* (1965) is a slightly predictable series entry with only its spectacular underwater scenes to make it stand out, but *From Russia With Love* (1963) would get the nod of many fans as the high point of the whole Bond pantheon. Its fantasy violence and easy sex were skilfully undercut by shafts of black humour and self-parody.

Young never really regained such giddy heights and many of his 1960s films were muddled European co-productions. He faired little better in Hollywood where he was resident for most of the 1970s making such aberrations as *The Klansman* (1974) and the bizarre *Inchon* (1981), although the earlier suspense thriller *Wait Until Dark* (1967) with Audrey Hepburn is handled with style. His later British films range from the heavy-handed period romance *Mayerling* (1968) to the undistinguished spy yarn *The Jigsaw Man* (1983). Young was never less than a highly professional craftsman who showed a particular skill with set-pieces, but with his three Bond films he helped to establish the most successful cinematic franchise British cinema has yet produced and thereby ensured his place in its story. He died in Cannes, France on 7 September 1994.

**British Feature Films:** *Corridor of Mirrors* (1948); *One Night With You* (1948); *Woman Hater* (1948); *They Were Not Divided* (1950); *Valley of Eagles* (1951); *Tall Headlines* (1952); *The Red Beret* (1953); *Storm Over the Nile* (1955); *That Lady* (1955); *Safari* (1956); *Zarak* (1956); *Action of the Tiger* (1957); *No Time to Die* (1958); *Serious Charge* (1959); *Too Hot to Handle* (1960); *Dr No* (1962); *From Russia With Love* (1963); *Thunderball* (1965); *The Amorous Adventures of Moll Flanders* (1965); *Triple Cross* (1966); *Mayerling* (1968); *The Jigsaw Man* (1984).

**Bibliography:** James Chapman, *Licence to Thrill: A Cultural History of the James Bond Films* (London: I. B. Tauris, 1999).

# British Feature Film Titles Cited

| | |
|---|---|
| *2001: A Space Odyssey* | Stanley Kubrick |
| *21 Days* | Basil Dean |
| *24 Hour Party People* | Michael Winterbottom |
| *28 Days Later* | Danny Boyle |
| *39 Steps, The (1935)* | Alfred Hitchcock |
| *39 Steps, The (1958)* | Ralph Thomas |
| *49th Parallel* | Michael Powell |
| *80,000 Suspects* | Val Guest |
| *8½ Women* | Peter Greenaway |
| *9 Songs* | Michael Winterbottom |
| | |
| *Abominable Snowman, The* | Val Guest |
| *Above us the Waves* | Ralph Thomas |
| *Academy Decides, The* | John Baxter |
| *Accident* | Joseph Losey |
| *Aces High* | Jack Gold |
| *Action of the Tiger* | Terence Young |
| *Admirable Crichton, The* | Lewis Gilbert |
| *Adventures of Baron Munchausen, The* | Terry Gilliam |
| *Ae Fond Kiss* | Ken Loach |
| *Against the Wind* | Charles Crichton |
| *Age of Consent* | Michael Powell |
| *Albert RN* | Lewis Gilbert |
| *Alf's Button* | Cecil Hepworth |
| *Alf's Button Afloat* | Marcel Varnel |
| *Alfie* | Lewis Gilbert |
| *Alien Love Triangle* | Danny Boyle |
| *All for Mary* | Wendy Toye |
| *All In* | Marcel Varnel |
| *All Night Long* | Basil Dearden |
| *All or Nothing* | Mike Leigh |
| *Alligator Named Daisy, An* | J. Lee Thompson |
| *Amorous Adventures of Moll Flanders, The* | Terence Young |
| *And Now the Screaming Starts!* | Roy Ward Baker |
| *Angel* | Neil Jordan |

| | |
|---|---|
| *Angela's Ashes* | Alan Parker |
| *Angelic Conversation, The* | Derek Jarman |
| *Animal Farm* | John Halas and Joy Batchelor |
| *Anna the Adventuress* | Cecil Hepworth |
| *Annie Laurie* | Cecil Hepworth |
| *Anniversary, The* | Roy Ward Baker |
| *Another Shore* | Charles Crichton |
| *Appointment in London* | Philip Leacock |
| *Appointment with Death* | Michael Winner |
| *Appointment with Venus* | Ralph Thomas |
| *Arcadians, The* | Victor Saville |
| *Arsenal Stadium Mystery, The* | Thorold Dickinson |
| *As Long as They're Happy* | J. Lee Thompson |
| *Ask a Policeman* | Marcel Varnel |
| *Assassination Bureau Limited, The* | Basil Dearden |
| *Assassination of Trotsky, The* | Joseph Losey |
| *Assignment K* | Val Guest |
| *Astonished Heart, The* | Terence Fisher |
| *Asylum* | Roy Ward Baker |
| *Au Pair Girls* | Val Guest |
| *Autumn Crocus* | Basil Dean |
| *Awakening, The* | Mike Newell |
| *Awfully Big Adventure, An* | Mike Newell |
| | |
| *Baby of Macon, The* | Peter Greenaway |
| *Baby on the Barge, The* | Cecil Hepworth |
| *Bad Blood* | Mike Newell |
| *Bad Timing* | Nicolas Roeg |
| *Band Waggon* | Marcel Varnel |
| *Bank Holiday* | Carol Reed |
| *Barnacle Bill* | Charles Frend |
| *Barry Lyndon* | Stanley Kubrick |
| *Basilisk, The* | Cecil Hepworth |
| *Battle of Britain* | Guy Hamilton |
| *Battle of the River Plate, The* | Michael Powell |
| *Battle of the Sexes, The* | Charles Crichton |
| *Beachcomber, The* | Muriel Box |
| *Beauty Jungle, The* | Val Guest |
| *Bed Sitting Room, The* | Richard Lester |
| *Bees in Paradise* | Val Guest |
| *Before Winter Comes* | J. Lee Thompson |
| *Before You Go* | Lewis Gilbert |
| *Bell-Bottom George* | Marcel Varnel |
| *Belles of St Trinian's, The* | Frank Launder |
| *Bells Go Down, The* | Basil Dearden |
| *Belly of an Architect, The* | Peter Greenaway |
| *Bend It Like Beckham* | Gurinder Chadha |
| *Better 'Ole, The* | George Pearson |
| *Better Late than Never* | Bryan Forbes |

| | |
|---|---|
| *Bhaji on the Beach* | Gurinder Chadha |
| *Big Blockade, The* | Charles Frend |
| *Big Job, The* | Gerald Thomas |
| *Big Sleep, The* | Michael Winner |
| *Biggest Bank Robbery, The* | Ralph Thomas |
| *Billion Dollar Brain* | Ken Russell |
| *Billy Liar* | John Schlesinger |
| *Billy the Kid and the Green Baize Vampire* | Alan Clarke |
| *Birds of a Feather* | John Baxter |
| *Birds of Prey* | Basil Dean |
| *Bitter Moon* | Roman Polanski |
| *Bitter Sweet* | Herbert Wilcox |
| *Black Jack* | Ken Loach |
| *Black Narcissus* | Michael Powell |
| *Black Sheep of Whitehall, The* | Basil Dearden |
| *Blackmail* | Alfred Hitchcock |
| *Blame It on the Bellboy* | Mark Herman |
| *Bleak Moments* | Mike Leigh |
| *Bless this House* | Gerald Thomas |
| *Blind Date* | Joseph Losey |
| *Blithe Spirit* | David Lean |
| *Blood Orange* | Terence Fisher |
| *Blue* | Derek Jarman |
| *Blue Danube, The* | Herbert Wilcox |
| *Blue Lagoon, The* | Frank Launder |
| *Blue Lamp, The* | Basil Dearden |
| *Blue Murder at St Trinian's* | Frank Launder |
| *Blue Scar* | Jill Craigie |
| *Bluebeard's Castle* | Michael Powell |
| *Body Said No!, The* | Val Guest |
| *Bofors Gun, The* | Jack Gold |
| *Bondman, The* | Herbert Wilcox |
| *Boom* | Joseph Losey |
| *Bostonians, The* | James Ivory |
| *Boy Friend, The* | Ken Russell |
| *Boy Who Stole a Million, The* | Charles Crichton |
| *Boy Who Turned Yellow, The* | Michael Powell |
| *Boys, The* | Sidney J. Furie |
| *Boys in Blue, The* | Val Guest |
| *Brassed Off* | Mark Herman |
| *Brave Don't Cry, The* | Philip Leacock |
| *Brazil* | Terry Gilliam |
| *Break in the Circle* | Val Guest |
| *Breakfast on Pluto* | Neil Jordan |
| *Bridal Path, The* | Frank Launder |
| *Bride and Prejudice* | Gurinder Chadha |
| *Brides of Dracula, The* | Terence Fisher |
| *Bridge on the River Kwai, The* | David Lean |
| *Bridge Too Far, A* | Richard Attenborough |

| | |
|---|---|
| *Brief Encounter* | David Lean |
| *Brighton Rock* | John Boulting |
| *Britannia Hospital* | Lindsay Anderson |
| *Brothers in Law* | Roy Boulting |
| *Browning Version, The (1951)* | Anthony Asquith |
| *Browning Version, The (1994)* | Mike Figgis |
| *Bugsy Malone* | Alan Parker |
| *Butcher Boy, The* | Neil Jordan |
| *Butterfly Kiss* | Michael Winterbottom |
| | |
| *Cage of Gold* | Basil Dearden |
| *Calling Bulldog Drummond* | Victor Saville |
| *Camp on Blood Island, The* | Val Guest |
| *Campbell's Kingdom* | Ralph Thomas |
| *Canterbury Tale, A* | Michael Powell |
| *Captain Boycott* | Frank Launder |
| *Captive Heart, The* | Basil Dearden |
| *Caravaggio* | Derek Jarman |
| *Card, The* | Ronald Neame |
| *Career Girls* | Mike Leigh |
| *Carla's Song* | Ken Loach |
| *Carlton-Browne of the F.O.* | Roy Boulting |
| *Carnival* | Herbert Wilcox |
| *Carrington VC* | Anthony Asquith |
| *Carry On Abroad* | Gerald Thomas |
| *Carry On Admiral* | Val Guest |
| *Carry On Again Doctor* | Gerald Thomas |
| *Carry On at Your Convenience* | Gerald Thomas |
| *Carry On Behind* | Gerald Thomas |
| *Carry On Cabby* | Gerald Thomas |
| *Carry On Camping* | Gerald Thomas |
| *Carry On Cleo* | Gerald Thomas |
| *Carry On Columbus* | Gerald Thomas |
| *Carry On Constable* | Gerald Thomas |
| *Carry On Cowboy* | Gerald Thomas |
| *Carry On Cruising* | Gerald Thomas |
| *Carry On Dick* | Gerald Thomas |
| *Carry On Doctor* | Gerald Thomas |
| *Carry On Don't Lose Your Head* | Gerald Thomas |
| *Carry On Emmanuel* | Gerald Thomas |
| *Carry On England* | Gerald Thomas |
| *Carry On Follow That Camel* | Gerald Thomas |
| *Carry On Girls* | Gerald Thomas |
| *Carry On Henry* | Gerald Thomas |
| *Carry On Jack* | Gerald Thomas |
| *Carry On Loving* | Gerald Thomas |
| *Carry On Matron* | Gerald Thomas |
| *Carry On Nurse* | Gerald Thomas |
| *Carry On Regardless* | Gerald Thomas |

| | |
|---|---|
| *Carry On Screaming* | Gerald Thomas |
| *Carry On Sergeant* | Gerald Thomas |
| *Carry On Spying* | Gerald Thomas |
| *Carry On Teacher* | Gerald Thomas |
| *Carry On Up the Jungle* | Gerald Thomas |
| *Carry On Up the Khyber* | Gerald Thomas |
| *Carve Her Name With Pride* | Lewis Gilbert |
| *Cash* | Zoltán Korda |
| *Casino Royale* | Val Guest |
| *Cast a Dark Shadow* | Lewis Gilbert |
| *Castaway* | Nicolas Roeg |
| *Catch Us If You Can* | John Boorman |
| *Chain, The* | Jack Gold |
| *Chain of Events* | Gerald Thomas |
| *Chalk Garden, The* | Ronald Neame |
| *Champagne* | Alfred Hitchcock |
| *Champagne Charlie* | Alberto Cavalcanti |
| *Chance of a Night-Time, The* | Herbert Wilcox |
| *Chaplin* | Richard Attenborough |
| *Charge of the Light Brigade, The* | Tony Richardson |
| *Chariots of Fire* | Hugh Hudson |
| *Charley Moon* | Guy Hamilton |
| *Checkpoint* | Ralph Thomas |
| *Chicken Run* | Nick Park |
| *Child in the House* | Cy Endfield |
| *Children Galore* | Terence Fisher |
| *Chorus of Disapproval, A* | Michael Winner |
| *Chu Chin Chow* | Herbert Wilcox |
| *Circus Friends* | Gerald Thomas |
| *City of Joy* | Roland Joffé |
| *Claim, The* | Michael Winterbottom |
| *Climbing High* | Carol Reed |
| *Clockwork Orange, A* | Stanley Kubrick |
| *Clouded Yellow, The* | Ralph Thomas |
| *Cock and Bull Story, A* | Michael Winterbottom |
| *Code 46* | Michael Winterbottom |
| *Cold Mountain* | Anthony Minghella |
| *Colditz Story, The* | Guy Hamilton |
| *Colonel March Investigates* | Cy Endfield |
| *Comeback, The* | Pete Walker |
| *Comfort and Joy* | Bill Forsyth |
| *Comin' Thro' the Rye (1916 & 1923)* | Cecil Hepworth |
| *Commitments, The* | Alan Parker |
| *Common Touch, The* | John Baxter |
| *Company of Wolves, The* | Neil Jordan |
| *Comrades* | Bill Douglas |
| *Cone of Silence* | Charles Frend |
| *Confessions of a Window Cleaner* | Val Guest |
| *Consider your Verdict* | Roy Boulting |

| | |
|---|---|
| *Dead of Night* | Alberto Cavalcanti, Charles Crichton, Basil Dearden, Robert Hamer |
| *Deadfall* | Bryan Forbes |
| *Deadlier Than the Male* | Ralph Thomas |
| *Deadly Bees, The* | Freddie Francis |
| *Death and the Maiden* | Roman Polanski |
| *Decameron Nights* | Herbert Wilcox |
| *Delicate Balance, A* | Tony Richardson |
| *Demi-Paradise, The* | Anthony Asquith |
| *Derby Day* | Herbert Wilcox |
| *Devil Rides Out, The* | Terence Fisher |
| *Devil's Disciple, The* | Guy Hamilton |
| *Devils, The* | Ken Russell |
| *Diamond Mercenaries, The* | Val Guest |
| *Diamond Skulls* | Nick Broomfield |
| *Diamonds Are Forever* | Guy Hamilton |
| *Dictator, The* | Victor Saville |
| *Die Screaming, Marianne* | Pete Walker |
| *Dirty Pretty Things* | Stephen Frears |
| *Dirty Weekend* | Michael Winner |
| *Distant Trumpet* | Terence Fisher |
| *Distant Voices, Still Lives* | Terence Davies |
| *Divided Heart, The* | Charles Crichton |
| *Doctor and the Devils, The* | Freddie Francis |
| *Doctor at Large* | Ralph Thomas |
| *Doctor at Sea* | Ralph Thomas |
| *Doctor in Clover* | Ralph Thomas |
| *Doctor in Distress* | Ralph Thomas |
| *Doctor in Love* | Ralph Thomas |
| *Doctor in the House* | Ralph Thomas |
| *Doctor in Trouble* | Ralph Thomas |
| *Doctor Zhivago* | David Lean |
| *Doctor's Dilemma, The* | Anthony Asquith |
| *Dog and the Diamonds, The* | Ralph Thomas |
| *Doll's House, A* | Joseph Losey |
| *Don't Look Now* | Nicolas Roeg |
| *Doss House* | John Baxter |
| *Downhill* | Alfred Hitchcock |
| *Dr Blood's Coffin* | Sidney J. Furie |
| *Dr Jekyll and Sister Hyde* | Roy Ward Baker |
| *Dr No* | Terence Young |
| *Dr Strangelove* | Stanley Kubrick |
| *Dr Terror's House of Horror* | Freddie Francis |
| *Dracula* | Terence Fisher |
| *Dracula Has Risen from the Grave* | Freddie Francis |
| *Dracula Prince of Darkness* | Terence Fisher |
| *Dragon of Pendragon Castle, The* | John Baxter |
| *Draughtsman's Contract, The* | Peter Greenaway |
| *Dreaming* | John Baxter |

| | |
|---|---|
| *Drowning by Numbers* | Peter Greenaway |
| *Drum, The* | Zoltán Korda |
| *Duke Wore Jeans, The* | Gerald Thomas |
| *During One Night* | Sidney J. Furie |
| | |
| *Earth Dies Screaming, The* | Terence Fisher |
| *Easy Virtue* | Alfred Hitchcock |
| *Edge of the World, The* | Michael Powell |
| *Educating Rita* | Lewis Gilbert |
| *Edward II* | Derek Jarman |
| *Elephant Boy* | Zoltán Korda |
| *Elizabeth of Ladymead* | Herbert Wilcox |
| *Elusive Pimpernel, The* | Michael Powell |
| *Emerald Forest, The* | John Boorman |
| *Emergency Call* | Lewis Gilbert |
| *Enchanted April* | Mike Newell |
| *End of the Affair, The* | Neil Jordan |
| *Endless Night* | Sidney Gilliat |
| *English Patient, The* | Anthony Minghella |
| *Entertainer, The* | Tony Richardson |
| *Escapade* | Philip Leacock |
| *Escape* | Basil Dean |
| *Eureka* | Nicolas Roeg |
| *Europeans, The* | James Ivory |
| *Eve* | Joseph Losey |
| *Evening with the Royal Ballet, An* | Anthony Asquith |
| *Evensong* | Victor Saville |
| *Evergreen* | Victor Saville |
| *Evil of Frankenstein* | Freddie Francis |
| *Evil Under the Sun* | Guy Hamilton |
| *Evita* | Alan Parker |
| *Excaliber* | John Boorman |
| *Expresso Bongo* | Val Guest |
| *Eye of the Devil* | J. Lee Thompson |
| *Eyes Wide Shut* | Stanley Kubrick |
| *Eyewitness* | Muriel Box |
| | |
| *Face the Music* | Terence Fisher |
| *Faithful Heart, The* | Victor Saville |
| *Fall of the House of Usher, The* | Ken Russell |
| *Fallen Idol, The* | Carol Reed |
| *Fame is the Spur* | Roy Boulting |
| *Family Life* | Ken Loach |
| *Family Way, The* | John and Roy Boulting |
| *Fanny by Gaslight* | Anthony Asquith |
| *Far from the Madding Crowd* | John Schlesinger |
| *Farmer's Wife, The* | Alfred Hitchcock |
| *Father Brown* | Robert Hamer |
| *Fatherland* | Ken Loach |

| | |
|---|---|
| *Ferry to Hong Kong* | Lewis Gilbert |
| *Figures in a Landscape* | Joseph Losey |
| *Final Appointment* | Terence Fisher |
| *Final Test, The* | Anthony Asquith |
| *Firepower* | Michael Winner |
| *Fires Were Started* | Humphrey Jennings |
| *First a Girl* | Victor Saville |
| *First Gentleman, The* | Alberto Cavalcanti |
| *Fish Called Wanda, A* | Charles Crichton |
| *Flame in the Streets* | Roy Ward Baker |
| *Flash Gordon* | Mike Hodges |
| *Flaw, The* | Terence Fisher |
| *Flesh and Blood Show, The* | Pete Walker |
| *Flood Tide* | John Baxter |
| *Floods of Fear* | Charles Crichton |
| *Follow Me!* | Carol Reed |
| *Folly to be Wise* | Frank Launder |
| *For Better, For Worse* | J. Lee Thompson |
| *For Them That Trespass* | Alberto Cavalcanti |
| *For Those in Peril* | Charles Crichton |
| *Force Ten From Navarone* | Guy Hamilton |
| *Foreign Body* | Ronald Neame |
| *Foreman Went to France, The* | Charles Frend |
| *Forget Me Not* | Zoltán Korda |
| *Fortune Is a Woman* | Sidney Gilliat |
| *Fortune Lane* | John Baxter |
| *Four Dimensions of Greta* | Pete Walker |
| *Four Feathers, The* | Zoltán Korda |
| *Four Musketeers, The* | Richard Lester |
| *Four Sided Triangle* | Terence Fisher |
| *Four Weddings and a Funeral* | Mike Newell |
| *Frankenstein and the Monster From Hell* | Terence Fisher |
| *Frankenstein Created Woman* | Terence Fisher |
| *Frankenstein Must Be Destroyed* | Terence Fisher |
| *Freedom of the Seas* | Marcel Varnel |
| *Freedom Radio* | Anthony Asquith |
| *French Dressing* | Ken Russell |
| *French Lieutenant's Woman, The* | Karel Reisz |
| *French Mistress, A* | Roy Boulting |
| *French Without Tears* | Anthony Asquith |
| *Frenzy* | Alfred Hitchcock |
| *Friday the Thirteenth* | Victor Saville |
| *Frieda* | Basil Dearden |
| *Friends* | Lewis Gilbert |
| *Frightmare* | Pete Walker |
| *From Russia With Love* | Terence Young |
| *Frozen Limits, The* | Marcel Varnel |
| *Full Metal Jacket* | Stanley Kubrick |
| *Full Treatment, The* | Val Guest |

| | |
|---|---|
| *Funeral in Berlin* | Guy Hamilton |
| *Funny Thing Happened on the Way to the Forum, A* | Richard Lester |
| *Further up the Creek* | Val Guest |
| | |
| *Galileo* | Joseph Losey |
| *Gambit* | Ronald Neame |
| *Games, The* | Michael Winner |
| *Gandhi* | Richard Attenborough |
| *Garden, The* | Derek Jarman |
| *Gasbags* | Marcel Varnel |
| *Gaslight* | Thorold Dickinson |
| *General, The* | John Boorman |
| *Gentle Gunman, The* | Basil Dearden |
| *Geordie* | Frank Launder |
| *George in Civvy Street* | Marcel Varnel |
| *Get Back* | Richard Lester |
| *Get Carter* | Mike Hodges |
| *Get Cracking* | Marcel Varnel |
| *Ghost in the Noonday Sun* | Peter Medak |
| *Ghost of St Michael's, The* | Marcel Varnel |
| *Ghoul, The* | Freddie Francis |
| *Girl from Maxim's, The* | Alexander Korda |
| *Girl in the News, The* | Carol Reed |
| *Girl Must Live, A* | Carol Reed |
| *Girl on Approval* | Charles Frend |
| *Girls Will Be Boys* | Marcel Varnel |
| *Give Us the Moon* | Val Guest |
| *Go-Between, The* | Joseph Losey |
| *Gold Diggers, The* | Sally Potter |
| *Golden Bowl, The* | James Ivory |
| *Golden Salamander, The* | Ronald Neame |
| *Goldfinger* | Guy Hamilton |
| *Gone to Earth* | Michael Powell |
| *Good Companions, The (1956)* | J. Lee Thompson |
| *Good Companions, The (1933)* | Victor Saville |
| *Good Die Young, The* | Lewis Gilbert |
| *Good Father, The* | Mike Newell |
| *Good Morning, Boys!* | Marcel Varnel |
| *Good Thief, The* | Neil Jordan |
| *Goodnight Vienna* | Herbert Wilcox |
| *Goose Steps Out, The* | Basil Dearden |
| *Gorgon, The* | Terence Fisher |
| *Gothic* | Ken Russell |
| *Grand Escapade, The* | John Baxter |
| *Great Expectations* | David Lean |
| *Great St Trinian's Train Robbery, The* | Frank Launder and Sidney Gilliat |
| *Green for Danger* | Sidney Gilliat |
| *Greengage Summer, The* | Lewis Gilbert |

| | |
|---|---|
| *Gregory's Girl* | Bill Forsyth |
| *Gregory's Two Girls* | Bill Forsyth |
| *Grey Owl* | Richard Attenborough |
| *Greystoke* | Hugh Hudson |
| *Guinea Pig, The* | Roy Boulting |
| *Gumshoe* | Stephen Frears |
| *Guns of Darkness* | Anthony Asquith |
| *Guns of Navarone, The* | J. Lee Thompson |
| *Gypsy and the Gentleman, The* | Joseph Losey |
| | |
| *Halfway House, The* | Basil Dearden |
| *Hamlet (1948)* | Laurence Olivier |
| *Hamlet (1969)* | Tony Richardson |
| *Hamlet (1996)* | Kenneth Branagh |
| *Hand in Hand* | Philip Leacock |
| *Hannibal Brooks* | Michael Winner |
| *Happiest Days of Your Life, The* | Frank Launder |
| *Happy Family, The* | Muriel Box |
| *Happy Is the Bride* | Roy Boulting |
| *Hard Day's Night, A* | Richard Lester |
| *Haunted* | Lewis Gilbert |
| *He Snoops to Conquer* | Marcel Varnel |
| *He Who Rides a Tiger* | Charles Crichton |
| *Heart of a Man, The* | Herbert Wilcox |
| *Hearts of Humanity* | John Baxter |
| *Heat and Dust* | James Ivory |
| *Heaven's Above!* | John and Roy Boulting |
| *Hell Drivers* | Cy Endfield |
| *Hell Is a City* | Val Guest |
| *Help!* | Richard Lester |
| *Helter Skelter* | Ralph Thomas |
| *Henry V (1944)* | Laurence Olivier |
| *Henry V (1989)* | Kenneth Branagh |
| *Here Comes the Sun* | John Baxter |
| *Hey! Hey! USA!* | Marcel Varnel |
| *Hi, Gang!* | Marcel Varnel |
| *Hidden Agenda* | Ken Loach |
| *Hide and Seek* | Cy Endfield |
| *High Bright Sun, The* | Ralph Thomas |
| *High Command* | Thorold Dickinson |
| *High Hopes* | Mike Leigh |
| *High Tide at Noon* | Philip Leacock |
| *High Treason* | Roy Boulting |
| *High Wind in Jamaica, A* | Alexander Mackendrick |
| *Highly Dangerous* | Roy Ward Baker |
| *Hindle Wakes* | Victor Saville |
| *His Excellency* | Robert Hamer |
| *Hit, The* | Stephen Frears |
| *HMS Defiant* | Lewis Gilbert |

| | |
|---|---|
| *Innocent Sinners* | Philip Leacock |
| *Innocents, The* | Jack Clayton |
| *Inquest* | Roy Boulting |
| *Insignificance* | Nicolas Roeg |
| *Inspector Calls, An* | Guy Hamilton |
| *International Velvet* | Bryan Forbes |
| *Intimate Stranger, The* | Joseph Losey |
| *Into the Blue* | Herbert Wilcox |
| *Into the West* | Mike Newell |
| *Intruder, The* | Guy Hamilton |
| *Ipcress File, The* | Sidney J. Furie |
| *Iron Duke, The* | Victor Saville |
| *Iron Maiden, The* | Gerald Thomas |
| *Iron Petticoat, The* | Ralph Thomas |
| *Isadora* | Karel Reisz |
| *Island of Terror* | Terence Fisher |
| *It Always Rains on Sunday* | Robert Hamer |
| *It Happened in Paris* | Carol Reed |
| *It's 2' 6" Above the Ground* | Ralph Thomas |
| *It's a Wonderful World* | Val Guest |
| *It's Love Again* | Victor Saville |
| *It's Trad, Dad!* | Richard Lester |
| | |
| *Jabberwocky* | Terry Gilliam |
| *Jacqueline* | Roy Ward Baker |
| *Jamaica Inn* | Alfred Hitchcock |
| *Jet Storm* | Cy Endfield |
| *Jigsaw* | Val Guest |
| *Jigsaw Man, The* | Terence Young |
| *Jimmy Boy* | John Baxter |
| *Joey Boy* | Frank Launder |
| *Johnny Frenchman* | Charles Frend |
| *Johnny on the Run* | Lewis Gilbert |
| *Jokers, The* | Michael Winner |
| *Joseph Andrews* | Tony Richardson |
| *Josephine and Men* | Roy Boulting |
| *Journey Together* | John Boulting |
| *Jubilee* | Derek Jarman |
| *Jude* | Michael Winterbottom |
| *Judgment Deferred* | John Baxter |
| *Juggernaut* | Richard Lester |
| *Juno and the Paycock* | Alfred Hitchcock |
| *Just William's Luck* | Val Guest |
| *Juvenile Liaison* | Nick Broomfield |
| *Juvenile Liaison 2* | Nick Broomfield |
| | |
| *Kentucky Minstrels* | John Baxter |
| *Kes* | Ken Loach |
| *Key, The* | Carol Reed |

| | |
|---|---|
| *Khartoum* | Basil Dearden |
| *Kid for Two Farthings, A* | Carol Reed |
| *Kidnappers, The* | Philip Leacock |
| *Kill Me Tomorrow* | Terence Fisher |
| *Killing Fields, The* | Roland Joffé |
| *Kind Hearts and Coronets* | Robert Hamer |
| *Kind of Loving, A* | John Schlesinger |
| *King and Country* | Joseph Losey |
| *King Arthur Was a Gentleman* | Marcel Varnel |
| *King's Cup, The* | Herbert Wilcox |
| *King's Rhapsody* | Herbert Wilcox |
| *Kipps* | Carol Reed |
| *Kitty* | Victor Saville |
| *Knack, The* | Richard Lester |
| *Krays, The* | Peter Medak |
| | |
| *L-Shaped Room, The* | Bryan Forbes |
| *Laburnum Grove* | Carol Reed |
| *Lady Godiva Rides Again* | Frank Launder |
| *Lady Is a Square, The* | Herbert Wilcox |
| *Lady Vanishes, The* | Alfred Hitchcock |
| *Lady with a Lamp, The* | Herbert Wilcox |
| *Ladybird, Ladybird* | Ken Loach |
| *Ladykillers, The* | Alexander Mackendrick |
| *Lair of the White Worm, The* | Ken Russell |
| *Land and Freedom* | Ken Loach |
| *Landlady, The* | Roy Boulting |
| *Last Load, The* | John Baxter |
| *Last Man to Hang?, The* | Terence Fisher |
| *Last of England, The* | Derek Jarman |
| *Last Page, The* | Terence Fisher |
| *Laugh It Off* | John Baxter |
| *Laughing Annie* | Herbert Wilcox |
| *Laughter in the Dark* | Tony Richardson |
| *Lavender Hill Mob, The* | Charles Crichton |
| *Law and Disorder* | Charles Crichton |
| *Lawrence of Arabia* | David Lean |
| *Leader, His Driver and the Driver's Wife, The* | Nick Broomfield |
| *League of Gentlemen, The* | Basil Dearden |
| *Lease of Life* | Charles Frend |
| *Leather Boys, The* | Sidney J. Furie |
| *Left Right and Centre* | Sidney Gilliat |
| *Legend of the Seven Golden Vampires, The* | Roy Ward Baker |
| *Legend of the Werewolf* | Freddie Francis |
| *Leo the Last* | John Boorman |
| *Lest We Forget* | John Baxter |
| *Let George Do It!* | Marcel Varnel |
| *Let Him Have It* | Peter Medak |
| *Let the People Sing* | John Baxter |

| | |
|---|---|
| *Liam* | Stephen Frears |
| *Libel* | Anthony Asquith |
| *Life and Death of Colonel Blimp, The* | Michael Powell |
| *Life for Ruth* | Basil Dearden |
| *Life Is a Circus* | Val Guest |
| *Life Is Sweet* | Mike Leigh |
| *Life With the Lyons* | Val Guest |
| *Light Up the Sky!* | Lewis Gilbert |
| *Lilacs in the Spring* | Herbert Wilcox |
| *Limelight* | Herbert Wilcox |
| *Limping Man, The* | Cy Endfield |
| *Lion Has Wings, The* | Michael Powell |
| *Lisztomania* | Ken Russell |
| *Little Ballerina* | Lewis Gilbert |
| *Little Damozel, The* | Herbert Wilcox |
| *Little People, The* | George Pearson |
| *Little Voice* | Mark Herman |
| *Live and Let Die* | Guy Hamilton |
| *Local Hero* | Bill Forsyth |
| *Lock, Stock and Two Smoking Barrels* | Guy Ritchie |
| *Lodger, The* | Alfred Hitchcock |
| *Lolita* | Stanley Kubrick |
| *London* | Herbert Wilcox |
| *London Belongs to Me* | Sidney Gilliat |
| *London Melody* | Herbert Wilcox |
| *Loneliness of the Long Distance Runner, The* | Tony Richardson |
| *Lonely Passion of Judith Hearne, The* | Jack Clayton |
| *Long Arm, The* | Charles Frend |
| *Long Day Closes, The* | Terence Davies |
| *Long Memory, The* | Robert Hamer |
| *Look Back in Anger* | Tony Richardson |
| *Look Up and Laugh* | Basil Dean |
| *Looking on the Brightside* | Basil Dean |
| *Looks and Smiles* | Ken Loach |
| *Lorna Doone* | Basil Dean |
| *Loss of Sexual Innocence, The* | Mike Figgis |
| *Love Lottery, The* | Charles Crichton |
| *Love on the Dole* | John Baxter |
| *Love on Wheels* | Victor Saville |
| *Love, Life and Laughter* | George Pearson |
| *Love's Labour's Lost* | Kenneth Branagh |
| *Loves of Joanna Godden, The* | Charles Frend |
| *Loves of Robert Burns, The* | Herbert Wilcox |
| *Loyalties* | Basil Dean |
| *Lucky Jim* | John Boulting |
| *Lucky Number, The* | Anthony Asquith |
| *Luna de Miel* | Michael Powell |
| *Lyons in Paris, The* | Val Guest |

| | |
|---|---|
| *Macbeth* | Roman Polanski |
| *Mad About Men* | Ralph Thomas |
| *Madame Pompadour* | Herbert Wilcox |
| *Madame Sousatzka* | John Schlesinger |
| *Madeleine* | David Lean |
| *Mademoiselle* | Tony Richardson |
| *Madwoman of Chaillot, The* | Bryan Forbes |
| *Maggie, The* | Alexander Mackendrick |
| *Magic Box, The* | John Boulting |
| *Magnet, The* | Charles Frend |
| *Mahler* | Ken Russell |
| *Man Between, The* | Carol Reed |
| *Man Friday* | Jack Gold |
| *Man in the Iron Mask, The* | Mike Newell |
| *Man in the Middle* | Guy Hamilton |
| *Man in the Moon* | Basil Dearden |
| *Man in the Sky, The* | Charles Crichton |
| *Man in the White Suit, The* | Alexander Mackendrick |
| *Man of Violence* | Pete Walker |
| *Man Who Could Cheat Death, The* | Terence Fisher |
| *Man Who Cried, The* | Sally Potter |
| *Man Who Fell to Earth, The* | Nicolas Roeg |
| *Man Who Haunted Himself, The* | Basil Dearden |
| *Man Who Knew Too Much, The* | Alfred Hitchcock |
| *Man Who Never Was, The* | Ronald Neame |
| *Man Who Wouldn't Talk, The* | Herbert Wilcox |
| *Man with the Golden Gun, The* | Guy Hamilton |
| *Mandy* | Alexander Mackendrick |
| *Mantrap* | Terence Fisher |
| *Manuela* | Guy Hamilton |
| *Manxman, The* | Alfred Hitchcock |
| *Marry Me* | Terence Fisher |
| *Mary Shelley's Frankenstein* | Kenneth Branagh |
| *Mask of Dust* | Terence Fisher |
| *Masquerade* | Basil Dearden |
| *Master Plan, The* | Cy Endfield |
| *Matter of Life and Death, A* | Michael Powell |
| *Maurice* | James Ivory |
| *Mayerling* | Terence Young |
| *Maytime in Mayfair* | Herbert Wilcox |
| *Me and Marlborough* | Victor Saville |
| *Medusa Touch, The* | Jack Gold |
| *Men of Sherwood Forest, The* | Val Guest |
| *Men of Two Worlds* | Thorold Dickinson |
| *Men of Yesterday* | John Baxter |
| *Michael and Mary* | Victor Saville |
| *Michael Collins* | Neil Jordan |
| *Midnight Express* | Alan Parker |
| *Midshipman Easy* | Carol Reed |

| | |
|---|---|
| *Million Pound Note, The* | Ronald Neame |
| *Millionairess, The* | Anthony Asquith |
| *Millions* | Danny Boyle |
| *Millions Like Us* | Frank Launder and Sidney Gilliat |
| *Mind Benders, The* | Basil Dearden |
| *Miracle, The* | Neil Jordan |
| *Mirror Crack'd, The* | Guy Hamilton |
| *Miss Julie* | Mike Figgis |
| *Miss London Ltd* | Val Guest |
| *Miss Pilgrim's Progress* | Val Guest |
| *Mission, The* | Roland Joffé |
| *Mist in the Valley* | Cecil Hepworth |
| *Mister Moses* | Ronald Neame |
| *Modesty Blaise* | Joseph Losey |
| *Mona Lisa* | Neil Jordan |
| *Money Means Nothing* | Herbert Wilcox |
| *Monster Club, The* | Roy Ward Baker |
| *Monty Python and the Holy Grail* | Terry Gilliam |
| *Moon Zero Two* | Roy Ward Baker |
| *Moonraker* | Lewis Gilbert |
| *Morgan: A Suitable Case for Treatment* | Karel Reisz |
| *Morning Departure* | Roy Ward Baker |
| *Morons from Outer Space* | Mike Hodges |
| *Morvern Callar* | Lynne Ramsay |
| *Moscow Nights* | Anthony Asquith |
| *Most Dangerous Man in the World, The* | J. Lee Thompson |
| *Mountain Eagle, The* | Alfred Hitchcock |
| *Mouse on the Moon, The* | Richard Lester |
| *Mr Drake's Duck* | Val Guest |
| *Mrs Henderson Presents* | Stephen Frears |
| *Much Ado About Nothing* | Kenneth Branagh |
| *Much Too Shy* | Marcel Varnel |
| *Mummy, The* | Terence Fisher |
| *Mumsie* | Herbert Wilcox |
| *Mumsy, Nanny, Sonny and Girly* | Freddie Francis |
| *Murder* | Alfred Hitchcock |
| *Murder at the Windmill* | Val Guest |
| *Murder by Proxy* | Terence Fisher |
| *Murder Without Crime* | J. Lee Thompson |
| *Music Hall* | John Baxter |
| *Music Lovers, The* | Ken Russell |
| *My Ain Folk* | Bill Douglas |
| *My Beautiful Laundrette* | Stephen Frears |
| *My Childhood* | Bill Douglas |
| *My Learned Friend* | Basil Dearden |
| *My Life so Far* | Hugh Hudson |
| *My Name is Joe* | Ken Loach |
| *My Teenage Daughter* | Herbert Wilcox |
| *My Way Home* | Bill Douglas |

| | |
|---|---|
| *Old Mother Riley in Business* | John Baxter |
| *Old Mother Riley in Society* | John Baxter |
| *Old Mother Riley's Ghosts* | John Baxter |
| *Oliver!* | Carol Reed |
| *Oliver Twist (1948)* | David Lean |
| *Oliver Twist (2005)* | Roman Polanski |
| *Once a Sinner* | Lewis Gilbert |
| *Once Upon a Dream* | Ralph Thomas |
| *Once Upon a Time in the Midlands* | Shane Meadows |
| *One Night With You* | Terence Young |
| *One of Our Aircraft Is Missing* | Michael Powell |
| *One That Got Away, The* | Roy Ward Baker |
| *Only Two Can Play* | Sidney Gilliat |
| *Only Way, The* | Herbert Wilcox |
| *Only When I Larf* | Basil Dearden |
| *Orders to Kill* | Anthony Asquith |
| *Orlando* | Sally Potter |
| *Our Man in Havana* | Carol Reed |
| *Our Mother's House* | Jack Clayton |
| *Out of the Clouds* | Basil Dearden |
| *Out of the Shadow* | Michael Winner |
| *Outcast of the Islands* | Carol Reed |
| | |
| *Painted Boats* | Charles Crichton |
| *Pair of Briefs, A* | Ralph Thomas |
| *Paper Orchid* | Roy Ward Baker |
| *Paranoiac* | Freddie Francis |
| *Parting Shots* | Michael Winner |
| *Party's Over, The* | Guy Hamilton |
| *Passage, The* | J. Lee Thompson |
| *Passage Home* | Roy Ward Baker |
| *Passage to India, A* | David Lean |
| *Passionate Friends, The* | David Lean |
| *Passionate Stranger, A* | Muriel Box |
| *Pastor Hall* | Roy Boulting |
| *Paul and Michelle* | Lewis Gilbert |
| *Peeping Tom* | Michael Powell |
| *Peg of Old Drury* | Herbert Wilcox |
| *Penny Paradise* | Carol Reed |
| *Penny Princess* | Val Guest |
| *Percy* | Ralph Thomas |
| *Percy's Progress* | Ralph Thomas |
| *Perfect Strangers* | Alexander Korda |
| *Performance* | Donald Cammell and Nicolas Roeg |
| *Peter's Friends* | Kenneth Branagh |
| *Phantom of the Opera, The* | Terence Fisher |
| *Pianist, The* | Roman Polanski |
| *Piccadilly Incident* | Herbert Wilcox |
| *Pillow Book, The* | Peter Greenaway |

| | |
|---|---|
| *Pink Floyd The Wall* | Alan Parker |
| *Pink String and Sealing Wax* | Robert Hamer |
| *Piper's Tune, The* | Muriel Box |
| *Place to Go, A* | Basil Dearden |
| *Play It Cool* | Michael Winner |
| *Please Turn Over* | Gerald Thomas |
| *Pleasure Garden, The* | Alfred Hitchcock |
| *Pool of London* | Basil Dearden |
| *Poor Cow* | Ken Loach |
| *Portrait from Life* | Terence Fisher |
| *Prayer for the Dying, A* | Mike Hodges |
| *Prick up Your Ears* | Stephen Frears |
| *Prime Minister, The* | Thorold Dickinson |
| *Prime of Miss Jean Brodie, The* | Ronald Neame |
| *Prince and the Showgirl, The* | Laurence Olivier |
| *Private Life of Don Juan, The* | Alexander Korda |
| *Private Life of Henry VIII, The* | Alexander Korda |
| *Private's Progress* | John Boulting |
| *Prospero's Books* | Peter Greenaway |
| *Proud Valley, The* | Pen Tennyson |
| *Prudence and the Pill* | Ronald Neame |
| *Psychopath, The* | Freddie Francis |
| *Public Nuisance No. 1* | Marcel Varnel |
| *Pulp* | Mike Hodges |
| *Pumpkin Eater, The* | Jack Clayton |
| *Pure Hell of St Trinian's, The* | Frank Launder |
| *Purely Belter* | Mark Herman |
| *Pygmalion* | Anthony Asquith |
| | |
| *Quartet* | James Ivory |
| *Quatermass and the Pit* | Roy Ward Baker |
| *Quatermass Experiment, The* | Val Guest |
| *Quatermass II* | Val Guest |
| *Queen, The* | Stephen Frears |
| *Queen of Spades* | Thorold Dickinson |
| *Queen's Affair, The* | Herbert Wilcox |
| *Queen's Guard, The* | Michael Powell |
| *Quest for Love* | Ralph Thomas |
| *Quiet Wedding* | Anthony Asquith |
| | |
| *Raging Moon, The* | Bryan Forbes |
| *Rainbow, The* | Ken Russell |
| *Rainbow Jacket, The* | Basil Dearden |
| *Raining Stones* | Ken Loach |
| *Raising a Riot* | Wendy Toye |
| *Raising the Wind* | Gerald Thomas |
| *Rake's Progress, The* | Sidney Gilliat |
| *Ramsbottom Rides Again* | John Baxter |
| *Ratcatcher* | Lynne Ramsay |

| | |
|---|---|
| *Rattle of a Simple Man* | Muriel Box |
| *Reach for Glory* | Philip Leacock |
| *Reach for the Sky* | Lewis Gilbert |
| *Real Bloke, A* | John Baxter |
| *Reckoning, The* | Jack Gold |
| *Red Beret, The* | Terence Young |
| *Red Shoes, The* | Michael Powell |
| *Remains of the Day, The* | James Ivory |
| *Rembrandt* | Alexander Korda |
| *Repulsion* | Roman Polanski |
| *Return from the Ashes* | J. Lee Thompson |
| *Return of the Musketeers, The* | Richard Lester |
| *Return of the Vikings* | Charles Frend |
| *Reveille* | George Pearson |
| *Revenge of Frankenstein, The* | Terence Fisher |
| *Revenge of the Blood Beast* | Michael Reeves |
| *Revolution* | Hugh Hudson |
| *Revolver* | Guy Ritchie |
| *Rich and Strange* | Alfred Hitchcock |
| *Richard III* | Laurence Olivier |
| *Riff-Raff* | Ken Loach |
| *Ring, The* | Alfred Hitchcock |
| *Ringer, The* | Guy Hamilton |
| *Ripe Earth* | Roy Boulting |
| *Rita, Sue and Bob Too* | Alan Clarke |
| *Robin and Marion* | Richard Lester |
| *Romantic Englishwoman, The* | Joseph Losey |
| *Room at the Top* | Jack Clayton |
| *Room for Romeo Brass, A* | Shane Meadows |
| *Room With a View, A* | James Ivory |
| *Rotten to the Core* | John Boulting |
| *Royal Cavalcade* | Marcel Varnel |
| *Royal Flash* | Richard Lester |
| *Ruddigore* | John Halas and Joy Batchelor |
| *Ruling Class, The* | Peter Medak |
| *Run for Your Money, A* | Charles Frend |
| *Runaway Bus, The* | Val Guest |
| *Runaway Princess, The* | Anthony Asquith |
| *Running Man, The* | Carol Reed |
| *Ryan's Daughter* | David Lean |
| | |
| *Sabotage* | Alfred Hitchcock |
| *Safari* | Terence Young |
| *Sailor From Gibraltar, The* | Tony Richardson |
| *Sailor's Return, The* | Jack Gold |
| *Salomé's Last Dance* | Ken Russell |
| *Sammy and Rosie Get Laid* | Stephen Frears |
| *Sammy Going South* | Alexander Mackendrick |
| *San Demetrio London* | Charles Frend |

| | |
|---|---|
| *Sanders of the River* | Zoltán Korda |
| *Sands of the Kalahari* | Cy Endfield |
| *Sapphire* | Basil Dearden |
| *Saraband for Dead Lovers* | Basil Dearden |
| *Saturday Night and Sunday Morning* | Karel Reisz |
| *Savage Messiah* | Ken Russell |
| *Say it with Flowers* | John Baxter |
| *Scapegoat, The* | Robert Hamer |
| *Scarlet Thread, The* | Lewis Gilbert |
| *Scars of Dracula* | Roy Ward Baker |
| *Schizo* | Pete Walker |
| *School for Scoundrels* | Robert Hamer |
| *School for Sex* | Pete Walker |
| *Scott of the Antarctic* | Charles Frend |
| *Scrooge* | Ronald Neame |
| *Scum* | Alan Clarke |
| *Sea Fury* | Cy Endfield |
| *Sea Shall Not Have Them, The* | Lewis Gilbert |
| *Seagulls over Sorrento* | John and Roy Boulting |
| *Séance on a Wet Afternoon* | Bryan Forbes |
| *Sebastiane* | Derek Jarman |
| *Second Mate, The* | John Baxter |
| *Second Victory, The* | Gerald Thomas |
| *Secret, The* | Cy Endfield |
| *Secret Agent* | Alfred Hitchcock |
| *Secret Ceremony* | Joseph Losey |
| *Secret Journey* | John Baxter |
| *Secret Partner, The* | Basil Dearden |
| *Secret People* | Thorold Dickinson |
| *Secrets and Lies* | Mike Leigh |
| *Seeing Stars* | Roy Boulting |
| *Serious Charge* | Terence Young |
| *Servant, The* | Joseph Losey |
| *Service for Ladies* | Alexander Korda |
| *Seven Days to Noon* | John and Roy Boulting |
| *Seven Nights in Japan* | Lewis Gilbert |
| *Seventh Dawn, The* | Lewis Gilbert |
| *Shadowlands* | Richard Attenborough |
| *Shallow Grave* | Danny Boyle |
| *Sheba* | Cecil Hepworth |
| *Shillingbury Blowers, The* | Val Guest |
| *Shining, The* | Stanley Kubrick |
| *Ship that Died of Shame, The* | Basil Dearden |
| *Shipbuilders* | John Baxter |
| *Shirley Valentine* | Lewis Gilbert |
| *Shoot to Kill* | Michael Winner |
| *Shooting Stars* | Anthony Asquith |
| *Show Goes On, The* | Basil Dean |
| *Silent Village* | Humphrey Jennings |

| | |
|---|---|
| *Simon and Laura* | Muriel Box |
| *Sing As We Go!* | Basil Dean |
| *Singer Not the Song, The* | Roy Ward Baker |
| *Single-Handed* | Roy Boulting |
| *Sink the Bismarck!* | Lewis Gilbert |
| *Sixty Glorious Years* | Herbert Wilcox |
| *Skin Game, The* | Alfred Hitchcock |
| *Skull, The* | Freddie Francis |
| *Sky Bike, The* | Charles Frend |
| *Sleeping Tiger, The* | Joseph Losey |
| *Slipper and the Rose, The* | Bryan Forbes |
| *Small Back Room, The* | Michael Powell |
| *Small Man, The* | John Baxter |
| *Smallest Show on Earth, The* | Basil Dearden |
| *Snake Woman, The* | Sidney J. Furie |
| *Snapper, The* | Stephen Frears |
| *Snatch* | Guy Ritchie |
| *So Long at the Fair* | Terence Fisher |
| *Soft Beds, Hard Battles* | Roy Boulting |
| *Soldier's Daughter Never Cries, A* | James Ivory |
| *Solitary Child, The* | Gerald Thomas |
| *Some Girls Do* | Ralph Thomas |
| *Some Like it Cool* | Michael Winner |
| *Son of Dracula* | Freddie Francis |
| *Song of the Plough* | John Baxter |
| *Song of the Road* | John Baxter |
| *Sorcerers, The* | Michael Reeves |
| *Sound Barrier, The* | David Lean |
| *Soursweet* | Mike Newell |
| *South American George* | Marcel Varnel |
| *South Riding* | Victor Saville |
| *Southern Love* | Herbert Wilcox |
| *Spaceways* | Terence Fisher |
| *Spanish Gardener, The* | Philip Leacock |
| *Spider and the Fly, The* | Robert Hamer |
| *Sport of Kings, The* | Victor Saville |
| *Spring in Park Lane* | Herbert Wilcox |
| *Spy in Black, The* | Michael Powell |
| *Spy Who Loved Me, The* | Lewis Gilbert |
| *Square Ring, The* | Basil Dearden |
| *Squibs* | George Pearson |
| *Stage Fright* | Alfred Hitchcock |
| *Stars Look Down, The* | Carol Reed |
| *State Secret* | Sidney Gilliat |
| *Steaming* | Joseph Losey |
| *Stepping Toes* | John Baxter |
| *Stolen Assignment* | Terence Fisher |
| *Stolen Face* | Terence Fisher |
| *Storm in a Teacup* | Victor Saville |

| | |
|---|---|
| *Storm Over the Nile* | Terence Young/Zoltán Korda |
| *Stormy Monday* | Mike Figgis |
| *Story of Gilbert and Sullivan, The* | Sidney Gilliat |
| *Stranger Came Home, The* | Terence Fisher |
| *Stranglers of Bombay, The* | Terence Fisher |
| *Street Corner* | Muriel Box |
| *Strip Poker* | Pete Walker |
| *Study in Scarlet, A* | George Pearson |
| *Subway in the Sky* | Muriel Box |
| *Summer Madness* | David Lean |
| *Sunday Bloody Sunday* | John Schlesinger |
| *Sunshine Susie* | Victor Saville |
| *Surviving Picasso* | James Ivory |
| *Suspect* | John and Roy Boulting |
| *Sweet Sixteen* | Ken Loach |
| *Swept Away* | Guy Ritchie |
| *Sword of Sherwood Forest* | Terence Fisher |
| *System, The* | Michael Winner |
| | |
| *Take My Life* | Ronald Neame |
| *Tale of Two Cities, A* | Ralph Thomas |
| *Tales from the Crypt* | Freddie Francis |
| *Tales of Hoffman, The* | Michael Powell |
| *Tales that Witness Madness* | Freddie Francis |
| *Talk of the Devil* | Carol Reed |
| *Talking Feet* | John Baxter |
| *Tall Headlines* | Terence Young |
| *Tamahine* | Philip Leacock |
| *Tango Lesson, The* | Sally Potter |
| *Tansy* | Cecil Hepworth |
| *Taste of Honey, A* | Tony Richardson |
| *Teckman Mystery, The* | Wendy Toye |
| *Tell England* | Anthony Asquith |
| *Tempest, The* | Derek Jarman |
| *Terence Davies Trilogy, The* | Terence Davies |
| *Tesha* | Victor Saville |
| *Tess* | Roman Polanski |
| *That Lady* | Terence Young |
| *That Sinking Feeling* | Bill Forsyth |
| *That's Carry On* | Gerald Thomas |
| *Theatre Royal* | John Baxter |
| *There Ain't No Justice* | Pen Tennyson |
| *There Is Another Sun* | Lewis Gilbert |
| *There's a Girl in My Soup* | Roy Boulting |
| *These Dangerous Years* | Herbert Wilcox |
| *They Came from Beyond Space* | Freddie Francis |
| *They Came to a City* | Basil Dearden |
| *They Can't Hang Me* | Val Guest |
| *They Flew Alone* | Herbert Wilcox |

| | |
|---|---|
| *True as a Turtle* | Wendy Toye |
| *True Glory, The* | Carol Reed |
| *Truly, Madly, Deeply* | Anthony Minghella |
| *Trunk Crime* | Roy Boulting |
| *Truth About Women, The* | Muriel Box |
| *Tulse Luper Suitcases, The* | Peter Greenaway |
| *Tunes of Glory* | Ronald Neame |
| *Turned Out Nice Again* | Marcel Varnel |
| *Twenty-Four Hours of a Woman's Life* | Victor Saville |
| *TwentyFourSeven* | Shane Meadows |
| *Twice Round the Daffodils* | Gerald Thomas |
| *Twisted Nerve* | Roy Boulting |
| *Two and Two Make Six* | Freddie Francis |
| *Two Deaths* | Nicolas Roeg |
| *Two Faces of Dr Jekyll, The* | Terence Fisher |
| *Two Left Feet* | Roy Ward Baker |
| *Two Living, One Dead* | Anthony Asquith |
| *Two Thousand Women* | Frank Launder |
| | |
| *Ultus: The Man from the Dead* | George Pearson |
| *Uncensored* | Anthony Asquith |
| *Under Capricorn* | Alfred Hitchcock |
| *Underground* | Anthony Asquith |
| *Unfinished Symphony* | Anthony Asquith |
| *Universal Soldier* | Cy Endfield |
| *Up the Creek* | Val Guest |
| *Upstairs and Downstairs* | Ralph Thomas |
| | |
| *Valentino* | Ken Russell |
| *Valiant, The* | Roy Ward Baker |
| *Valley of Eagles* | Terence Young |
| *Vampire Happening* | Freddie Francis |
| *Vampire Lovers, The* | Roy Ward Baker |
| *Van, The* | Stephen Frears |
| *Vatel* | Roland Joffé |
| *Vault of Horror* | Roy Ward Baker |
| *Venetian Bird* | Ralph Thomas |
| *Vengeance* | Freddie Francis |
| *Vera Drake* | Mike Leigh |
| *Vicious Circle, The* | Gerald Thomas |
| *Victim* | Basil Dearden |
| *Victoria the Great* | Herbert Wilcox |
| *Violent Playground* | Basil Dearden |
| *VIPs, The* | Anthony Asquith |
| | |
| *W Plan, The* | Victor Saville |
| *Walkabout* | Nicolas Roeg |
| *Waltzes from Vienna* | Alfred Hitchcock |
| *War Lover, The* | Philip Leacock |

| | |
|---|---|
| *War Requiem* | Derek Jarman |
| *Warm Corner, A* | Victor Saville |
| *Watch your Stern* | Gerald Thomas |
| *Waterloo Road* | Sidney Gilliat |
| *Way Ahead, The* | Carol Reed |
| *Way to the Stars, The* | Anthony Asquith |
| *We Dive at Dawn* | Anthony Asquith |
| *We Joined the Navy* | Wendy Toye |
| *We'll Smile Again* | John Baxter |
| *Weak and the Wicked, The* | J. Lee Thompson |
| *Weaker Sex, The* | Roy Ward Baker |
| *Weapon, The* | Val Guest |
| *Wedding Rehearsal* | Alexander Korda |
| *Welcome to Sarajevo* | Michael Winterbottom |
| *Went the Day Well?* | Alberto Cavalcanti |
| *West 11* | Michael Winner |
| *What Would You Do, Chums?* | John Baxter |
| *When Dinosaurs Ruled the Earth* | Val Guest |
| *When You Come Home* | John Baxter |
| *Where the Spies are* | Val Guest |
| *'Where's That Fire?'* | Marcel Varnel |
| *While the Sun Shines* | Anthony Asquith |
| *Whiskey Galore!* | Alexander Mackendrick |
| *Whisperers, The* | Bryan Forbes |
| *Whistle Down the Wind* | Bryan Forbes |
| *White Countess, The* | James Ivory |
| *Who?* | Jack Gold |
| *Who Done It?* | Basil Dearden |
| *Who's Your Lady Friend?* | Carol Reed |
| *Whom the God's Love* | Basil Dean |
| *Wicked Lady, The* | Michael Winner |
| *Wild and the Willing, The* | Ralph Thomas |
| *Wild Heather* | Cecil Hepworth |
| *Wildcats of St. Trinian's, The* | Frank Launder |
| *William Comes to Town* | Val Guest |
| *Wind Cannot Read, The* | Ralph Thomas |
| *Windom's Way* | Ronald Neame |
| *Wings of Danger* | Terence Fisher |
| *Winslow Boy, The* | Anthony Asquith |
| *Witches, The* | Nicolas Roeg |
| *Witchfinder General* | Michael Reeves |
| *Withnail and I* | Bruce Robinson |
| *Wittgenstein* | Derek Jarman |
| *Woman Hater* | Terence Young |
| *Woman in a Dressing Gown* | J. Lee Thompson |
| *Woman in Question, The* | Anthony Asquith |
| *Woman in White, The* | Herbert Wilcox |
| *Woman of Straw* | Basil Dearden |
| *Woman to Woman* | Victor Saville |

| | |
|---|---|
| *Women in Love* | Ken Russell |
| *Wonderful Life* | Sidney J. Furie |
| *Wonderful Things* | Herbert Wilcox |
| *Wonderland* | Michael Winterbottom |
| *Wrong Box, The* | Bryan Forbes |
| | |
| *Yanks* | John Schlesinger |
| *Yellow Balloon, The* | J. Lee Thompson |
| *Yellow Canary* | Herbert Wilcox |
| *Yellow Rolls-Royce, The* | Anthony Asquith |
| *Yes* | Sally Potter |
| *Yes Mr Brown* | Herbert Wilcox |
| *Yesterday's Enemy* | Val Guest |
| *Yield to the Night* | J. Lee Thompson |
| *You Must be Joking!* | Michael Winner |
| *You Only Live Twice* | Lewis Gilbert |
| *Young and Innocent* | Alfred Hitchcock |
| *Young Lovers, The* | Anthony Asquith |
| *Young Mr Pitt, The* | Carol Reed |
| *Young Ones, The* | Sidney J. Furie |
| *Young Soul Rebels* | Issac Julien |
| *Young Winston* | Richard Attenborough |
| | |
| *Zarak* | Terence Young |
| *Zardoz* | John Boorman |
| *Zed and Two Noughts, A* | Peter Greenaway |
| *Zulu* | Cy Endfield |